HOPE
When the World Falls Apart

DANIEL AND REVELATION'S MESSAGE OF HOPE

Russell Burrill

SEMINARS UNLIMITED
P.O. Box 66, Keene, TX 76059

Edited by Ken McFarland
Cover art direction, design by Ed Guthero, Melissa Renken
Cover photo by permission of Corbis
Cover illustration by Lars Justinen

Unless otherwise indicated, all Bible quotations are from the
New King James Version of the Bible (NKJV), copyright © 1982
by Thomas Nelson, Inc., Nashville, Tennessee.

Bible quotations credited to NASB are from the New American
Standard Version of the Bible, copyright © 1977 by the Lockman
Foundation, La Habra, California.

The author assumes responsibility for the accuracy of all facts,
statistics, and quotations as cited in this book.

ISBN: 1-882704-01-0

Contents

Acknowledgments

I would like to acknowledge the many people who have helped put this manuscript together. My secretary, Alice McIntyre, along with my wife, Cynthia, spent many hours poring over the manuscript and offering suggestions as to where I could be clearer in my wording. I am deeply grateful for their help and suggestions. I also would like to thank Carl Johnston of Seminars Unlimited for making the publication of the manuscript a priority. Throughout my ministry, there have been countless individuals who have shared insights with me that have shaped my thinking in many of the prophetic areas. I wish to acknowledge their contribution as well.

About the Author

Russell Burrill is the director of the North American Division Evangelism Institute, located at Andrews University in Berrien Springs, Michigan. He teaches at the Andrews University Theological Seminary, where he holds the faculty rank of professor. He is in much demand as a speaker and trainer and has lectured on the prophecies of Daniel and Revelation across the United States and in many other countries. Russell is the author of the popular Bible study series—the Prophecy Seminar—and has written numerous other books and magazine articles.

He was converted through the ministry of the Voice of Prophecy with H.M.S.Richards, Sr. Having discovered Christ as the center of all prophecy, he began to share the prophecies with others. He continues to proclaim Christ in the prophecies through various prophecy meetings, as well as teaching young ministers how to share Christ in the prophecies. This book is the result of many requests to put in writing some of the great prophetic subjects proclaimed in his various prophecy seminars.

He and his wife, Cynthia, have two children and five grandchildren. He and his wife enjoy hiking, biking, and camping, where they can enjoy God's great outdoors. They maintain a vibrant hope in the coming of Jesus as the ultimate answer to humanity's needs and look forward to that day when all prophecies will find their consummation in the return of Jesus.

Foreword

If you keep even halfway current with the news, you know that our world seems to be falling apart all around us. Just when we think things can't get worse, they do. Terrorists and warlords are determined to destroy our peace and freedom.

And even as the world we live in grows more frightening, we feel increasingly overwhelmed as well with the mounting stresses of our daily lives. It's as if some sinister force is pushing us—and our homes and families—to the breaking point. Our own personal worlds, too, seem to be coming apart. Plenty of fear, conflict, and stress—but where's the hope?

In these pages, author Russell Burrill insists that we need not abandon ourselves to despair. Why? Because when the world around us falls apart, there is hope. When our own personal world falls apart, there is hope. When it seems as if evil is winning, there is hope. There is hope, because the force for good revealed in the Bible books of Daniel and Revelation is the all-powerful Creator and King of the universe.

God knew that those of us living near the very end of time—just before the return of Jesus to this earth—would be overwhelmed and frightened by the power of evil. That's why through His prophets, He told us to hang on to hope, because good is about to win. Hang on to hope, because God has more power than all the forces of terrorism and evil. Hang on to hope, because peace is about to become permanent.

When the world around you falls apart—when your own world falls apart—don't let go of your hope till you've read this book. Tie a knot. Hang on. God is going to win this great battle between good and evil!

Lonnie Melashenko
Speaker-Director
The Voice of Prophecy
World's second-oldest religious broadcast

Author's Preface

Our world will never be the same again. The events of September 11, 2001 forever changed our lives. In this new world, where terrorists can strike unannounced and kill thousands of innocent people, one may be wondering how to find hope and peace when a bomb could be hiding in the next building we enter. We can increase security at airports and other government buildings, but we will no longer feel safe.

The twenty-first century, with its unstable world, reminds all of us that time is growing old for this planet. The darkness of our times only amplifies the need to be focused on the great hope that awaits the born-again believer at the coming of Jesus. That is why this book focuses on hope. In an age of hopelessness, the advent hope still must resonate in the hearts of the followers of Christ. Too often, books on prophecy have emphasized the despair of last-day events. That is not my intent here. Instead, it is my desire that readers of this book will find hope as they study the great prophecies of Daniel and Revelation. It is my hope that those who read these pages will discover a vibrant hope in the Christ who is the center of all our hopes.

As we study together the prophecies of Daniel and Revelation, we will discover that the message of these two great prophetic books is indeed one of hope. Behind all the beasts and symbols is a revelation of the ultimate hope-giver—Jesus Christ. These great prophetic scriptures will reveal to us that God is still in charge of the planet. Things may seem to be out of control, but God assures us that He is still in charge.

God has nothing to do with acts of terrorism. They are the

work of Satan, the great instigator of evil. In the following pages, we will find that God does not always step in and prohibit Satan from doing evil. He allows the fires to come, but the promise of Scripture is that He will go through the fire with us. Problems will arise, bad things will happen, yet God goes through these trials with us. He weeps with us. He does not always deliver us from disaster, but He strengthens us to endure life's tragedies.

God was with the victims of September 11, and He will be with us as we face life's tragedies. This is the ultimate message of the books of Daniel and Revelation. It is a message of hope—the message of this book.

It is my hope and desire that as you read this book, you too will discover the peace that only God can bring. It is my desire that you too will find this hope—a hope built solidly upon a relationship with Jesus Christ and acceptance of Him who alone provides eternal life through faith and not by any works which we might be able to accomplish. Only through a relationship with Jesus can one find meaning and hope in this world. May this hope encourage you when your own world falls apart.

SECTION I

1

God's Final Message of Hope

Terrorism, crime, political crises, natural disasters, and uncertainty greet the inhabitants of Planet Earth today. Change has become so widely accepted that if circumstances aren't changing, people become nervous, assuming something is wrong. In the last twenty-five years we have experienced more innovations than in the previous 2,500 years. Technological advances occur with such rapidity that the latest gadget is already outdated before it is even sold. To give a specific example would outdate this book before it could be published. Terrorist activities and widespread change in our world have created a generation of people uncertain about the future—a generation of pessimists and world-class skeptics. People today lack hope for tomorrow, and many are unable to grasp the future direction of the world.

Add to this all the political changes that have occurred on the planet over the last few years, and even deeper uncertainty is created. In the past, Americans have been brought together by a common enemy (the former Soviet Union). However, today that common enemy, the terrorist network, is unseen. There is only one gigantic superpower left in the world—the United States of America, the object of the terrorist venom. What will the world be like as the United States continues to dominate the political landscape around the world? There are some negatives in being the world's only military and economic superpower, such as becoming the target of terrorist attacks and the supplier of money for developing nations around the world.

Yet in spite of the obstacles, forecasters still predict a world under America's dominance in the twenty-first century. The twentieth century was dubbed "the American century," but the twenty-first promises to be dominated even more by America. Writing at the end of the twentieth century, Bob Whiteset declared:

> The United States will possess even more global influence in the next century, become a nation without peer, enabling it to influence as never before economic and political events around the globe. Yet along with this comes a caveat. Without an accompanying ethical foundation, the United States' newly enhanced power can become perverted and misguided. To address this dilemma, America must first recognize that it will continue to be what Friedman calls "the center of (political and ethical) gravity" in the next century. Then to wield this bourgeoning power, ethically, America must have a heightened sense of a moral compass.

> The church must provide the magnetism for this compass in the form of ethical teaching, pragmatic application, authentic prayer, and moral example. Strides in technology will dictate that America picks up this ethical mantle whether it wants it or not. This is not a time for silence from our pulpits or from our lives. The world is facing a dangerous future with America's hand upon the rudder, and the direction America steers will be dictated by the response of America's church.—Bob Whiteset, "Another American Century," *Strategies for Today's Leaders,* November-December, 1997.

God has not been caught off guard by all these powerful changes occurring in our post-modern society. Ages ago, to a lonely prophet on Patmos, God communicated the message of the book of Revelation. The message of that book not only reveals world conditions that exist in our day but provides Christians with hope for the future, in knowing that God is in control of human history. The rise and fall of nations is not accidental. Behind it all is the unseen hand of the Almighty guiding the course of human history toward its ultimate climax.

The prophetic books of Daniel and Revelation were designed by God to bring hope and meaning to Christians in all ages, but especially to those living at the close of the age. Full of beasts and symbols, these books have at times been confusing to many Christians. The grotesque beasts even appear scary to those not familiar with biblical symbolism. However, it is helpful to realize that the beasts are merely God's cartoon characters, representing the various nations of prophecy. Much as modern nations have used animals as symbols of political entities, such as the Russian bear or the United States eagle, so God has used these animals to represent different nations. The scriptures themselves hold the key to understanding the symbols. For example, Daniel 7:25 indicates that prophetic beasts represent political kingdoms. Revelation 17:16 utilizes water to represent multitudes of people, while Ezekiel 4:6 intimates that a prophetic day could be interpreted as a literal year.

One has to be careful when applying meaning to the symbols. Only when appearing in highly apocalyptic-type prophecies which utilize obvious symbolic language, can these meanings be attached to the symbols. In most places in scripture, water means water, a beast means an animal, and a day means a literal day. In all cases where prophetic imagery is intended, the context makes it very clear that the word is used in symbolic meaning.

Many of the symbols of the book of Revelation are drawn from the Old Testament. In fact, there are over 2,000 allusions to the Old Testament in the book of Revelation alone. To attempt to interpret the book of Revelation without consulting the Old Testament allusions is likely to result in faulty interpretation.

The Bible does not focus on general political history. Nations and kingdoms only appear in scripture as they affect

God's covenant people. The scriptures are a historical account of redemption. God is not merely demonstrating His fore-knowledge by giving us the history of the world in advance. God is simply revealing to His people the powers that will oppress them in any age of the earth. Thus in interpreting prophecy, one should look for a connection to God's covenant people to discover fulfillment of the prophecy. It is not just a political event, but a political event that affects the covenant people. Many people wonder why China and India are not predicted in the Bible. They simply did not affect the covenant people politically, so there was no place for them in the re-demptive history of God's people. God cares for these nations, but they are not major players in *redemptive* history—they are not entered into the prophetic jigsaw puzzle unless they affect the covenant people.

God's Message in Uncertain Times

In this age of uncertainty and perplexity, God sends one final message to Planet Earth. That message is centered in the heart of the book of Revelation under the symbol of three angels flying in mid-heaven with the final message to the in-habitants of this tumultuous age.

> Then I saw another angel flying in the midst of heaven, having the everlasting gospel to preach to those who dwell on the earth—to every nation, tribe, tongue, and people— saying with a loud voice, "Fear God and give glory to Him, for the hour of His judgment has come; and worship Him who made heaven and earth, the sea and springs of water."

> And another angel followed, saying, "Babylon is fallen, is fallen, that great city, because she has made all nations drink of the wine of the wrath of her fornication." Then a third angel followed them, saying with a loud voice, "If anyone wor-ships the beast and his image, and receives his mark on his forehead or on his hand, he himself shall also drink of the

wine of the wrath of God, which is poured out full strength into the cup of His indignation. He shall be tormented with fire and brimstone in the presence of the holy angels and in the presence of the Lamb. And the smoke of their torment ascends forever and ever; and they have no rest day or night, who worship the beast and his image, and whoever receives the mark of his name." Here is the patience of the saints; here are those who keep the commandments of God and the faith of Jesus. Revelation 14:6-12.

When earth's political arena arrives at the final rebellion against God, as described in the preceding chapter, this mighty message of the three angels is to triumph in its grand proclamation to the inhabitants of earth. Interestingly, this final message is a gospel message, a message centered in the gospel of free grace that has been at the heart of Christianity since its inception.

No new gospel is needed for the end time—just a mighty proclamation of the same everlasting gospel. The remedy for the human condition has not changed. Humankind's greatest need is still the everlasting gospel. It is everlasting in the sense that it is changeless. It is the same gospel proclaimed by the great Old Testament prophets, as well as Jesus Himself, the twelve apostles, and, of course, the same gospel preached by Paul. The gospel does not change throughout the ages. It still speaks to the hearts of earth's final generation.

The gospel is the good news that Jesus Christ has forgiven me of my sins through His ultimate sacrifice on Calvary's cross. It proclaims clearly that there is nothing I can do to receive this matchless gift except to reach out and receive it. Never is it mine by human works, but always solely by the grace of God. That is the heart cry of this final message to be given to the planet.

The uniqueness of this final proclamation is sensed by the context in which it is proclaimed here in Revelation 14. Verse 7 declares that "the hour of His judgment has come," when this message of the everlasting gospel is to be given. It is a judgment-hour message centered in the eternal grace of Christ. Judgment in this passage is not in conflict with the gospel of grace. In Revelation, as we shall see later, judgment is always good news to the righteous. The greatest choruses of praise spring forth from God's people because of judgment. Judgment is not a fearful event for the redeemed—it is a joyous salvation experience.

We notice also that the warnings against the fall of Babylon and the mark of the beast are included in these three angels' messages. They too must be seen as part of the gospel of free grace. Remember the text declares that the gospel says judgment is here—that Babylon is fallen, and watch out for the mark of the beast. To correctly understand the amazing warnings, one must see them in the setting of the everlasting gospel, for that is the biblical setting in which they are given.

Revelation is not primarily about beasts and harlots—the book of Revelation is primarily about Jesus. The very first verse in the book declares it to be "the revelation of Jesus Christ" (Revelation 1:1). Thus one will misunderstand the book if one does not view it from a Christ-centered perspective. Even this stern warning about the mark of the beast is misunderstood if it is not seen as a revelation of Jesus. This book contains one of the greatest revelations of Jesus ever given to the human race. It is the underlying principle for interpreting the entire book.

The Need of the Everlasting Gospel

God declares that the greatest need of human beings at the end time is the everlasting gospel. Why does our race need such a message at this climactic hour? Only by understanding the fall of humanity can we grasp our great need of the everlasting gospel. Genesis 1:26 declares: "Then God said, 'Let Us make man in Our image, according to Our likeness.'" Humanity's exalted origin is the image of God. The race was made in His likeness. In all aspects of our nature, we bear the divine image. The three areas of humanity's nature have been described as the physical, mental, and spiritual (including the social) dimensions. In each of these we were created in the image of God. The physical, mental, and spiritual aspects reflected the divine image.

The sad tale of Genesis is that the divine image was marred by the introduction of sin into the human race. Genesis 3:1-6 reveals not only the fall but the loss of this divine image in all three of the human dimensions:

> Now the serpent was more cunning than any beast of the field which the Lord God had made. And he said to the woman, "Has God indeed said, 'You shall not eat of every tree of the garden'?" And the woman said to the serpent, "We may eat the fruit of the trees of the garden; but of the fruit of the tree which is in the midst of the garden, God has said, 'You shall not eat it, nor shall you touch it, lest you die.'" Then the serpent said to the woman, "You will not surely die. For God knows that in the day you eat of it your eyes will be opened, and you will be like God, knowing good and evil." So when the woman saw that the tree was good for food, that it was pleasant to the eyes, and a tree desirable to make one wise, she took of its fruit and ate. She also gave to her husband with her, and he ate.

Verse 6 is especially significant. "When the woman saw that the tree was good for food." Food, obviously, is dealing with the physical nature of humanity. God said that this tree was not good for food, yet she now saw it as good for food. The human physical nature was thus marred and altered from the divine image.

Second, she saw "that it was pleasant to the eyes." Eyes are used in scripture to symbolize the spiritual nature (Revelation 3:18). Now humanity's spiritual nature was marred by sin. Third, she saw that it was a "tree desirable to make one wise." Now the third dimension of humanity—the mental area—became marred by the deceitfulness of sin.

Humanity, created in the divine image physically, mentally,

and spiritually, now experienced an image marred by sin. As a result, temptations from without found an answering chord within the human heart, and the feet turned imperceptibly to evil. The natural result of this marring of the divine image was that it was very logical for our first parents to reach out, take the fruit, and eat. Eating the fruit was not the sin. Sin already existed (Genesis 3:6) in the heart before the first sinful act. Eating the fruit was thus the natural consequence of the fallen nature that now existed in humanity as this divine image was marred in all areas: physical, mental, and spiritual.

Sin is a disease of the whole being. Sin is not just outward acts of disobedience committed by a fallen race. As the result of the fall, humanity lives with sin as a part of the human experience, inherent in the nature of humanity. The result is as Isaiah describes it:

> From the sole of the foot even to the head, there is no soundness in it, but wounds and bruises and putrefying sores; they have not been closed or bound up, or soothed with ointment. Isaiah 1:6.

The solution to the sin problem is not just reforming the life. The very heart of humanity must be changed. The image of God, marred by sin in the beginning, must be restored. Provision must be made for the race to recapture the lost image. The sin problem does not merely deal with outward acts of disobedience; therefore, the sin problem can only be eradicated by a total change in the nature of humanity. That kind of change is impossible for the human race to conceive by itself. That's why Jesus had to come.

The Second Adam

Humanity's incapacity to change its nature demanded a solution outside of the human race. Enter Jesus, the divine

Son of God. Clothing His divinity in humanity, He appeared as the second Adam. Treading the same ground that Adam and Eve walked, He must be tempted in all ways that humans are tempted. Every aspect of His nature must be put to the test, making it possible for Him to gain the victory in all the human dimensions. He must gain the victory for humanity —physically, mentally, and spiritually—in order that the human race, through the acceptance of His meritorious life offered in man's place on Calvary, can have the divine image fully restored.

Matthew 4 describes the conflict as Jesus, the second Adam—standing as representative of the new humanity— faced the tempter straight on:

> Then Jesus was led up by the Spirit into the wilderness to be tempted by the devil. And when He had fasted forty days and forty nights, afterward He was hungry. Now when the tempter came to Him, he said, "If You are the Son of God, command that these stones become bread." But He answered and said, "It is written, 'Man shall not live by bread alone, but by every word that proceeds from the mouth of God.'" Verses 1-4.

Amazingly, Satan immediately hit Christ at the very point where Eve was tempted—appetite. Jesus, as the second Adam, must gain the victory physically for the human race at the very point where the original pair failed. This first temptation was uniquely crafted by Satan to fit the person of Christ, tempting His human nature physically as Eve had been tempted in Eden. Whereas the original pair failed the test, Jesus resisted the temptation to the physical nature, thereby providing a substitutionary victory for the human race. The divine image could now be restored physically.

Verses 5-7 describe the second temptation. Satan took Christ to the temple mount, tempting Him to jump off the cliff so the angels would rescue Him, thus asserting Himself as the promised Messiah. No greater temptation can come to a person's mind than presumptuous pride, which is the very heart of the second temptation. Jesus failed to accept Satan's temptation of the mind, thus gaining the victory for the human race in the mental dimension.

Finally, in the third temptation (verses 8-10), Satan offered Jesus all the kingdoms of the world for one simple acknowledgment of worship. This was the test to the spiritual nature, but Jesus staunchly refused to yield to this mighty temptation, declaring that only God is worthy of worship. Even in the spiritual nature, Satan is unsuccessful in causing Christ to fail.

Jesus emerged from the temptations a victor. Satan has been vanquished; conquered. The second Adam was successful at every point where Eden's parents failed. Sin had been conquered. What humanity had been unable to accomplish in their fallen state, Jesus had now done for them. The bridge between humanity and God was now forever forged by the second Adam. In all three of the human dimensions—physical, mental, and spiritual—Jesus had forever gained the victory. It was complete.

The Gospel's Restoration of the Image of God

What Adam lost, Christ restored. Because of His sacrificial death, the gospel of Christ envisions the full restoration of humanity to the image of God by the acceptance of Jesus as both Savior and Lord. The parting words of the Promised One summed up the mission of His followers. They were to go forth and make disciples of all people (Matthew 28:16-20). Their sole objective was to disciple people into becoming fully devoted followers of Jesus Christ—people in whom Jesus was the top priority in every area of their life: the physical, the mental, and the spiritual dimension.

Revelation 14:6, 7 reveals that the preaching of that gospel of radical discipleship is still to be proclaimed in the setting of the final judgment hour. This message is not just the gospel of Jesus as Savior, it also includes Jesus as total Lord of one's life in all three of the human dimensions. Accepting Him as Savior is the first step. Following that is the willingness to turn over one's life to Him as Lord. Every aspect of the person's life becomes subject to the Lordship of Christ.

Revelation 14:6 proclaims the gospel, but verse 7 has the angel announcing three injunctions: "Fear God," "give glory to Him," and "worship Him." Just as Adam and Eve fell physically, mentally, and spiritually and Jesus restored the divine image in those same three areas, now the final message to the earth announces that God desires His people to fully make Christ Lord of their physical, mental, and spiritual natures.

Scripture has already defined that the injunction to fear God is dealing with the mental areas of one's life. "The fear of the Lord is the beginning of knowledge" (Proverbs 1:7). In this final age of the earth, filled with abundant mind pollution, God sends a message to earth's inhabitants to bring their minds into harmony with the Lordship of Christ. As Paul declared, Christians are to think on those things that are honest, just, pure, lovely, and of good report (Philippians 4:8). Accepting Jesus as Savior and Lord means that He is now in control of our minds. We can no longer afford to put the junk of television, the Internet, and movies into our minds. Born-again Christians are called upon to bring their minds fully under the control of Jesus, who has now become the Lord of their minds.

The expression "give glory to Him" is reflective of Paul's counsel in 1 Corinthian 10:31, where he counsels Christians to eat and drink to the glory of God. Or as he further declares in 1 Corinthians 6:19, 20, our bodies are God's temple. Since we have been purchased by Calvary, we must glorify God in our bodies. Here is the call to surrender the control of the physical passions such as sex and appetite to Christ and allow Him to fully become Lord of our physical nature.

The final injunction "worship Him" is an obvious reference to the spiritual dimension of our lives. It is a clarion call from the heart of the ascended Lord to make Christ the sole object of our worship. Christians can no longer worship money, sex, or power. The ultimate Lordship of Christ over the spiritual dimension demands the sole worship of Christ in all areas of our being.

Thus this first angel mightily proclaims the message in the end times that Christ must be accepted as both Savior and Lord. Having received the grace of Christ in one's life, the Christian is now willing to allow Christ to have absolute control of all three dimensions: the physical, the mental, and the spiritual. He who gained victory in all these areas in the wilderness of temptation, now wants us to claim His victory in all the dimensions of our being.

The Second Angel

Following quickly on the heels of the first angel, the second angel sounds the awesome message that Babylon is fallen. Babylon, in Revelation's symbolism, represents all the forces arrayed against God's people. Just as ancient Nebuchadnezzar's Babylon oppressed the Hebrews, so modern-day Babylon will seek to oppress Christians in the final days of earth's history. (We will study Babylon more deeply in chapter 6.)

Babylon is presented to us in a fallen condition. She is fallen because she has departed from the gospel of free grace and has sought to save herself by her works. The foundation of all false religion is a righteousness that can be achieved by sheer human effort. God's warning about Babylon's fallen condition must be heeded, since it is the opposite of the first angel's message—calling people to accept Jesus fully as Savior and Lord.

The Third Angel

The third angel follows with the most fearful warning of all Scripture—the exhortation to neither receive the mark of the beast nor to worship the beast. Clearly the main issue in last-day events will focus on worship. While the first angel loudly calls for humanity to worship the Creator, the third angel confirms that message with the vivid call to not worship the beast. Two kinds of worship are contrasted in these three angels' messages: humanistic worship of the creature (beast)—and genuine worship of the Creator.

People Who Accept the Message of the Three Angels

While Revelation 14:6-12 sounds forth earth's final warning, Revelation 14:1-5 describes the people who respond to the messages of these three angels. They are referred to as the 144,000. It is not our purpose in this chapter to explore in detail the identity of these 144,000. It is easy to lose our focus and concentrate on whether this is a literal or symbolic number and miss the meaning of the passage. This writer is convinced that the number is highly symbolic. Others may disagree, but this is not the thrust of the passage.

Revelation 14:1-5 is describing a people who have responded to the message of the three angels. The passage clearly reveals that these people have been thoroughly discipled and have truly accepted the Lordship of Christ in their lives. Verse 1 declares that they have the Father's name written on their foreheads—they belong totally to God in Christ. Jesus is Lord of every area of their life. His precious blood has redeemed them. That's why verse 4 declares that they follow the Lamb wherever he goes. They are totally enraptured with Jesus. His Lordship is manifested in all areas of their lives.

Christ is such a part of these people's lives that the passage concludes with the unbelievable declaration that in their mouth was found no guile, for they are without fault before the throne of God. Obviously, this does not mean they are without fault in their own righteousness, but they are fully clothed in the righteousness of Christ, and only His righteousness is reflected in the lives of these last-day followers of the Lamb. The word translated *guile* in the King James Version basically means "fish bait." In their mouth was found no fish bait. Fish bait, of course, is not what it appears to be on the outside. Instead of a delicious meal, there is a hook inside. But in these redeemed people, there is no fish bait—they are totally transparent in everything. That kind of declaration can only be made of people who have allowed Jesus to become absolute Lord of their lives.

God's final message to the inhabitants of Planet Earth is not really any different than the radical message He gave during the first century. It is a clarion call from a God who loved the human race so much that He sent His Son to die for them. It is a call to accept Jesus as Savior and absolute Lord. God is not calling earth's inhabitants to an easy religion, but to one of total commitment to Jesus. Earth's final call is the call to radical discipleship.

To respond to this message means to develop a deep, lasting, abiding relationship with the Lord Jesus Christ. It demands the reordering of life's priorities to reflect the fact that Jesus has taken first place, which is reflected in the areas of time, talent, money, and lifestyle. Such a priority is only gained by spending time with Jesus in a deep relationship. So God calls you, dear reader, to open your heart to the most joyous relationship you have ever experienced—one of radical discipleship with Jesus Christ. Will you be one of His radical disciples in earth's final hours?

2

Hope for Humanity

Humanity struggles to find hope on this darkened planet called Earth. But where is such hope to be found? In various New Age philosophies, eastern meditations, yoga, Buddhism? Or is our hope best found in Jesus, the Christ? Each of these religions or modern philosophies tout theirs as the only way to find peace and meaning in life. Yet, are their claims real? Can they be trusted to deliver the ultimate hope of all—an eternity with the great God of the universe?

Why do Christians feel that the claims of Christ are vastly superior to the claims of Buddha? Why does hope in Jesus bring more peace to people than do days of meditating or contemplating the philosophies and practices of New Age ideas? How can I be sure that Jesus, as the only Savior from sin, is the sole place to put my hope and trust? In this chapter we will examine several Old Testament prophecies about the coming of the Messiah, written long before Jesus walked the planet. It will be our attempt to discover whether or not Jesus really fulfilled these amazing prophecies given by the ancient Jewish prophets.

Seven hundred years before the birth of Christ, the prophet Isaiah predicted that the Messiah would be born of a virgin: "Therefore the Lord Himself will give you a sign: Behold, a virgin will be with child and bear a son, and she will call His name Immanuel" (Isaiah 7:14, NASB). The virgin birth, sung about every Christmas, was actually predicted 700 years before it happened. Isaiah is clear that the One born here was to be called *Immanuel*, which means "God with us." Amazingly, Isaiah not only predicted the virgin birth of Christ but also declared that the One born of the virgin was actually God in human flesh.

Five hundred years before Jesus saw Bethlehem's manger, the prophet Micah predicted the birth would occur in Bethlehem:

> But you, Bethlehem Ephrathah, though you are little among the thousands of Judah, yet out of you shall come forth to Me the One to be Ruler in Israel, whose goings forth are from of old, From everlasting. Micah 5:2.

Out of the hundreds of cities in ancient Israel, the prophet just happened to pick the right city where Jesus was born. This is no coincidence. Divine foreknowledge has given us this additional evidence of the Messiahship of Jesus.

Both Isaiah and Malachi leave no doubt that the One they predicted was God. Isaiah calls Him Immanuel ("God with us"); while Micah proclaims that His works emanate from eternity. These two prophets are declaring that Jesus is not just a prophet or a good man who taught great moral lessons and performed mighty deeds—they are proclaiming that He is fully and equally God. He has always existed, they declare—from eternity. You see, there never was a time when Christ did not exist. He does not have a beginning—He is the beginning. That is why He is called God.

In other words, the One born in Bethlehem did not originate there, but preexisted in eternity with God the Father. The New Testament makes the bold claim that Jesus was the Creator (Colossians 1:16), the Alpha and the Omega (the first and last letters of the Greek alphabet), indicating that Jesus is both the beginning and the ending (Revelation 1:8). The apostle John boldly proclaims Jesus to be God:

> In the beginning was the Word, and the Word was with God, and the Word was God. He was in the beginning with

God. All things were made through Him, and without Him nothing was made that was made. He was in the world, and the world was made through Him, and the world did not know Him. John 1:1-3, 10.

Please note this awesome claim that the Bible makes for Jesus: He is the origin of all things. Of course, God the Father was involved in creation, but the biblical writers make the bold assertion that Jesus was the One who was intimately involved in the creation of this planet. Only one equal with God could be given the credit for creating something that only the hands of the Infinite God could produce. Jesus is not presented in scripture as just a manifestation of God or a being sent from God. He is fully and equally God in every particular.

This is the astounding claim of the biblical writers, as well as the testimony of the prophets of the Old Testament—that the Christian Jesus is the Creator-God. This Jesus did not first appear as a babe in Bethlehem's manger, but preexisted with God the Father from the very beginning. He was not inactive in this preexistent state but very involved in the creation of the earth. He was also personally involved with His Old Testament people, the Jews. In 1 Corinthians 10:1-4, the apostle Paul even makes the bold claim that Jesus was the One who led Israel out of Egypt and into the Promised Land. Paul declared Jesus to be the One in the pillar of cloud by day and the pillar of fire by night who led the Israelites out of Egypt; He is the One who provided manna in the wilderness and was the Rock who provided the refreshing water in the desert.

When God called Moses at the burning bush to be the one to lead the Israelites out of Egypt under the mighty direction of God, he asked this God who called him to identify Himself by name. The answer came: "'I AM WHO I AM.' And He said, 'Thus you shall say to the children of Israel, 'I AM has sent me to you'" (Exodus 3:14). The God who led Israel out of Egypt was known as the "I AM" God. What an amazing name for God—not the God of the past or future, but the ever-present God.

Jesus, when attacked by the religious leaders of His day, made an astounding statement in John 8:58, 59: "Jesus said to them, 'Most assuredly, I say to you, before Abraham was, I AM.' Then they took up stones to throw at Him."

Hear this amazing claim of Jesus. He proclaimed Himself to be the I AM, the God of the Old Testament, the One who led Israel out of Egypt. To the Jews of that era such a statement was blasphemous, so they were ready to stone Him. Indeed, it would have been blasphemy if it were not true.

Some would attempt to create a difference between the God of the Old Testament and the God of the New Testament, but Jesus makes it clear: He represents the Father. If you know Jesus, you will know the Father, for they are of the same essence. The God of the Old Testament is not a vengeful tyrant and the God of the New Testament the forgiving God—they are both the same God. Yet the claim of Christ is unmistakable: He is God.

Not only was Jesus fully God, but He was also fully human. He looked like any other human being while on earth. God in Christ actually came down to our level in order to reach us where we are. Trying to reveal Himself as a God from the heavens had too many limitations, so He came and lived among us that we might see God in human flesh. That is who Jesus is.

Christians normally speak of the one God as manifested in three persons: Father, Son, and Holy Spirit—or the Trinity, as Christians usually refer to this amazing three in one. It sometimes seems difficult to understand how God could be One and yet be Three.

Of course, this is the mystery of godliness. If God could be fully understood by the finite minds of humans, then He would cease to be God. This biblical God is so far above us that in our human minds we can never fully fathom Him, yet there are some ways we can better understand this unique relationship.

One of them is by considering the human family. The Bible declares, for example, that when a man leaves father and mother and is joined to his bride, the two become one flesh. They are still two people, but they are now one in the fullest sense of the word. Marriage is a reflection of the unity of the Godhead.

Just as husband and wife are two separate people united to form one family, so God the Father, God the Son, and God the Holy Spirit are three separate persons, yet totally united to form the family of the One God. They are unified in character and purpose; therefore, they act as One.

In human experience, we have time manifested as past, present, and future, but still, all is time. Energy takes the form of solids, liquids, and gases, but all is energy. So Jesus sent His disciples forth to make disciples among all nations, baptizing them in the one name of the Father, Son, and Holy Spirit (Matthew 28:19). Even in the great commission, you find the three persons of the Godhead expressed as one.

The Mission of Christ Who is God

The Old Testament not only foretold that the Messiah was to be God living among humans, but even the mission of the Messiah was fully declared 700 years before the advent of Christ occurred. One of the greatest Old Testament Messianic prophecies is found in the fifty-third chapter of Isaiah. Notice some of these astounding predictions:

> He was despised and forsaken of men, a man of sorrows and acquainted with grief; and like one from whom men hide their face, He was despised, and we did not esteem Him. Surely our griefs He Himself bore, and our sorrows He carried; yet we ourselves esteemed him stricken, smitten of God, and afflicted. But He was pierced through for our transgressions, He was crushed for our iniquities; the chastening for our well-being fell upon Him, and by His scourging we are healed. All of us like sheep have gone astray, each of us has turned to his own way; but the Lord has caused the iniquity of us all to fall on Him. Isaiah 53:3-6, NASB.

The Bible never predicted that the Messiah would be coming as an earthly deliverer, as the Jews of the first century expected. The book of Isaiah is very exact on the mission of Christ. He was to come as a sin-deliverer. His purpose was to rescue humankind from the greatest bondage that has ever afflicted the human race: the bondage of sin. Even His rejection by the multitudes is clearly predicted in this passage. Amazingly, the substitutionary death of the Messiah is also clearly foretold in this powerful prophecy—He was "pierced through for our transgression;" God has placed "our iniquities on Him."

The sinless Son of God was to have the sins of humankind placed on Him. He was to die as a substitute, to free humanity of the curse of sin. This remarkable prediction is the foundation of the great truth of the gospel: humans are saved solely by the grace of this loving God, who gave Himself to die in our place. His death on the cross was not for Himself, but for us. We need not pay the penalty of our sins if we accept His substitutionary death.

Isaiah 53:7 continues by predicting that the Messiah would be led like a dumb sheep to the slaughter and would not even open His mouth to defend Himself. Of course, when Jesus stood before Pilate, falsely accused and condemned, the Bible declares that He did not even open His mouth in defense, just as Isaiah had predicted (Matthew 27:11-14). Even Pilate marveled at the full composure of Jesus under what Pilate knew to be false charges.

Isaiah 53:9 declares that the Messiah will make His grave with a rich man. According to the New Testament account, this was accurately fulfilled by the rich man Joseph of Arimathea, who went to Pilate and begged to be given the body of Christ to bury in his own tomb. However, according to the Roman custom of the time, people who died on the cross were such terrible criminals that they were not supposed to be given a decent burial, but instead their bodies were to be thrown out on Gehenna, the rubbish heap at Jerusalem, for the vultures to devour and the flames of the dump to consume. But

Pilate responded to Joseph and granted His request for an exception—to allow Jesus to be buried in the rich man's cave. Pilate's very exception fulfilled Isaiah's amazing prediction 700 years earlier.

Isaiah 53 ends with verse 12 reasserting the importance of Christ's substitutionary death, declaring that He was numbered with the transgressors, bore the sin of many, and thus interceded for transgressors. There can be no doubt that only Jesus fulfilled every specification of this marvelous Old Testament prophecy regarding the mission of the Messiah. If only those living in the first century had taken the time to examine the claims of Christ in view of the prediction of Isaiah 53, they might not have rejected Him when He came.

Prediction of His Death

Isaiah 53 may have predicted the substituionary nature of the Messiah's mission, but other Old Testament passages speak equally of the details concerning His death. For example, Psalm 41:9 predicted that He would be betrayed by one who ate with Him, and Zechariah 11:12 adds that the betrayer would be paid thirty pieces of silver. Any examination of the events leading up to the arrest of Christ makes it clear that Judas, one of the twelve disciples, who indeed ate with Him, was the one who betrayed Him. And for this despicable act, he was paid exactly thirty pieces of silver by the religious leaders, thus creating another remarkable fulfillment of prophecy.

One thousand years before the birth of Christ, the psalmist David predicted the following concerning the death of the Messiah:

> For dogs have surrounded Me; the congregation of the wicked has enclosed Me. They pierced My hands and My feet; I can count all My bones. They look and stare at Me. They divide My garments among them, And for My clothing they cast lots. Psalm 22:16-18.

Imagine, 1,000 years before the birth of Christ, scripture proclaimed the exact manner of His death: crucifixion. Crucifixion was a Roman invention. It did not exist in David's time, yet He accurately describes how Messiah's hands and feet were to be pierced as Jesus was nailed to Calvary's cross. The uplifting of Christ on the cross in all His shame is foretold as they look and stare at Him.

David predicted that not a bone of the Messiah would be broken. His was to be a perfect sacrifice. Yet the Roman soldiers, in attempting to hasten the death of those on the cross, proceeded to break the legs of the two thieves, but when they came to Jesus, they discovered the man in the middle was already dead. So no bone was broken, just as David had predicted (John 19:31-33). Once again, another prophecy was ratified, proving anew that Jesus was the Christ.

Furthermore, David predicted that beneath the cross the soldiers would cast lots for His clothing. John described the scene among the soldiers at the foot of the cross. They took His garments and, rather than tear them up, they indeed cast lots for them, just as David predicted (John 19: 23-25).

The Most Amazing Prophecy

All these prophetic fulfillments boggle the mind. God gave abundant evidence that Jesus was indeed the predicted One who was to come as humankind's Redeemer. The prophetic record unfolds this amazing story of prophecy after prophecy being fulfilled exactly in this Jesus of Nazareth. However, the most amazing of the many Old Testament prophecies of the Messiah is the one given in the prophetic book of Daniel.

Daniel lived between 500 and 600 years before the coming of Christ. He was a young Jewish man taken captive to Babylon by the world ruler, Nebuchadnezzar. Daniel, after passing several tests that we will examine later, eventually became prime minister of the ancient Babylonian empire under Nebuchadnezzar. While a political prisoner, he was actually given a position of political rulership in Babylon. Yet he still longed for the time when his people, the Jews, could return from their captivity in Babylon and once again inhabit Palestine. In this setting God gave Daniel several prophetic visions, which are recorded in the book of Daniel. One of these is the amazing prediction that God gave him of the coming of the Messiah. Notice this prediction:

> Seventy weeks are determined for your people and for your holy city, to finish the transgression, to make an end of sins, to make reconciliation for iniquity, to bring in everlasting righteousness, to seal up vision and prophecy, and to anoint the Most Holy. Know therefore and understand, that from the going forth of the command to restore and build Jerusalem until Messiah the Prince, there shall be seven weeks and sixty-two weeks; the street shall be built again, and the wall, even in troublesome times. And after the sixty-two weeks Messiah shall be cut off, but not for Himself; and the people of the prince who is to come shall destroy the city and the sanctuary. The end of it shall be with a flood, and till the end of the war desolations are determined. Then he shall confirm a covenant with many for one week; but in the middle of the week He shall bring an end to sacrifice and offering. And on the wing of abominations shall be one who makes desolate, even until the consummation, which is determined, is poured out on the desolate. Daniel 9:24-27.

As noted in chapter one, a day in prophecy equals one literal year (Ezekiel 4:6). Seventy weeks (70 x 7) is 490 days, or prophetic years. Here God gave Daniel the assurance that He, a merciful God, had not rejected His people but would give them another chance to return to Palestine, rebuild the city and the temple, and once again attempt to reach the world for God. Yet God tells Daniel that there is a limit of 490 years for them to get their act together. God bears long with His wayward people, but there comes a time when God says enough is enough.

The next verse (Daniel 9:25) grants Daniel the beginning date for this amazing prophecy. It is to commence with the decree to rebuild Jerusalem. There were several such decrees that allowed the Jewish people to return to Israel and rebuild the temple. The most important of these was the decree of Artaxerxes given in the year 457 B.C., one of the clearest dates in ancient history. Thus from 457 B.C. there would be 490 years, ending in A.D. 34, allotted to Daniel's people to come into line and fulfill God's mission for them.

Then the angel Gabriel gave the astonished Daniel the announcement that from this decree (457 B.C.) until Messiah the Prince would come, would be seven weeks, then an additional 62 weeks, or a total of 69 weeks—one week shy of the seventy allotted in the prophecy. The 69 weeks would equal 483 literal days or prophetic years, bringing us to the year A.D. 27 for the coming of this Messiah the Prince.

Note that the prophecy is not about the birth of Messiah, but the coming of the Messiah. *Messiah* is the Hebrew name; the Greek equivalent is *Christ*, and the English is *Anointed One*. Jesus was anointed for His ministry at His baptism. Thus this fascinating prophecy is predicting the very year of the baptism and inauguration of the ministry of Christ. At Christ's baptism, the Holy Spirit came upon Him in the form of a dove, anointing Him for His ministry.

What year was Jesus baptized? Luke 3:1 declares that it was the fifteenth year of the reign of Tiberius Caesar. That year was A.D. 27, the very year predicted through the prophet Daniel. Jesus and only Jesus arrived on time, just as the prophecy had specified. Right after that, Jesus began His ministry with the startling words: "The time is fulfilled" (Mark 1:15). Later on, Paul declared: "But when the fullness of the time came, God sent forth His Son" (Galatians 4:4, NASB). The true Messiah must arrive in A.D. 27. Others who claim to be this One from God arrived either too early or too late. Only Jesus fulfilled this amazing prophecy exactly.

However, the prophecy did not just give us the coming of Christ. Daniel 9:26 goes on to declare that this Messiah is to be cut off, or to die. Then Daniel added the sad note that the people of this prince would ultimately destroy the sanctuary and the city of Jerusalem because of their stubborn rejection of the Messiah when He came. Thus in A.D. 70, Titus invaded Jerusalem. The temple was such a masterpiece of architecture that he gave orders to his soldiers to preserve it. Yet the stubborn resistance of the people forced him ultimately to destroy both the city and the temple forever, thus fulfilling the sad feature of this prophecy.

Verse 27 reiterates the message of the previous verse. Messiah will make a covenant with the people for one more week—the final week of the 70 allotted to Israel. In the middle of the week, 3½ years later, Messiah is to bring an end to the sacrificial system. The ministry of Christ lasted exactly 3½ years. In the spring of A.D. 31, Jesus went to the cross and died. At His death, the curtain in the sacred temple separating the holy and most holy places was torn in two from top to bottom by an unseen hand, indicating the end of the sacrificial system. No longer would animal sacrifices be needed. Jesus, the Lamb of God, had offered the only sacrifice that counts: He gave Himself on the cross for our sins. His death and His death alone had brought an end to the sacrificial system. Jesus had died on time.

What an amazing God! Jesus came on time. He died on time. No one else could fulfill these predictions as Jesus did. That is why Jesus is unquestionably the Messiah of prophecy. There can be no doubt now about His claims. Buddha cannot claim to have met such exact predictions. Only Jesus can; but that's not all. He proved it again by rising from the dead.

This is why Christians can have such hope in this mixed-up world of the twenty-first century. That hope is not based on fantasy. It is based on facts that cannot be controverted. Jesus fulfilled every specification of the Old Testament prophecies of the coming of the Messiah, even to coming and dying on time.

One cannot, therefore, escape the claims of this Christ. Neither Buddhism, Hinduism, Islam, transcendental meditation, yoga, or New Age philosophies can make the claims of Christianity. Christ is alive. Christ is divine. Christ is human. Christ died for us. Christ fulfilled every prediction. He is the Son of God. He *IS* God. You cannot ignore the claims of this Christ. He is real. Why not decide right now to give your life over completely to this Jesus, who will give you a hope that no other religion of the world can offer—hope backed up by One who is God and who rose from the dead? Will you accept Him into your life now?

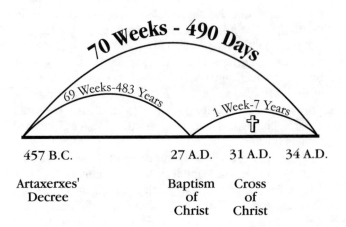

3

Hope in the Midst of Cultic Activity

The twenty-first century seems plagued by cultic activity. Cults and the world of the occult seem to dominate our world today. Innocent individuals at times seem to get caught up in all these cultic movements. Do the prophetic scriptures offer any hope to help us remain true to the Christ of scripture when cultic activity abounds? The answer is a definite Yes. Over the next several chapters, we will begin to explore the prophetic book of Daniel. In it we will find hope, peace, and security, as the prophetic message is unfolded to us. Even when God's people get mixed up with cults, God, through the prophetic scriptures, provides a way out.

One of the most disastrous cults to hit the American continent was that of the Branch Davidians in Waco, Texas, in the decade of the 1990s. David Koresh, the cultic leader, believed himself to be a second Messiah, sent to earth because the first Messiah, Jesus, failed in His mission by not sinning. So God had sent David to experience sin, so that God would know what sin was like.

Under this unbelievable theology, Koresh countenanced all kinds of immorality.

Time magazine reported, "He began to teach that all the women in the world belonged to him and only he had the right to procreate" (March 15, 1993). He then declared that all marriages in his cultic compound were null and void and that if a man had sex with his wife, he would be committing adultery. Only Koresh was allowed to have sex, and he could have it freely, even with young girls barely in their teens.

Amazingly, men willingly turned their wives over to him. To an outsider, his beliefs seemed so far-fetched one can only wonder about the sanity of the people who followed him.

Yet these followers were not ignorant people. One of them even had a law degree from Harvard University. The second in command at Waco, James Schneider, had a theology degree from the University of Hawaii. These were college graduates— intelligent people. Even Jim Jones, the cultic despot of the 70s, had medical doctors and other educated people who committed suicide with him in Guyana. Evidently, education is no safeguard from the dominion of the cults.

Many individuals feel immune from cult involvement simply because they are too highly educated to get mixed up in them, but history proves that educated people are at times especially vulnerable to the kingdom of the cults.

How did Koresh gain such control over the minds of these people? *Time* magazine reported that he rationed food, deprived newcomers of their bank accounts and possessions, and created an "us" versus "them" mentality with the outside world by making people listen to endless hours of his preaching.

Finally, he claimed that he alone understood and could interpret the Bible, yet he kept changing his interpretation. He would forbid his people to eat a certain food one week, and then the next week it would be all right to eat it, but something else was forbidden.

These changing restrictions were designed to teach people to obey Koresh absolutely. There was no reason for these restrictions other than to develop total control over the minds of his followers.

What Is a Cult?

There are certain common characteristics found in most cults. Cults are hard to identify simply because the word has been so misused. For example, any group that might seem strange, different, or unusual may be labeled as a cult. Since the word carries such a stigma, just calling a group a cult causes many people to turn away. We must be careful not to label something a cult just because it is new or different. However, there are some common characteristics found in most cultic groups. Here are three such characteristics.

First, one strong, charismatic leader, who demands absolute obedience to his authority, usually dominates cults. No one can question the leader. This person is seen as almost incapable of error. Second, cults usually try to limit or control people's contact with the outside world. In extreme cases, like that of Koresh, followers move to the cult headquarters and are not allowed to leave. In Koresh's case, he took control of all bank accounts, so that his people could not leave.

In other cases, cults threaten physical harm if a member leaves. In less extreme cases, the cult leader will simply tell people not to read any religious material except that which emanates from the cult and not to listen to any other religious leader. Third, many cults major in prophetic interpretation and create very bizarre explanations. They usually end up setting dates for the end of the world.

Cults are not limited to the religious realm, nor are they new on the human scene. Cults have been actively at work from ancient times. Then, people were actually forced into cults, whereas today people seem to enter them voluntarily, not initially realizing what they are getting into, only to discover too late that they have entered the dominion of the cults.

How to Avoid Joining a Cult

Strange as it may seem, the best way to avoid joining one of these end-of-the-world cults is to understand the prophetic scriptures. Since so many of these modern cults are dealing with prophecy, it is imperative today that people understand the prophetic voice of the scriptures. Since most people are grossly ignorant in this area, they end up believing the cults because they have not been exposed to any other interpretation of prophecy.

Biblical prophecy does not attempt to give us all the details of the future. Instead, biblical prophecy portrays the grand outline of events. It gives the general direction of world events as they affect the covenant people but does not attempt to provide us with all the intricate details. Many people wish to know more than what God has revealed in the Bible, so they end up listening to the cults. These cults offer to give more information than the Bible reveals. If one is not satisfied with what God has safely revealed to us about the future, one can easily be drawn into the dominion of the cults.

We can learn how to deal with present-day cultic activity by examining the story of Daniel, the ancient biblical prophet, who was forced to become a part of the cultic activity of ancient Babylon. He did not willingly choose to enter the Babylonian cult, yet even when being forced to conform, Daniel revealed ways that God's people can avoid having their minds controlled by a cultic leader.

Daniel and the Cult of Babylon

The book of Daniel opens with Daniel as a young lad between 16 and 18 years of age, being hauled out of his home and taken in captivity to ancient Babylon, a place filled with all kinds of occult activity. Not only did ancient Babylon display all the trappings of a cult, but this cult was also highly involved in the occult spirit world. It was not an easy place for one who had been brought up to serve the Lord Jehovah.

No sooner does Daniel arrive in the Babylonian capital, than his reeducation begins. Nebuchadnezzar, the king and cultic leader, examines the captives and chooses the brightest and the best for reeducation at the cultic university of Babylon. Among those chosen were Daniel and three of his friends (Daniel 1:3, 4). Next, the king attempts to control what they eat by demanding that they must all eat at the table provided by the king himself. At first this seems to be a gracious concession. They were not to eat like slaves but like kings. However, for these Jewish youths, it proved an acid test of how they would live under cultic rule.

Young people brought up in Jewish culture followed certain dietary restrictions, such as not eating pork (Leviticus 11:2-10). Nebuchadnezzar would have no such scruples. Furthermore, Jewish youths were very careful about what they drank. They were familiar with the words of Solomon that said, "Wine is a mocker, strong drink is a brawler, and whoever is led astray by it is not wise." Proverbs 20:1. To try to live for God among the strong cultic attractions of ancient Babylon could not be accomplished if these young men were inebriated most of the time or eating all the king's junk food. Nebuchadnezzar wanted to control their minds, and they would be more controllable under the influence of alcohol. Thus the table of the king proved to be part of the controlling power of the cultic Babylonians.

Daniel 1:6 further indicates that the king sought to give each of these Jewish lads new names to indicate their new allegiance to the gods of Babylon. Thus Daniel's name, meaning, "God is my judge," was changed to *Belteshazzar,* indicating allegiance to the Babylonian god Bel. All of this activity was an attempt to brainwash the young Hebrews into submission to the cult of Babylon.

Such high-pressure tactics demanded an immediate response from Daniel and his friends. If they were to avoid the kingdom of the cults, in their minds, they knew they must remain loyal to God, so they immediately requested an exemption. Such an exemption was unheard of. You don't request an exemption from a cultic leader, especially one who has the power of life and death over you. Yet so strong was their desire to remain loyal to God that the Bible declares that:

> Daniel made up his mind that he would not defile himself with the king's choice food or with the wine which he drank; so he sought permission from the commander of the officials that he might not defile himself. Daniel 1:8, NASB.

What courage! Refusing to eat what the king demanded to be eaten could have resulted in death, but to Daniel, following God and being obedient to Him was more important than life itself.

This verse is one of the key verses in the entire book of Daniel. It is one of the great truths that this book will emphasize as we examine its sacred pages. It is a book pregnant with meaning for the last days of earth's history. God will have a people who love Christ so much that they will not disobey Him even when a government orders them to disobey. They are so appreciative of the fact that Christ has saved them solely by His grace, that they would not dishonor Christ by disobeying Him even in the smallest of issues. Daniel's obedience was not a legalistic obedience. It sprang from a heart in deep relationship with the King of the universe.

The astonishing thing is that Daniel and his friends, requesting the simple Judean diet of vegetables and water, were granted the exception. They were given ten days to prove that they were not diminished for opposing the practices of the cult. At the end of ten days, the Bible reported that they were ten times better than all those who ate the king's junk food. You can't go wrong following God's plan. He always rewards those who are faithful to Him.

Another Test

Daniel and his friends, after surviving this first test, continued to face additional tests. Interestingly, of all the Hebrew youth taken in captivity, the scripture only mentions Daniel and his friends as having not compromised their faith. Later, when major issues of compromise appear, only these four Hebrew youth who passed this simple test on diet in chapter 1 were able to pass the big tests on worshiping the image and praying, in Daniel 3 and 6. There may have been others who did not compromise, but these are the only ones the Bible mentions. Those who are faithful in small tests end up being faithful in the big tests that come.

Daniel 2 opens with Nebuchadnezzar having a dream. When he awakes, he cannot remember it. The dream troubles him, because he knows that it revealed things about the future. Later, we discover that it was the God of heaven who gave Nebuchadnezzar the dream. This is fascinating. The Hebrew God did not limit Himself to the Hebrews. He could have given the dream just to Daniel, but instead He chose to work through this cultic leader, Nebuchadnezzar. Why? Because of the infinite heart of God, who desires all people to be saved and come to a knowledge of Him. The only reason for giving the dream to this heathen monarch was to reach him. Evidently, God even wants to save the cultic leaders and bring them to Him.

No one is beyond the reach of God. We cringe at the existence of despotic rulers who exploit and destroy their people, but this chapter teaches us that God still loves the Adolf Hitlers, the Saddam Husseins, and the Osama bin Ladens of this world and wants to bring them to Him.

The only problem with the dream is that Nebuchadnezzar can't remember it the next morning. Of course, if he could have remembered it, Daniel would never have been called in, and Nebuchadnezzar would not have come in contact with the Giver of the dream: God. This king, however, does not know God, so he calls in his sacred brain trust: the magicians, the astrologers, the sorcerers, and the Chaldeans (Daniel 2:2). These were the trusted advisors to the Babylonian monarch. God is attempting to do something else here. The Babylonians gloried in their wisdom. God is about to discredit the wisdom of Babylon and reveal the superiority of the wisdom of God.

Who composed this brain trust? First were the magicians, who professed ability to interpret the future by the shape of an animal's liver. The astrologers attempted to interpret the future by the placement of the stars in the heavens. The sorcerers foretold the future by consulting the dead, while the Chaldeans attempted to forecast future events by the way numbers fell together. Note that all these advisors were exponents of false prophecy. In this setting of many false prophets and false prophecy, God sends His message on genuine prophecy.

The king orders them to tell him the dream, which they are obviously unable to do, even though they profess to interpret the future. Nebuchadnezzar, in a fit of rage, orders them all to be killed. Just like David Koresh, ordering the fire that killed his followers, so Nebuchadnezzar plays the role of the cultic leader. However, it is not just this brain trust that is ordered to be killed; anyone who had been given education by Babylonian standards is to be executed. That order includes Daniel and his friends.

Quickly, Daniel comes to the rescue, requesting time to pray to His God for the interpretation of the dream. The anxious Nebuchadnezzar decides to hold back the execution one day while Daniel prays. This is just the opening God had prepared for Daniel: Nebuchadnezzar is now reachable for the kingdom of God. So that night as Daniel sleeps, God reveals to him the same dream He had given to Nebuchadnezzar the night before.

The next morning, Daniel immediately makes his way to the palace with the good news that the execution must be halted because God has given him the dream. Can you imagine this: These occult leaders of ancient Babylon's brain trust end up owing their very lives to this prophet from Judea? One would think they would have appreciated him; instead, they were jealous.

Note the purpose of the dream and what it reveals as Daniel gives us the main thrust of this important vision:

> Daniel answered and said: "Blessed be the name of God forever and ever, for wisdom and might are His. And He changes the times and the seasons; He removes kings and raises up kings; He gives wisdom to the wise and knowledge to those who have understanding. He reveals deep and secret things; He knows what is in the darkness, and light dwells with Him. Daniel 2:20-22.

In the midst of all this false prophecy, God gives us the true understanding of prophecy. God is in control of human events. The world is not spinning recklessly out of control. Nothing happens that God has not prepared for. God gives us the assurance that no matter what happens, He has foreseen it all, and He is in control. What a reassuring message to a young man in the midst of captivity in cultic Babylon. Sometimes, people feel that they should avoid studying prophecy because of all the false prophecy in today's world. However, Daniel reminds us that in spite of all the horrific false prophecy of Babylon, God's answer to this cultic activity was to provide biblical prophecy, giving His people the true understanding of the future.

Nebuchadnezzar's Dream

Quickly, Daniel makes his way to the palace and appears before the king with the good news that God has given him the dream. Nebuchadnezzar, sitting on the edge of his seat, is all ears, ready to listen to this prophet of the Jewish God. God now had Nebuchadnezzar's full attention. The message here is not so much about the future as it is about God seeking a lost person to get his attention so that He might reveal Himself to him. What God did for Nebuchadnezzar, He wishes to do for all of us today. How thankful we can be that God searches us out and reveals Himself to us! Note as Daniel gives the king God's dream:

You, O king, were watching; and behold, a great image! This great image, whose splendor was excellent, stood before you; and its form was awesome. This image's head was of fine gold, its chest and arms of silver, its belly and thighs of bronze, its legs of iron, its feet partly of iron and partly of clay. You watched while a stone was cut out without hands, which struck the image on its feet of iron and clay, and broke them in pieces. Then the iron, the clay, the bronze, the silver, and the gold were crushed together, and became like chaff from the summer threshing floors; the wind carried them away so that no trace of them was found. And the stone that struck the image became a great mountain and filled the whole earth. Daniel 2:31-35.

Can you imagine the excitement as Nebuchadnezzar quickly recognizes the description of what he had dreamed the previous night? How impressed he must have been with this Jewish prophet who could reveal the secret things of his head. Note again that Daniel does not take personal credit. Daniel 2:28 reveals that Daniel gives full credit to God for this dream.

Daniel understands that this event was not about the future; it was about reaching Nebuchadnezzar. Even when asked to give the interpretation, Daniel does not interpret but declares, "We will tell the interpretation of it" (verse 36). Another great principle of prophetic interpretation is here given. Let the scripture or God Himself give the interpretation. Human beings are not to be like David Koresh, developing their own interpretation; instead, we are to let the prophecies explain themselves, as God gives us the interpretation.

> You, O king, are a king of kings. For the God of heaven has given you a kingdom, power, strength, and glory; and wherever the children of men dwell, or the beasts of the field and the birds of the heaven, He has given them into your hand, and has made you ruler over them all—you are this head of gold. Daniel 2:37, 38.

What a message! Nebuchadnezzar did not conquer by his ingenuity; God had placed Him on the throne. Kingdoms rise, kingdoms fall, but God is in control. That is the message to this heathen monarch of antiquity. Of course, at first it may have seemed like flattery, to think that God had made Him such a great ruler. However, Daniel is quick to remind him that another kingdom is coming (verse 39). While the kingdom of silver would be inferior to gold, the kingdom that followed Babylon in 539 B.C.—the kingdom of the Medes and the Persians—would be inferior to Babylon. This heathen monarch thought his dynasty would be immortalized forever, but Daniel sends him the opposite message—another kingdom is coming.

In quick succession, verses 39-43 explain the rapid rise and fall of the world's powers for the rest of the world's history. Babylon is followed by the silver kingdom of Media Persia; which in turn would be overrun by Alexander the Great, the Grecian kingdom of brass; only to be followed by the iron monarchy of Rome, the fourth empire.

These are the four great empires that will affect the Jewish people over the next five hundred years. Other ancient empires existed, but since scripture is giving salvation history, only the empires that affect the covenant people are predicted. The Jews were oppressed by Babylon, then by Persia, then by the Greeks, and finally by the Romans, who in turn nailed the Jewish Messiah, Jesus, to the cross.

After the fourth empire, God declares through Daniel that the feet of the image are made of a mixture of iron and clay— elements that do not cling to each other—representing the divisions of the Roman empire (verses 41-43). In A.D. 476, the Roman empire collapsed as a result of the invasion of Germanic tribes from the north that eventually broke the Roman empire into ten divisions. These divisions in turn became the forerunners of the modern nations of Europe. As a result, the European continent has remained divided politically for the last fifteen hundred years.

During these centuries, would-be world conquerors have attempted to unite Europe politically, but every such action has failed. The prophecy declared: "They will mingle with the seed of men; but they will not adhere to one another, just as iron does not mix with clay" (Daniel 2:43). Through conquest, as well as marriage alliances, attempts have been made to unite Europe, but the prophecy has held true to this very day.

Verse 44 gives us the climax. There is one more kingdom coming—God's kingdom. In the days of divided Europe, the end time, God Himself will establish a kingdom. It will not be a takeover of earthly kingdoms. Daniel declares that the kingdom of the stone smashes the image, grinds it to powder, and the wind blows it all away. Then the stone becomes the great mountain that fills the whole earth. Thus God's kingdom will last forever.

In just a few short verses, Daniel has given us the entire history of the world: four great empires, followed by a divided Europe, and ultimately the establishment of the kingdom of God at the second coming of Christ. This is the big picture. This is the direction the world is headed. These are the big events. We are living today in the toes of the image. The next big event is the establishment of the kingdom of the stone. We need not fear the future, because we know where the future is going. God is in control. God is in charge.

This great prophecy was not given merely to show us the history of the world. It was recorded in scripture so we could know that God knows where the world is headed and that He is in control. It was given to Nebuchadnezzar to let him know that God, not Nebuchadnezzar, is in control of the world, and this God who controls the world wishes to establish a relationship with us, His creation. Even in these prophecies, we see this great God who desires a relationship with His people.

Daniel 2 is the first of four great prophecies found in the book of Daniel. They are in chapters 2, 7, 8, 9, and 10 through 12. Daniel 2 lays the foundation that all future prophecies will build on. Each succeeding prophecy will go over this same sequence of empires, but each one will add new details, completing for us a broader look at the world's future. The area that will be expanded to the fullest extent is the area near the time of the end. The prophecy of Daniel 2 is called an "outline prophecy" because it outlines the big picture of human history upon which the other prophecies will repeat and expand. They will use different symbols, but the meaning will be the same.

Prophecy and the Cults

Many modern cults are majoring in prophecies about the time of the end.

God's people cannot be ignorant of Bible prophecies. In the midst of all this false prophecy in ancient Babylon, God gave the true understanding of prophecy. So today, in spite of all the false prophecy offered up by the cults, we must study biblical prophecy and see the big picture as God gave it. Thus we will not be deceived by the cultic activity of the twenty-first century.

How does one avoid joining a cult today? Three simple precautions will help people avoid the kingdom of the cults today. Daniel may not have had a choice, but we do. Therefore make certain that you follow these simple guidelines to avoid the cults that seek to conquer you today.

First, study the Bible yourself. Don't take any preacher's word for it. Check him out. Look up texts that are quoted to make certain that the texts say what the preacher declares them to say. God gave you a mind. Don't subject yourself to just one or two preachers. Study the Bible yourself. Some people get spiritual food only by listening to preachers; they fail to study the Bible on their own. Such become wide open for deception. Preachers usually don't intentionally deceive, but they must be tested by the Word of God. If the preacher declares something to be true, and the Bible indicates the opposite is true, then you must obey scripture. Even if many preachers agree on an issue, that doesn't make it right. The only thing we can trust is the Word of the living God. Check it out. Be a real Bible student, and know the Bible for yourself. That is the best safeguard available against deception.

Second, be leery of any group that forbids contact outside of the group. For example, if you find yourself in a group where you are told to listen only to preachers belonging to that group or to read only literature produced by that group, be careful—you may be entering the dominion of the cults. Cults wish to control what goes into your mind. They are fearful that if you get exposed to ideas contrary to the cult, you might leave. To prevent that, they seek to control your mind. Remember, God gave you a mind. He expects you to use it. So don't limit your reading to literature from only one group. Read opposite opinions, and then make a decision based on what you believe the Bible is saying. At times, put aside all literature written by uninspired people. Take just your Bible, and read it for yourself. Make certain you have a devotional time with just the Bible and no other literature. Then you will know what the Bible says without being influenced by other people.

Third, be wary of any group that is currently predicting a time for the end of the world. The Bible indicates that no one knows the day or the hour of Christ's return (Matthew 24:36). While we cannot know the exact time of His return, we can know that it is near. The cults attempt to go beyond the nearness of His return and give you exact timetables. Anyone who does so is in violation of the words of Jesus, who declared that no one knows the time.

The danger of cults is all around us today. The Bible even warns us about these wolves in sheep's clothing that are bent on our destruction or are in it for the love of money. Never rest easy, for many will be deceived. Jesus even indicated that deceptions in the last days will be so great that they will deceive the very elect of God, if that were possible (Matthew 24:24). You are not immune.

In 2 Corinthians 11:13-15, the Bible indicates that Satan will come as an angel of light to deceive us. We are in warfare—a cosmic conflict between the forces of good and evil. This conflict is far more serious than any cosmic struggle created by "Star Wars." It is the greatest drama of the ages—the great controversy between Christ and Satan that has been going on for the last six thousand years on this planet.

Satan never approaches us professing to have evil to give us. In 2 Corinthians 11, scripture declares that he claims to be giving us truth. No preacher or cultic leader is ever going to tell you he is giving you error. That is why you must test everything by the unerring standard of the Bible. That, and that only, is your line of defense in these deceptive times in which we currently live. Note the implements of warfare that the Christian is to stockpile in anticipation of the deceptions of the last days:

> Stand therefore, having girded your waist with truth, having put on the breastplate of righteousness, and having shod your feet with the preparation of the gospel of peace; above all, taking the shield of faith with which you will be able to quench all the fiery darts of the wicked one. And take the helmet of salvation, and the sword of the Spirit, which is the word of God. Ephesians 6:14-17.

David Koresh had it all wrong. The armaments that we are to stockpile are not guns and ammunition, but the spiritual values of the gospel, truth, and the Word of God. Get deep into God's Word, and you will be safe against the powers of darkness that will seek to deceive you in these last days.

The only way you can make it in these final deceptive times is to have a deep personal relationship with Jesus Christ. He is the One we talked about in chapter 2. He is the One who desires to really get to know us. He is the One we must spend time getting to know if we want to be secure in the last days. This means we must spend quality time with Him and with His Word. Make certain you really know God and Jesus. Deception is in the very air we breathe today, but the greatest deception to hit the planet is not a David Koresh or a Jim Jones. The greatest deception is yet to come, and it is fully unmasked in the prophecies of Daniel and Revelation that we will explore together. Don't be deceived. Know God, know the Bible, and spend quality time in a personal relationship with Jesus. That is the best defense against the wiles of the evil one.

4

Hope in Difficult Times

I t is never easy to serve God. Life is full of trials and tests that sometimes exhaust us as we seek to find meaning amidst life's tumultuous storms. Modern life seems to offer us more frustration than that experienced by previous generations. Yet throughout the ages, humankind has always struggled with the complexities of living. Difficult times come even for those who seek to follow Christ.

It would have been wonderful if all my problems disappeared when I became a Christian, but that is not reality. If it were, then people would become Christians for the wrong reasons. The Christian life does not provide an end to the conflicts of this life, but it does provide safety amid the storms of life. God has not always promised us smooth sailing, but He has assured us a safe arrival.

When one examines the history of the people of God, one quickly discovers that those who served God endured multitudinous trials and tribulations. Life for many was one constant struggle, during which some gave their lives as a consequence of standing firm for God. God does not always deliver us from our problems. He does, however, assure us that He will go through these problems with us.

The book of Daniel is divided into two parts: the historical and the prophetic sections. There are four major prophecies in the prophetic section (chapters 2, 7, 8, 9, and 10 through 12). The rest of the book, the historical section, contains stories of Daniel and his friends in Babylon. Many who seek to understand the prophecies of Daniel jump over the stories and attempt to interpret the prophecies alone. However, the stories are not independent of the prophecies. Rather, the stories illustrate through real life in ancient Babylon the issues that God's people will face as foretold in the prophecies.

Daniel 7 may talk about the little horn that seeks to dominate and destroy the people of God, but the stories of Daniel illustrate that Nebuchadnezzar's Babylon was seeking to do the same thing to God's people in ancient Babylon. Thus, the stories illustrate what the prophecies are foretelling. A correct interpretation of the prophecies is impossible unless one understands this relationship of the stories to the prophecies. Remember that the book of Daniel is a whole. It was written as one book and must be interpreted as one book.

Not only do the stories illustrate Daniel's prophecies; they also illustrate Revelation's prophecies. Most of the symbols in the book of Revelation are drawn from these stories in the book of Daniel. In this chapter we will notice in particular the relationship between Revelation 13 and its call to worship the image of the beast in the last days; and Daniel 3, where Shadrach, Meshach, and Abednego also are forced to worship the image Nebuchadnezzar set up. One cannot understand either the worship of the beast or the mark of the beast in Revelation 13 without fully understanding their relationship to Daniel 3.

The tests that came to God's people in ancient Babylon will be repeated in the last generation as the world is commanded to bow down to the image of the beast. The only ones who stood firm in ancient Babylon were those who had continued to maintain their deep, abiding, relationship with God. Likewise, only those who have developed such a deep relationship with Jesus will be able to remain faithful in the final crisis of the ages. The methods Daniel and his friends used to cope with their difficult times can help God's people today deal with the difficult days coming to earth's final generation. The record of the three friends of Daniel coping with the crisis of their day will help us deal with the crisis soon to come to Planet Earth. It will provide us, as it did them, with hope in the midst of crisis.

The Call to Worship the Image

Daniel 2 concluded with Nebuchadnezzar acknowledging the biblical God of the Jews as the only true God. He had been fascinated by the image that the Hebrew God had shown him in vision. At first, he seems humbled by this vision and the thought that other kingdoms would eventually conquer his kingdom. However, this humility is short-lived. It isn't long before Nebuchadnezzar is making plans to ensure that his kingdom will last forever.

The symbol of the endurance of Babylon was to make the image all of gold, instead of just the head. Obviously, when you change the symbol, you change the meaning. Sometimes people feel they can change just a little bit of what God has revealed, as long as it is a small point, but there are no minimum points with God. Even changing such a small thing as the head of gold to the image of gold implied a direct defiance of the revelation of God.

Whenever one falls from the worship of God, the result is nearly always self-worship. This was Nebuchadnezzar's problem. At first, he had worshiped Daniel's God, but his religion was only a "head" acknowledgement, not a heart wholly committed to God. The inevitable result was to start worshiping the creature rather than the Creator.

In all this, we continue to see the patience of God. After having been given the astonishing vision of Daniel 2, Nebuchadnezzar should have been obedient to God, but like so many today, he soon slipped away from his experience with God. This seems to be the natural state of humanity. People come to Christ, they are faithful to Him, but then some seem to slip away from God and Christ and lose their way, just as Nebuchadnezzar did.

However, God does not forsake Nebuchadnezzar. He goes after him even when he is living in defiance of God by erecting this enormous statue to worship. God is about to give him one of the greatest revelations of God in the entire Old Testament. Catch this picture of God. He does not give up on us. We can't go so far into sin that God cannot and will not find us. No matter how far away from God we may stray, He still goes after us. He is a seeking God, ever attempting to find that which is lost and bring it home. Nowhere is this more demonstrated than in the third chapter of Daniel.

The Image Is Set Up

Nebuchadnezzar the king made an image of gold, whose height was sixty cubits and its width six cubits. He set it up in the plain of Dura, in the province of Babylon. And King Nebuchadnezzar sent word to gather together the satraps, the administrators, the governors, the counselors, the treasurers, the judges, the magistrates, and all the officials of the provinces, to come to the dedication of the image which King Nebuchadnezzar had set up. So the satraps, the administrators, the governors, the counselors, the treasurers, the judges, the magistrates, and all the officials of the provinces gathered together for the dedication of the image that King Nebuchadnezzar had set up; and they stood before the image that Nebuchadnezzar had set up. Daniel 3:1-3.

This enormous image was ninety feet high and nine feet wide. It must have been an imposing sight when it was erected on the flat plain with no other object to obscure the view. People from all over the world were commanded to be present for this dedication. There had been a rebellion in Nebuchadnezzar's empire, according to archeological records. In order to create loyalty to the king, rulers from all over the world were invited to Babylon for a loyalty ceremony. Daniel 3 is probably the only record of what occurred in this particular ceremony.

One wonders how many other Jews were present for this ceremony. The Bible only mentions three—the ones who remained loyal to God. No one knows where Daniel was. He evidently wasn't there for the ceremony. Probably his loyalty was not questioned, since he was serving as prime minister for

Nebuchadnezzar at the time. However, there is some indication that the king of Judah, who was still reigning at this time, made a trip to Babylon. No reason is given, but one can only surmise that the king may have been in the crowd that had been commanded to bow down. Evidently he must have bent the knee, for he is not mentioned as being thrown into the furnace. One can only imagine the pressure that the king's presence must have placed upon the three Hebrews. If the king bows down, why don't you? Yet they decided to follow God even if the king did not.

The Command to False Worship

Then a herald cried aloud: "To you it is commanded, O peoples, nations, and languages, that at the time you hear the sound of the horn, flute, harp, lyre, and psaltery, in symphony with all kinds of music, you shall fall down and worship the gold image that King Nebuchadnezzar has set up; and whoever does not fall down and worship shall be cast immediately into the midst of a burning fiery furnace." So at that time, when all the people heard the sound of the horn, flute, harp, and lyre, in symphony with all kinds of music, all the people, nations, and languages fell down and worshiped the gold image which King Nebuchadnezzar had set up. Daniel 3:4-7.

Here was a test of loyalty to the king, required of all citizens of the empire. There were five aspects to this decree mentioned in the text:

1. A powerful world leader compelled people to worship.

2. The basic issue facing God's people was obedience to human law (the law of the king) or to God's law (the Ten Commandments, which forbad God's people to worship images).

3. It was a universal decree, binding on people from every nation on the planet.

4. To enforce the decree, the state united with the religious power of ancient Babylon.

5. The penalty for refusing to worship the image was death.

Later on in this chapter, we will discover that these same five aspects of the decree in ancient Babylon are repeated in the final decree given to worship the image of the beast in Revelation 13. Remember, Revelation cannot be understood without understanding Daniel.

The Hebrews Refuse to Worship the Image

Therefore at that time certain Chaldeans came forward and accused the Jews. They spoke and said to King Nebuchadnezzar, "O king, live forever! You, O king, have made a decree that everyone who hears the sound of the horn, flute, harp, lyre, and psaltery, in symphony with all kinds of music, shall fall down and worship the gold image; and whoever does not fall down and worship shall be cast into the midst of a burning fiery furnace. There are certain Jews whom you have set over the affairs of the province of Babylon: Shadrach, Meshach, and Abed-Nego; these men, O king, have not paid due regard to you. They do not serve your gods or worship the gold image which you have set up." Daniel 3:8-12.

Imagine the pressure brought on these young men to compromise their faith and bow down. It must have been difficult to stand alone when the whole world bowed down and worshiped the image. It is so easy to go with the flow and keep pace with the majority. Yet the majority is often wrong. One cannot decide matters of faith based on majority opinion. Worshiping God is not by majority vote.

Here in this chapter, the two major issues of the book of Daniel—worship and obedience—come together. Now the three Hebrews are commanded to worship falsely, but to do so would put them in opposition to the commandments of God and render them disobedient to God. Obviously, God is the higher authority. This is much easier to recognize with words than with actions, when the result of obeying God is death. However, in matters of faith, we must obey God rather than any human being. No human being has authority to legislate contrary to the Word of God. While Christians should be honest and obedient citizens, if the laws of the state are in conflict with the law of God, the Christian must always choose God's law over state legislation.

Some may have even suggested that the three young men merely bow down, but not worship the image. However, everyone would have noticed and thought they had worshiped the image. They determined that their ultimate loyalty could never be compromised, so when the music sounded, they stood tall for God. Those who obey like this in times of crisis will always stand out from the crowd, but that will not bother them, for they know where their ultimate loyalty lies.

People were watching these three young men who knew about their loyalty to God, and now they wanted to see how the Hebrews would stand up under the threat of death. Would they compromise? The record is clear: no compromising with the three Hebrews. The ones in charge of watching that section quickly made their way to the king with the news that the Hebrews had refused to bow down. Immediately, the king summoned them to appear before him and answer for their disloyalty.

The Appearance Before the King

Then Nebuchadnezzar, in rage and fury, gave the command to bring Shadrach, Meshach, and Abed-Nego. So they brought these men before the king. Nebuchadnezzar spoke, saying to them, "Is it true, Shadrach, Meshach, and Abed-

Nego, that you do not serve my gods or worship the gold image which I have set up? Now if you are ready at the time you hear the sound of the horn, flute, harp, lyre, and psaltery, in symphony with all kinds of music, and you fall down and worship the image which I have made, good! But if you do not worship, you shall be cast immediately into the midst of a burning fiery furnace. And who is the god who will deliver you from my hands?" Daniel 3:13-15.

Imagine that—Nebuchadnezzar actually gave them a second chance. Evidently he believed in fair play. He wanted to see for himself if they would refuse to obey. He was not willing to put people to death just on the word of informers. He had to see their disobedience in action. Maybe he even thought they didn't understand the consequences, so he repeated it, just in case it got lost in the translation.

Nebuchadnezzar does not understand why they refuse to obey. He knows they are Hebrews, and this image is like the one that the Hebrew God gave him. He had only changed it a little bit—why wouldn't they bow down? To Nebuchadnezzar, it was such a small matter of compromise. Certainly their God would understand why they did it when their lives were at stake. Certainly God is not that particular. Nebuchadnezzar did not realize that there are no small issues with God. Sin is sin, whether we think it is a big one or a little one. To compromise on one small point ultimately will lead to compromise on much larger issues. He who is faithful in that which is least will be faithful in the big issues of life.

Remember, this story illustrates what God's last-day people will face. They too will be asked to compromise their faith in an area that many feel is a small thing. But like the three Hebrews, they will not compromise on any point that is in disobedience to God. Loyalty to God in the small things is what causes you to be loyal in the larger issues.

Interestingly, the only ones who remained true in this test on worship—which is a big issue for Christians—are those who remained loyal on the "smaller" issue of what they ate, as recorded in chapter 1. That is why Christians must never compromise their faith on small things if they want to be obedient on the larger issues.

These faithful Hebrews did not need Nebuchadnezzar's second chance. They had already counted the cost and made their decision. All the threats of Nebuchadnezzar to yield could not command their attention. They did not need to hear the music again. The decision was already made before they ever came to the plain of Dura.

The Response of the Three Hebrews

Shadrach, Meshach, and Abed-Nego answered and said to the king, "O Nebuchadnezzar, we have no need to answer you in this matter. If that is the case, our God whom we serve is able to deliver us from the burning fiery furnace, and He will deliver us from your hand, O king. But if not, let it be known to you, O king, that we do not serve your gods, nor will we worship the gold image which you have set up." Daniel 4:16-18.

These three verses are probably the highest level of faith expressed in the entire Old Testament. These words sprang forth from those who had entered into a very deep relationship with their God. They are the expressions of a mature faith. This passage is the center of the entire message of the book of Daniel. It is a message expressing total trust and confidence in the God they served.

They knew that they served a God who was able to deliver them from Nebuchadnezzar's burning furnace, but they did not serve Him in hopes of deliverance. Whether God delivered or not was a separate issue from whether they would obey Him or not.

What deep faith is here expressed! They had absolute confidence in the power of their God to deliver them from Nebuchadnezzar's hand. They simply did not know whether or not He would exercise that power.

Whether God delivered or not was irrelevant. Their confidence and trust in their God did not depend on their deliverance. God knew what was best, and they trusted Him. This indeed is the height of Old Testament faith. What happened to them was not crucial, but it was crucial that each of them took a stand for God.

Some people today agree to serve God if God first works out all things in their lives. For example, a young man is working in an adult bookstore. He comes under conviction that he should serve God and recognizes that his present occupation is not conducive to spiritual growth. So he makes a decision to serve God, *if* God can work it out to find him a new job. That is not biblical faith. Now, sometimes God honors embryonic faith like this, but God wants us to serve Him regardless of the consequences.

With a mature faith, the young man would quit his job, whether God found him another job or not. Following Jesus does not depend on God working everything out. When one studies the history of God's people, one quickly discovers that many times God does not work things out, but He is honored by His people who serve Him anyway.

In the final crisis that is coming on the planet, God's people will again be asked to follow Christ unquestionably. God will not need to work out every detail before they obey. When they see what God says, those who have a deep relationship with Jesus will immediately step out and follow Him, regardless of the consequences. They will not bring dishonor upon the name of God by waiting to obey. If God says it, that is all that is needed—they will follow and obey.

The Mighty Deliverance

Then Nebuchadnezzar was full of fury, and the expression on his face changed toward Shadrach, Meshach, and Abed-Nego. He spoke and commanded that they heat the furnace seven times more than it was usually heated. And he commanded certain mighty men of valor who were in his army to bind Shadrach, Meshach, and Abed-Nego, and cast them into the burning fiery furnace. Then these men were bound in their coats, their trousers, their turbans, and their other garments, and were cast into the midst of the burning fiery furnace. Therefore, because the king's command was urgent, and the furnace exceedingly hot, the flame of the fire killed those men who took up Shadrach, Meshach, and Abed-Nego. And these three men, Shadrach, Meshach, and Abed-Nego, fell down bound into the midst of the burning fiery furnace. Then King Nebuchadnezzar was astonished; and he rose in haste and spoke, saying to his counselors, "Did we not cast three men bound into the midst of the fire?" They answered and said to the king, "True, O king." "Look!" he answered, "I see four men loose, walking in the midst of the fire; and they are not hurt, and the form of the fourth is like the Son of God." Daniel 3:19-25.

The deliverance of the Hebrews is a spectacular event, yet it almost seems anticlimatic. The height of the chapter was reached with their decision. Their answer was not predicated upon their deliverance, so even if they had been slain, they would have given a powerful witness for God, just as many martyrs of the past have done. But in this case, God chose to bring spectacular deliverance to His people.

The three Hebrews are tied up and thrown into the fire. The soldiers who threw them in are slain by the heat of the furnace. No one could claim the fire was not hot enough. No sooner do they get into the fire than Nebuchadnezzar jumps up and with an astonished look cries out that the ones who have been thrown in bound are now loose and walking amid the flames. The only thing the fire consumes is the rope that binds them. The fire frees them.

With his bewildered eyes, Nebuchadnezzar notices not three men in the furnace, but four, and the fourth he declares to be like the "Son of God." The Bible does not say exactly who the fourth was, but it certainly was a divine figure. Whether it was the actual preincarnate Son of God, Jesus Christ, or His angel, is really not significant. The important point is that God went into the fire with them.

The truth pouring forth from Daniel 3 is not that God always delivers. He doesn't. Yet we still should serve Him. He may not miraculously deliver us from times of trouble, but He goes through the trial with us. That is why many Christians being burned at the stake could die singing praises to their God, even though they were not delivered, because they knew and felt the presence of the unseen God with them in the midst of their troubles.

In the same way today, Christians don't always have all their problems worked out. The Christian does not have fewer problems than the non-Christian. The difference is that Christians know God is carrying them through the trial. If God be for us, then who can be against us?

Likewise, in earth's final conflict, the people of God will not be spared the final time of trouble. They, like the three Hebrews, will not know whether God will deliver them or not, yet they still will serve Him. They still will go through the trial, trusting God and knowing that He will go through it with them. Yet, like the three young men, in the midst of that final great tribulation, God's people will be delivered. They are not delivered before tribulation, but in the midst of it.

> At that time Michael shall stand up, the great prince who stands watch over the sons of your people; and there shall be a time of trouble, such as never was since there was a nation, even to that time. And at that time your people shall be delivered, every one who is found written in the book. Daniel 12:1.

So God's last-day people will be delivered in the midst of earth's final conflict. They will not be delivered from it, but will be rescued in the midst of it. In the rescue of the three Hebrews, we catch another glimpse of God. He is a God who comes close to people. He goes through trouble with them and delivers them.

Another question confronts us in this story. Why did God allow them to go into the fire? He could have delivered them from it. Why did the Son of God appear in the midst of the flames? Was it to assure the Hebrews that God was with them? I doubt it. They already knew He was there; they did not need further outward assurances of God's presence. Why then the appearance? It was for the sake of Nebuchadnezzar. Here again we see God making another attempt to win Nebuchadnezzar to Himself. How patient God is! He never gives up on us. God still wants to reach those who seemingly defile Him the most, in order to bring them to Him.

God will do whatever it takes to reach people. This is one of the greatest revelations of the Old Testament, and here again we see it displayed on behalf of a heathen king. God never gives up on people, and neither should we. Sometimes God has to let us get to the very bottom of rebellion, but down there in the gutter, God comes, ready to pick us up and restore us to wholeness again. Don't miss this exciting picture of the character of God—the God who never gives up on any of us. If He did this to reach Nebuchadnezzar, He will do it for you as well. Remember, you can never go so far from God that He cannot and will not find you. Will you hear His voice? You have never done anything for which God cannot forgive you. Will you let Him?

Revelation 13 and the Image

Revelation 13 pictures a time when the whole world will be invited to worship the image of the beast. No one will be able to buy or sell without the mark of the beast. It will be as unpopular then to refuse the mark of the beast, as was the refusal of the three Hebrews to bow down. The important point then will be the same as the three Hebrews faced. It will not be a question of whether or not God will deliver. The real question will be whether or not each of us will take our stand for Christ and His truth regardless of whether we live or die.

Only a few will refuse to worship the image of the beast.

God's people may feel all alone in this crisis hour. They may feel that everyone has forsaken them, just as the three Hebrews probably felt when they arrived on the plains of Dura. These last-day Christians may even see several of their fellow Christians compromise, just as the three Hebrews probably saw fellow Jews and the King of Judah bow down to the image. The faithful will receive ridicule and scorn, as the three Hebrews did, but they will not yield their faith or compromise on any point. Finally, the death decree will be passed, even as in Babylon, but still they will not yield their faith. They will not be concerned as to whether they live or die. Their concern will be the honor of their God. They would not bring dishonor on His name by compromising their faith.

God's people in this hour must express their total faith in God's plan, not knowing whether they will live or die. They will make the same decision the three Hebrews did in Daniel 3:17, 18. No power on earth can force them to yield their conscience. Their deliverance is not their major concern. They know that they serve a God who can deliver, but they have left that decision in the hands of God.

Just as God stepped in to supernaturally deliver His people out of the fiery furnace, so He will supernaturally step in during this final time of trouble and deliver His people from the death decree that has been passed when the command is given to worship the image of the beast (Revelation 14:14).

Just as the Son of God walked with the three Hebrews in the fiery furnace, so God's faithful people will have the assurance that God will walk with them through this final time of trouble. As a result of their faithful witness at this time, the whole world will be brought to a final decision for God, just as the fiery furnace brought Nebuchadnezzar to a knowledge of the true God in ancient Babylon. Remember, God's ultimate purpose is to bring all who will come, to faith in Him; and He will do so through the presence of God with His people in the midst of earth's final struggle.

The issues in the final conflict will revolve around our worship of God. Note that the three Hebrews had to choose between worshiping the Creator and worshiping the image. But the issue was clearly worship. So in Revelation 13, the same issue appears. Revelation 13:12 warns against worshiping the beast, but those who resist are those who respond to the first angel's message and worship the Creator (Revelation 14:7). The issues of the final conflict revolve around who we will worship—the beast, or the Creator? The whole world will be divided into two camps based on who is worshiped.

The only ones who are able to worship the Creator instead of the beast in this final crisis are those who have a deep personal relationship with Jesus. Our concern today must be to build this deep relationship so we can make our decision for Christ in the final crisis and not end up worshiping the image of the beast.

The question that must concern us today is our faithfulness to God in that hour. Can we make that solid decision right now to follow God and Jesus Christ regardless of what family and friends may say? If we can't decide to follow Him now when it is relatively easy to follow Christ, how can we ever expect to decide when the whole world follows the beast in opposition to the truth of the Word of God?

Remember, the question is not whether God will work everything out so that life will return to normal. God can do that. The real question is whether we will serve Him no matter what happens. By developing a deep relationship with Jesus, we can be prepared to serve Him faithfully.

5

The Basis of Hope

God is incredibly patient. He has virtually pulled out all the stops in order to bring Nebuchadnezzar to a knowledge of who He truly is. Despite the revelations which God has given to this king—the prophetic dream of Daniel chapter 2 and the fiery furnace revelation of the Son of God—Nebuchadnezzar does not acknowledge Daniel's God as the true God. Nebuchadnezzar still wants to be first—even above God.

It would have been quite understandable had God given up on this rebellious king long before the events of chapter 4. Notice, though, the patience and longsuffering of the biblical God. Even though Nebuchadnezzar persists in living for himself, and even though he does not serve God after the Lord's repeated attempts to reveal Himself to this heathen king, God does not stop trying. God's patience toward this ancient monarch can assure each one of us today of His patience with us. He does not give up on us easily.

However, there comes a time when God says enough is enough. This will be discussed in the next chapter.

The Christian's hope is founded upon the patience of God and His great passion that all people come to accept Him. Chapter 4 of Daniel's prophetic book reveals God's third attempt to reach to the very core of Nebuchadnezzar's heart and bring Him to an acceptance of the biblical God. Sometimes God has to let people get all the way down into the gutter of society, just as He did with Nebuchadnezzar. Yet God never allows us to go the gutter alone; He goes there with us.

Daniel 4 tells the story of the haughty monarch boasting about the great city of Babylon that he had built. Nebuchadnezzar is displaying the very essence of sin—pride. It is more than mere pride, however, it is a boastful pride that takes full credit for all that had been accomplished. It is a pride that leaves God completely out of the picture. Yet before pronouncing judgment, God warns of what will happen if the king fails to acknowledge his Creator as the source of everything.

Imagine this: God gives him another dream. Again, Nebuchadnezzar calls in the Babylonian wise men—the brain trust. Here is the second discrediting of humanism as the source of truth. This time, he can remember the dream, but he can't interpret it.

Neither are all the wise men able to interpret the dream. In chapter 2 they had proclaimed that if he would tell them the dream, they would give the interpretation. Now he tells them the dream, but there is still no interpretation from human sources.

Quickly, Daniel comes to the rescue. The dream gives the king God's final warning message for him. If he would not acknowledge God after all that God had done to reveal Himself to him, Nebuchadnezzar would become insane for seven years, living with the wild beasts and eating grass. Get the picture of God again. He called Nebuchadnezzar through two positive experiences. The first was the dream of the image predicting the future and revealing that God controlled the future. Second, as Nebuchadnezzar erected the golden image representing his kingdom as the one that controlled the world, God did not denounce him. Instead, God gave Nebuchadnezzar a revelation of Himself amidst the flames of persecution.

These were positive approaches which did not denounce Nebuchadnezzar. God usually first calls us positively, and, if we don't respond, He will finally appeal to us through threats of the consequences of our actions. The heathen king is now having revealed to him the ultimate consequences of his failure to allow God to rule his life. At first Nebuchadnezzar appears to heed the counsel of Daniel, but then the haughty king gives in to the temptation of pride. One year later, he is back to his boasting. And the consequences fall—he becomes like a wild animal, eating grass, and humbled to the very core for seven years. He cannot even rule his kingdom; he is just like one of the many beasts of the field.

After seven years, his sanity returns, and he finally and fully acknowledges the God of Daniel as his Lord. He apparently gives his life completely to the biblical God. The last we read of Nebuchadnezzar in scripture is his humble acknowledgement that God is the One in charge of human life—the One who sets up kings and tears them down. God is in control of this planet. Scripture leaves Nebuchadnezzar as a saved individual, one who had gone from self-centeredness to God-centeredness.

This is the essence of what it means to be a saved person. It is important to determine who is at the center of one's life: God, or self. It took God three tries, but He finally enlightened Nebuchadnezzar.

Just as God was patient with Nebuchadnezzar and continually sought to reach him through both positive and negative means, so God is attempting to bring us to a knowledge of Himself and to our acknowledgment that He is truly in control of our lives.

We are not captains of our own destiny—God is truly in charge of our lives. We commonly call this remarkable change "conversion," and that is what it is: turning from a self-centered life to a God-centered life. We may not fully make it the first or second time, but God does not give up on us; He keeps working with us as long as we will listen to His pleading voice.

Only when we reach the point where we commit our lives unreservedly to Him, just as Nebuchadnezzar did, will we experience the real peace in our lives that God so desperately wants to give us. The basis of this peace is a full acknowledgement that this patient, biblical God is the absolute ruler of our lives.

The Human Situation

Our human condition is much like that of this ancient king. We are so caught up in what we have accomplished. Self-centeredness marks the very essence of most of our lives. We live for ourselves. We have turned away from the one source of help—God. We seek to run our own lives, yet we are miserable. We cover it well, masking our lack of peace with all the latest gimmicks and toys that society can invent. We do it to impress everyone else that we truly "have it all together," but down deep inside, we know differently.

We even put on masks, convincing ourselves that we are better than other people, so we should go to heaven someday because of this goodness we have in our hearts. We may boast of what we give to charity, or convince ourselves that we have not done any great sin. We actually become very good at convincing ourselves of our own righteousness. This is the pit from which God delivered Nebuchadnezzar. Self-righteousness leaves us with no peace.

Notice what the Bible says about the human situation. We saw it in Daniel 4, as God condemned Nebuchadnezzar's self-righteousness, but God spells it out for us in detail throughout the scripture:

"For all have sinned and fall short of the glory of God" (Romans 3:23).

"There is none righteous, no, not one" (Romans 3:10).

"The heart is deceitful above all things, and desperately wicked; who can know it?" (Jeremiah 17:9).

All humanity is in the same boat—we are all sinners. No one is righteous. In spite of all our great achievements on this planet, none of us can claim self-righteousness. We are all blighted by sin. Not only is scripture declaring us all to be sinners, but Jeremiah even declares that we deceive ourselves in this area. We convince ourselves that we are righteous, when, in fact, we are sinners. In other words, we cannot trust our own thinking—it deceives us.

The deception of self-righteousness is so great that it even entraps many who profess to have given their lives to God and Christ. They freely give their lives to Christ and then try to boost their standing with God through their own deeds. The lure of doing something to atone for our sins is so strong that over half the people who attend church every week still think they are saved by what they do. That is true across all denominations. No matter how clear the theology of a church may be, the power of self-righteousness seems to overwhelm even those with the correct biblical understanding that we are not saved by what we do. It is so strong that some will even profess with their mouths that they are not saved by their works, then proceed to act as if their works are saving them.

Some people simply believe that as long as they live a good, moral life, they will be saved. Not so. Scripture declares that one sin is sufficient to keep one out of heaven, and no amount of right living can make right even one sin that a person has committed. Instead, the Bible declares that "The wages of sin is death" (Romans 6:23). Here is one wage that inflation never changes. It is always the same. If you sin, you must die eternally. This is not talking about the human death we all face, but the final death of sinners in the lake of fire. This is the final, dire punishment for sin.

In order to be saved by our own righteousness, we would have to go from the cradle to the grave and never commit one sin. No human, except Christ, has ever done that. Self-righteousness is an impossibility. Some people think that if they sin, they just need to be good for a while to make up for it. The point is, you can't make up for it. The consequence of any sin, however small, is death.

Suppose twenty years ago a man had no money, and his family was in dire need. In desperation, he broke into a store and stole $10,000. Even though a careful investigation was carried out, he was never discovered until twenty years later. The man is brought to trial. As he stands before the judge, he declares: "Your honor, it is true that I took the money twenty years ago, but since that time, during all these twenty years, I have not stolen anything. All my friends will testify that I have lived an exemplary life for twenty years." Will twenty years of right living atone for that crime of burglary? Of course not. The man is guilty and must pay the penalty for his sin. Now, the human judge may offer some leniency for good behavior, but he will still have to pay the debt to society.

So it is with the law of God. No amount of right living can make right one act of sin we have committed when we broke God's law. Thus every single person on the planet stands in the sight of God as a sinner in desperate need of help. We cannot save ourselves. We, by our own efforts, cannot cross the gulf that sin has created. Anyone who thinks that the works they do can make them righteous is harboring a false hope. The basis of our hope is not self-righteousness, but rather, a God-provided righteousness.

It is a righteousness provided outside of ourselves and is only available to us when we finally acknowledge that self-righteousness will not get us to heaven. Jeremiah, the prophet makes it very clear:

"Can the Ethiopian change his skin or the leopard its spots? Then may you also do good who are accustomed to do evil?" (Jeremiah 13:23).

Here God unequivocally declares that it is absolutely impossible to be good in one's own strength. It is ridiculous even to think of a leopard removing its spots with spot remover or a person changing the color of his or her skin. Yet this is the analogy God uses to inform us that we cannot become righteous by ourselves and our good works. The message of scripture is clear: we cannot do anything about our miserable, lost situation. We stand guilty before the King of the universe. Until we recognize this fact, there is not one thing that can be done. We cannot pay the debt that sin has produced, because the penalty is death. If we paid it, we could not live. Where, then, lies our hope?

Many hot summers ago, a doctor—one of the famous Mayo brothers—was traveling in one of those unpredictable early automobiles. As often happened in the early part of the twentieth century, his car got a flat tire. This was a common occurrence, so it wasn't unusual for Dr. Mayo to be stuck in the country. Leaving the car in the road, he made his way to the nearest farmhouse, seeking help. While there, the farmer's wife noticed that the good doctor looked tired and thirsty and offered him a glass of cold buttermilk. He partook of the hospitality. Eventually, help came, and he went on his way. The incident was forgotten.

Years later, the farmer's wife became seriously ill. Finally, she was taken to the famous Mayo clinic in Rochester, Minnesota. There she underwent a very serious operation. For weeks, she teetered between life and death, but finally began to improve and was finally sent home. The farmer was worried about how he would pay the huge hospital bill that he knew was coming. This was before the days of good health insurance, and his resources were limited.

One day, as he opened the mailbox, he noticed the bill from the Mayo Clinic. With trembling hands, he tore open the envelope and pulled out a bill for over $15,000.00. His heart sank. In the early days of the twentieth century, that was a lot of money. It was more than he had. Even if he sold his farm, he could not pay the bill—it was beyond his capacity. Then he noticed that scrawled across the bottom were these words: "Paid in full by two glasses of cold buttermilk."

What the farmer was unable to do for himself, Dr. Mayo did for him. So it is with us and God. We stand guilty and in debt before the Judge of the universe, but scrawled across the bill in blood are the words, "Guilty, but paid in full by the nail-scarred hands of Calvary." We are unable to pay our sin debt, but God, through Jesus, has already paid it all for us. That debt was paid so well that nothing we might do could add to what Christ has already done for us.

The Remedy of God

The most famous of Bible texts reminds us of this great gift, provided by a loving and merciful God: "For God so loved the world that He gave His only begotten Son, that whoever believes in Him should not perish but have everlasting life" (John 3:16).

Here we see the holy God and sinful humanity, and between them, a great gulf caused by sin. Humanity cannot bridge the huge canyon that sin has created. Yet God Himself came down to earth, paid the penalty for humankind's sins, and thus made the cross a bridge, spanning the chasm created by sin and reuniting humanity with God

The only way sinners can be reunited with God is to grasp hold of this cross—the bridge over the abyss of sin. We cannot build the bridge; we can only accept the one provided by God Himself. You see, Jesus didn't just die, He died for you and me. On Calvary, He paid the full price of sin. He suffered in our place. The apostle Paul speaks of this divine transfer that occurs because of the cross: "For He made Him who knew no sin to be sin for us, that we might become the righteousness of God in Him" (2 Corinthians 5:21).

What an amazing accomplishment! Jesus, the only perfect person who ever lived, agreed to become responsible for my sins and your sins—the sins of the whole world. God placed those sins on Him. He suffered the wrath of God upon sin for us. He paid the penalty, so we wouldn't have to pay it and die.

As a result, my sins have been placed on Jesus, and His life of perfect, absolute righteousness has been placed to my account in the record books of heaven. Now, when God looks at me, He doesn't see all my sins. Instead, He sees the perfect righteousness of Jesus Christ. A divine transfer! My sins for His righteousness! What a marvelous remedy Jesus offers! No wonder the scripture declares this to be the amazing grace of God: "For by grace you have been saved through faith, and that not of yourselves; it is the gift of God, not of works, lest anyone should boast" (Ephesians 2:8, 9).

Grace, grace—amazing grace! Only the grace of God saves me. I did not deserve this. It was not given because of anything I did. Grace was provided by a loving God reaching out to a helpless sinner like me. I can't earn this grace. Nothing that I do can merit this grace. It is FREE! How often, though, people try to earn this grace. A man was assassinated on the streets of Barcelona, Spain. When they removed the clothes from his body, they found that he had many pins stuck in him. Why? Because he thought that if he inflicted enough pain in his body, God would forgive him and save him. This is not true. Nothing we do can earn this great salvation provided for us by a loving God.

No amount of right living, no long pilgrimages, no bodily affliction—nothing can earn the forgiveness of God and the right to enter heaven. Only by accepting Jesus can one be saved from the consequences of sin. Jesus has bridged the gap. We cannot add to His sacrifice. That is why scripture declares that there is no other name, given among men, whereby we can be saved; only the name of Jesus (Acts 4:12).

We are truly saved by grace alone. It is not grace, plus our works. It is grace, grace, and only grace that can save. Where, then, do good works fit in? They do not save—they are the fruit, the results, of salvation. When one has been so radically redeemed by this loving God who has provided salvation for us, one wants to live in obedience to this God, not for the sake of being saved, but because one has already been saved. Works are the fruit, not the means, of salvation.

In the illustration of Dr. Mayo, the farmer could never repay the famous physician for what he had done. If the good doctor came to visit again, I am sure he would have been offered another glass of buttermilk. The farmer would not be attempting to pay the doctor back, but would simply be letting him know how much he appreciated and loved him for what he had done. So it is with us and God. Our works cannot repay God. They merely, in a faulty way, reveal that we appreciate the great salvation provided for us in Christ. That is why Jesus said if we love Him, we will keep His commandments (John 14:15).

The remedy for sin was provided outside of us, not dependent on any works that we have done.

> But now the righteousness of God apart from the law is revealed, being witnessed by the Law and the Prophets, even the righteousness of God, through faith in Jesus Christ, to all and on all who believe. For there is no difference; for all have sinned and fall short of the glory of God, being justified freely by His grace through the redemption that is in Christ Jesus. Romans 3:21-24.

It seems that accepting the fact that we cannot save ourselves is the most difficult thing for self-centered humanity to do. We somehow want to view ourselves as having something to do with our own salvation. That is why the foundation of every false religion is salvation by works. Yet scripture is overwhelmingly clear. Absolutely nothing can be added to what Christ has done for us. It is a free gift (Romans 6:23). The wages we earn are death, but God gives us His perfect gift. Gifts are not earned, wages are—and the only way to receive a gift is to reach out and take it.

Salvation has been provided through Christ for every child of Adam. There is enough for all. Yet all do not receive, because they do not reach out and take salvation. It is not enough to be informed that Christ has provided this remedy—we must also reach out and accept this great Jesus into our lives. We must taste and see that salvation by grace alone is our only ticket to heaven. This is the only basis of peace for our lives.

How People Come to Jesus

How can we avail ourselves of the bridge to heaven? The bridge crossing the gulf of sin is not something we can build. That bridge is a person—Jesus Christ. To be saved, one must accept a person—not a church, not a doctrine, but a person. That person is Jesus.

There are nine steps that a person usually experiences in coming to Jesus. As we present them, we will be dissecting the process. There is the danger that some may think these are complicated steps. They are not. They do not even take a long time. They can happen in a matter of minutes. Yet these are steps that usually happen when one comes to Christ.

God takes the first step—He draws us to Himself. Jesus declared that if He were lifted up on Calvary's cross, He would draw all people to Him (John 12:32). He was lifted up, and He does draw all people to Him. Each of us, at some point in our life, will feel the drawing power of God. Just as Nebuchadnezzar felt God tugging at his heart, everyone will have this experience. Yet, not everyone will respond to God's invitation. God has given us the freedom of choice.

The second step is the human response to this divine drawing. Each person must respond by accepting Jesus into their life. It is not a work we do—it is giving God permission to enter our life. He does not enter uninvited. This happened to the Philippian jailer in Acts 16. The earthquake shook the prison, and the doors were opened. Through this experience, the jailer realized that God was speaking to him, and he responded, came to Paul, and asked: "Sirs, what must I do to be saved?" (Acts 16:30). Paul replied: "Believe on the Lord Jesus Christ, and you will be saved, you and your household" (Acts 16:31).

The human response to God's drawing is to believe on Jesus. The word *believe* does not mean simply to acknowledge that God exists, but it conveys the meaning of trusting absolutely in God.

To believe is to trust Christ and not self. It is to move from trying to accomplish one's own salvation to trusting fully in Christ as one's divine Substitute. Thus God takes the first step—He draws us; but humanity must take the second step—believe in Jesus by responding to the awesome drawing power of God. The second step is to respond by permitting Christ to fully enter our life. That is the only basis of our salvation.

The third step in this simple process is demonstrated by the prophet Isaiah as he experienced the drawing power of God in his life and responded. Immediately, God revealed Himself to Isaiah by contrasting the holiness of God with the sinfulness of humanity:

> In the year that King Uzziah died, I saw the Lord sitting on a throne, high and lifted up, and the train of His robe filled the temple. Above it stood seraphim; each one had six wings: with two he covered his face, with two he covered his feet, and with two he flew. And one cried to another and said: "Holy, holy, holy is the Lord of hosts; the whole earth is full of His glory!" And the posts of the door were shaken by the voice of him who cried out, and the house was filled with smoke. Isaiah 6:1-4.

God is holy. Humanity is unholy. After acknowledging Him, God wants us to understand clearly that we cannot save ourselves. We cannot equal His holiness. Here again, God is taking the initiative to reveal to us His holiness and our great need of Him. Of course, there is the human response to this revelation. We must recognize that what God says about our sinfulness is true. That is what Isaiah did in verse 5:

> So I said: "Woe is me, for I am undone! Because I am a man of unclean lips, and I dwell in the midst of a people of unclean lips; for my eyes have seen the King, the Lord of hosts." Isaiah 6:5.

This is step four. Humanity must recognize its need and the contrast that exists between the holy God and sinful mankind.

The fifth step follows quickly. As we see the contrast between the holy God and our sinful self, God brings repentance to us. Contrary to what many believe, repentance is not a human work. It is a God-given gift. "When they heard these things they became silent; and they glorified God, saying, 'Then God has also granted to the Gentiles repentance to life'" (Acts 11:18).

Only God can grant repentance. It is not something that

the human heart can generate.

What is repentance? Repentance means turning away from sin in sorrow. Yet the natural state of humanity is to crave sin, to love sin, to enjoy sin. Humankind does not naturally loathe sin and want to escape from it. We are often drawn quite willingly into sin. Taking a sinful heart and implanting within it a new nature so that the things once loved are now hated, is a deliberate act of God and a divine miracle. This is why scripture declares that we cannot repent of ourselves. It is God who grants us repentance.

Biblical repentance is not merely sorrow for sin. Many people are sorry for their sins when they get caught. Others abuse their bodies for decades with tobacco and then feel sorry that they smoked. They are sorry for the consequences of their sin. True biblical repentance, however, is to be sorry for the sin itself, because that sin sent Jesus to the cross. Only God can bring about that kind of repentance.

Step six is the human response to the repentance God provides. We confess the sins that God is causing us to repent of. "He who covers his sins will not prosper, but whoever confesses and forsakes them will have mercy" (Proverbs 28:13).

As God brings repentance, we confess the sins to God. Some people worry that perhaps there is one sin they cannot remember, and they will be lost because they cannot confess that one sin. However, God does not save us on the basis of our memories. If there is a sin that needs to be confessed, God will bring it to our minds. Otherwise, we can rest assured, remembering that it is God who brings repentance, and only then comes our response of confessing the sins for which He caused repentance.

Step seven follows very quickly. "If we confess our sins, He is faithful and just to forgive us our sins and to cleanse us from all unrighteousness" (1 John 1:9). What an awesome God! He causes us to repent. We respond and confess, and He immediately forgives us. Not only does He forgive us, but John declares that He totally cleanses us from all unrighteousness. We who were sinful now stand in the sight of a holy God just as if we had never sinned. We are not forgiven, yet still damaged. We are forgiven and totally restored as if the sin had never happened.

Having partaken of this marvelous grace of God, the natural response of the human heart is to obey Him. This is seen in the experience of Saul on the Damascus road. God draws Saul through the bright light. Saul responds positively. God reveals the contrast between sinful humanity and a holy God. Saul recognizes that God is right. God brings repentance to Him, Saul confesses, and God forgives. Recognizing all that God has done, Saul responds: "Lord, what do You want me to do?" (Acts 9:6).

The natural response of the human heart to receiving this awesome salvation is to be obedient to Him. It is not obedience designed to pay God back, but a loving response to what this gracious God has done for us. Yet even this loving obedience is an impossible task. Humans are forever incapable of obeying God in their human strength. God desires this positive response of willingness to obey, but God reminds us quickly in the ninth and final step that it is God who empowers us to obey (John 1:12). Even our loving obedience is not an effort that merits anything—it is simply a loving response to what God has already done, and it is He who empowers us even to make this response (Philippians 2:13).

Note that salvation is completely from God and not from any human work. In each of these steps, God has done all the work. All that humanity does is respond by allowing God to work each life. He never forces us. He just invites. Our part is to respond.

At every stage in the process, we are simply responding to the work God is doing in our life. As a result, God instills in us a new heart—a heart that puts God in the center of our life. Jesus calls this the new birth and declares that without it no one gets to heaven (John 3:3).

Is God drawing you, dear reader, at this very moment? Is He inviting you to receive Jesus into your life? Are you willing to respond to the power of that Infinite love? All it takes on your part is a willingness to allow Him into your life. Jesus never forces anyone, but He does stand outside the door of your heart, gently knocking for admittance (Revelation 3:20). Sufficient pardon has been provided for every child of Adam, but that pardon is not valid in your life until you reach out and receive it.

In the *Supreme Court Records*, volume 7, by Peters, the case of George Wilson is recorded. George had been sentenced to death for his crimes. His friends had sought clemency from the governor of the state and finally received it. However, when George Wilson heard the news, he refused to accept it, declaring that he did not want the governor's pardon. His friends were not to be put off by his refusal, and they took the case all the way to the Supreme Court of the United States, where the court ruled that a pardon is not valid unless it is accepted. George Wilson went to his death needlessly, because of his refusal to accept the governor's pardon. No one needs to go to an eternal death. We can choose eternal life by accepting the pardon so freely offered to us by Jesus, who has already paid the price of our redemption.

It was April 19, 1995. The place was Oklahoma City, Oklahoma. The event was the twelfth annual mayor's prayer breakfast at 6:30 a.m. at the Myriad Convention Center. Numerous federal workers had joined the twelve hundred people present for the occasion. The speaker was Richard Senstermacher, a Ford Motor Company executive. Instead of a standard devotional, Senstermacher preached a salvation message. He stressed that life is uncertain and that the most important thing one can do is to accept Christ as Savior. As he concluded, he urged everyone to stand and join him in praying the sinner's prayer. Those who had accepted Christ were asked to fill out a card. The response was tremendous.

At 8:30 a.m., the meeting adjourned, and people left for their places of business. Senstermacher lingered a while longer. As he and others rode the elevator to the parking lot, a powerful bomb exploded at the federal building. Driving north from the convention center, Senstermacher discovered he was driving on a lot of broken glass. He turned off the street to avoid the glass, only to discover that he had driven to the very site of the explosion. Some of the people now beneath the smoking rubble had just prayed the sinner's prayer with him a few moments ago. They had died secure in the arms of Jesus.

Life is so uncertain. That is why you cannot afford to put off your decision to invite Jesus Christ into your heart right now. You have nothing to lose and everything to gain by accepting Him as your Savior and Lord. Why not bow your head right now and repeat the sinner's prayer below and invite Jesus into your heart?

Dear Jesus:
Thank You for drawing me to You. I respond and accept You as my personal Savior. Please come into my heart right now. Thank You. Amen.

6

The End of Hope

God is patient with humanity. He does not give up easily. Just look at the repeated attempts God made to reach Nebuchadnezzar, who was in the total darkness of heathenism. But there comes a time when God says enough is enough. It happens with individuals as well as nations and the earth as a whole. Even though God was patient with the inhabitants of Sodom and Gomorrah, time ran out. God patiently waited for 120 years as Noah preached, until time ran out and the flood came.

God bears long with our refusal to follow Him completely and accept Him as our Lord and Savior, but the time comes when God says He will wait no longer. God offers us hope, yet there is a limit to God's endurance. This is clearly illustrated for us by the fall of Babylon in Daniel 5.

Revelation's symbolism makes abundant use of the fall of Babylon. Notice the repeated warnings:

> And another angel followed, saying, "Babylon is fallen, is fallen, that great city, because she has made all nations drink of the wine of the wrath of her fornication." Revelation 14:8.

> So he carried me away in the Spirit into the wilderness. And I saw a woman sitting on a scarlet beast which was full of names of blasphemy, having seven heads and ten horns. The woman was arrayed in purple and scarlet, and adorned with gold and precious stones and pearls, having in her hand a golden cup full of abominations and the filthiness of her

fornication. And on her forehead a name was written: MYS-TERY, BABYLON THE GREAT, THE MOTHER OF HARLOTS AND OF THE ABOMINATIONS OF THE EARTH. Revelation 17:3-5.

And he cried mightily with a loud voice, saying, "Babylon the great is fallen, is fallen, and has become a dwelling place of demons, a prison for every foul spirit, and a cage for every unclean and hated bird! For all the nations have drunk of the wine of the wrath of her fornication, the kings of the earth have committed fornication with her, and the merchants of the earth have become rich through the abundance of her luxury." And I heard another voice from heaven saying, "Come out of her, my people, lest you share in her sins, and lest you receive of her plagues." Revelation 18:2-4.

Obviously, to understand these fearful warnings of Revelation, one must clearly understand what is meant by the fall of Babylon. The symbolism here is drawn from the description of the fall of ancient Babylon in Daniel 5.

God always appeals positively to people before He uses negative warnings. However, sometimes the only thing that will reach us is a negative warning. We discovered when we studied Revelation 14 in chapter 1 that God calls the last generation positively through the first angel's message, calling us to be restored to the image of God. If that fails, God continues with the second message, warning us about the fall of Babylon.

In the book of Daniel, we discover this same sequence. God tried to reach Nebuchadnezzar positively through the dream of the image and the experience of the fiery furnace. When that failed, God's love was so great for Nebuchadnezzar that He finally allowed him to go insane in order to reach him. God will do whatever it takes, but there is a limit. Daniel 5 bears that out.

Many years have passed. Daniel, who was about 18 to 20 years of age when he first came to Babylon, is now around 90 years of age. Nebuchadnezzar is dead and has been for some time. His grandson, Belshazzar, is on the throne, reigning as co-regent with his father, Nabonidus, who is away from the capital when the events of chapter 5 occur. Belshazzar's mother is the daughter of Nebuchadnezzar. All during this time, Daniel had faithfully witnessed in Babylon about the true God. The Babylonian leadership was no longer ignorant of His supremacy. They had adequate opportunity to follow the path of Nebuchadnezzar and accept Him, but they did not.

Daniel 5 opens as Belshazzar conducts a feast in honor of all the gods and goddesses of Babylon. It was not the right time to have a feast. Cyrus, leading the Medes and the Persians, had already surrounded the city of Babylon and was preparing to take the city, but the Babylonians were feasting when their world was about to end. They felt secure within the boundaries of their city.

They might well have felt so secure. The massive walls were so thick that no battering ram could knock them down. Sufficient water flowed through the city, as the river Euphrates actually meandered its way right under the walls and into the city. There was plenty of food and water to withstand any siege. So why be concerned? Those doomsday heralds should not be believed. Babylon would last forever.

Yet someone should have noticed that the Medes and Persians had been busy digging an alternative channel for the Euphrates. If they noticed, it didn't seem to awaken the Babylonians. They were too busy preparing for the big feast. Little did they realize that this was to be their very last night on earth. God bears long, but there comes an end.

The feast began. Everyone who was anyone was there. It was the event of the year. Wine flowed freely. And then, under the influence of the alcohol, Belshazzar does the unthinkable:

> While he tasted the wine, Belshazzar gave the command to bring the gold and silver vessels which his father Nebuchadnezzar had taken from the temple which had been in Jerusalem, that the king and his lords, his wives, and his concubines might drink from them. Then they brought the

gold vessels that had been taken from the temple of the house of God which had been in Jerusalem; and the king and his lords, his wives, and his concubines drank from them. They drank wine, and praised the gods of gold and silver, bronze and iron, wood and stone. Daniel 5:2-4.

Sometimes people feel that God will overlook things because they were drunk and did not know what they were doing. This passage refutes that clearly. The Babylonians were drunk but were still accountable for their blasphemous actions. This act of violating the vessels dedicated solely to the worship of the God of heaven, by using them in heathen worship, is what brings down God's wrath on ancient Babylon.

It is almost as if God could tolerate their heathen worship when done in ignorance, but now that they had seen the light, God can no longer wink at their defiance. What appears to be the most damaging thing they do is their attempt to mix heathen worship with the worship of God. He cannot stand the mixture—one or the other, but don't mix the two. This defiant act of mixing paganism with the worship of God finally causes Him to bring down the curtain on ancient Babylon.

In the midst of their feasting and drunken revelry, an unseen hand appears and begins writing on the wall. The music stops, the trembling hands drop their wine glasses, and all over the banquet hall knees are shaking with fear (Daniel 5:5), 6. Something momentous is happening, and even though they are drunk, they know that all is not well.

Quickly, Belshazzar attempts to stay in control. He summons the famous Babylonian brain trust. It seems he would have learned that this group has no power when the God of heaven intervenes. He certainly had been brought up on the stories of Nebuchadnezzar's vain attempts to find answers apart from God.

We have seen the progressive discrediting of the wisdom of Babylon in these stories. In chapter 2, they could not recall the dream. In chapter 4, they could not interpret the dream, even though it was given. And now, they can't even read the writing on the wall. God is simply painting the picture clearly that the wisdom of Babylon cannot interpret the things of God. God is the only source of true wisdom and understanding.

With the wise men unable to read the writing, the king becomes more concerned. But soon his mother, the queen, enters the banquet hall with a message:

> There is a man in your kingdom in whom is the Spirit of the Holy God. And in the days of your father, light and understanding and wisdom, like the wisdom of the gods, were found in him; and King Nebuchadnezzar your father—your father the king—made him chief of the magicians, astrologers, Chaldeans, and soothsayers. Inasmuch as an excellent spirit, knowledge, understanding, interpreting dreams, solving riddles, and explaining enigmas were found in this Daniel, whom the king named Belteshazzar, now let Daniel be called, and he will give the interpretation. Daniel 5:11, 12.

Who was this queen mother? She was the daughter of Nebuchadnezzar. Growing up in the home of converted Nebuchadnezzar, she knew all about Daniel and his God. Perhaps she too followed Him. One wonders why she wasn't at the banquet. Perhaps it was because she refused to participate in those things that defied the God of heaven. She soon hears about the writing and comes in very quickly with a message—call Daniel.

Soon Daniel is standing before Belshazzar and being told he can be third ruler of Babylon, a significant position when one considers there were already two rulers: Belshazzar and Nabonidus. But Daniel refuses all offers of rewards. He was not there for a reward—he was there as a messenger of the Almighty whose hand had just written on the wall of the banquet hall. After all, what good is the reward? God's message was heralding the end of Babylon. He would be third ruler for only a few hours!

Belshazzar attempts to plead ignorance, claiming he might have even heard of Daniel (Daniel 5:13-16). Of course, he knew who Daniel was. You could not have lived in ancient Babylon without knowing Daniel. He was prime minister under Nebuchadnezzar. Everyone knew Daniel, and everyone knew what Daniel stood for. But Daniel does not allow him to hold on to his claim of ignorance:

> O king, the Most High God gave Nebuchadnezzar your father a kingdom and majesty, glory and honor. And because of the majesty that He gave him, all peoples, nations, and languages trembled and feared before him. Whomever he wished, he executed; whomever he wished, he kept alive; whomever he wished, he set up; and whomever he wished, he put down. But when his heart was lifted up, and his spirit was hardened in pride, he was deposed from his kingly throne, and they took his glory from him. Then he was driven from the sons of men, his heart was made like the beasts, and his dwelling was with the wild donkeys. They fed him with grass like oxen, and his body was wet with the dew of heaven, till he knew that the Most High God rules in the kingdom of men, and appoints over it whomever He chooses. But you his son, Belshazzar, have not humbled your heart, although you knew all this. And you have lifted yourself up against the Lord of heaven. They have brought the vessels of His house before you, and you and your lords, your wives and your concubines, have drunk wine from them. And you have praised the gods of silver and gold, bronze and iron, wood and stone, which do not see or hear or know; and the God who holds your breath in His hand and owns all your ways, you have not glorified. Daniel 5:18-23.

Note that Daniel holds the king accountable for what he already knew. Belshazzar may have tried to feign ignorance, but Daniel cut right to the heart. Belshazzar knew and still persisted in defying the great God of heaven. The act most despicable was his use of the vessels of God in heathen worship. God might tolerate ignorant heathen worship, but not the worship of God mixed with heathenism.

It is this despicable act of mixing paganism with the worship of God that finally brings down the wrath of God on ancient Babylon. Hope runs out for ancient Babylon. God has borne long with this nation and given it many opportunities for repentance, but there is a limit, and Babylon has reached that limit. Thus Babylon will fall. That is the announcement Daniel is about to give.

The climax is reached. All that is left is for Daniel to read the writing on the wall, which he does in verses 25-30. The handwriting declares it clearly: God has waited long, but Babylon is found wanting. Therefore, the kingdom of silver will now be set up. Can you imagine the hush over that banquet crowd as the writing is interpreted?

However, there is no time to recover from the shock of the announcement. Already, the Medes and the Persians had entered the city, and the fall of Babylon had begun. That very night, October 12, 539 B.C., mighty Babylon fell.

How did Cyrus accomplish it? As already noted, his soldiers had dug an alternate channel for the Euphrates River. On this night, he switched the river into the new channel, thus drying it up as it went through Babylon. That effectively should have cut off the water supply to those inside the city, which would have forced the city to yield in a short time.

However, the drunken Babylonians felt so secure in their walled city that they had left the gates under the wall open where the Euphrates ran through. Thus it was easy for Cyrus to send his soldiers under the wall and into the city.

This scenario, describing the fall of ancient Babylon, should seem very familiar to anyone who has read the book of Revelation. Revelation 16 describes what happens in the sixth plague to hit the earth at the end time: "Then the sixth angel poured out his bowl on the great river Euphrates, and its water was dried up, so that the way of the kings from the east might be prepared" (Revelation 16:12).

The passage then proceeds to describe the battle of Armageddon—earth's final battle. In Revelation 16, we see the Euphrates being dried up, the coming of the kings of the east, and mighty spiritual Babylon falling and dividing into three parts. Obviously, one cannot understand the final battle of Armageddon without understanding the symbolism from which it is drawn here in Daniel 5.

Likewise, in Daniel 5, we note the fall of Nebuchadnezzar's Babylon, accomplished by Cyrus, who the Bible describes as the "righteous man from the east" (Isaiah 45:1)—the one who was to deliver God's people held in Babylonian captivity (Isaiah 41:2-4). You also see this accomplished by the drying up of the same Euphrates. The link between the two events is obvious.

It is not our intention to attempt to interpret the battle of Armageddon in this chapter. That will be reserved for a later section. Here, it is our purpose to note the strong correlation between the two and the need to be careful as we interpret to make certain we understand Revelation 16 in light of the symbolism found in Daniel.

Revelation's Babylon

Much of Revelation's symbolism is built around Babylon. Yet it is not merely Babylon, it is always *fallen* Babylon. Any mention of the symbol of Babylon in the New Testament Revelation revolves around the fact that Babylon is fallen. It is the heart cry of the second angel's message in Revelation 14:8. The cry of Babylon's fall is then repeated in Revelation 18:1-3. The whole seventeenth chapter of Revelation describes this horrific entity called Babylon, while Revelation 18:4 calls God's people to get out of Babylon.

One cannot clearly understand the message of the book of Revelation without a clear understanding of the role of this final Babylon. Yet the Babylon of Revelation cannot be Nebuchadnezzar's Babylon. It had been a heap of ruins for over five hundred years before Revelation was written. Obviously, Revelation is using the term *Babylon* in a symbolic sense. And the meaning of the symbol must come from its source—the Old Testament.

What caused Old Testament Babylon to become fallen in

God's sight? There were several problems that Daniel 5 has especially highlighted for us. First, Babylon had oppressed God's people by taking them captive. Second, Babylon was caught up in self-glorification and her own riches. Third, Babylon defied God by mixing paganism with the worship of God. These are the factors that brought ancient Babylon into remembrance before God and caused her to fall.

Now notice Revelation 17 and the characteristics of spiritual Babylon. First, spiritual Babylon is caught up in self-glorification and riches (Revelation 17: 2, 4). Second, she oppressed God's people by killing them (Revelation 17:6). Third, like her ancient predecessor, she mixed elements of paganism into the worship of the true God. That is why she is called a harlot, full of immorality (Revelation 17:1, 2, 5). In fact, notice that the issues in Daniel 5 are repeated in Revelation 17 in describing the fall of spiritual Babylon. This is why both powers are referred to as Babylon. In both instances, the act of mixing paganism with the worship of God is the defining issue. We have already noticed it as we studied Daniel 5, but in Revelation 17 it is the issue that is mentioned again and again. The defining characteristic of spiritual Babylon is harlotry.

A harlot is one who has illicit relationships. It is putting together two people who do not belong together. In the spiritual sense, it would be to mix paganism with Christianity, or truth with error. The two do not mix. The tragedy of spiritual Babylon is that she has not only mixed truth and error together, but she has pawned off her immorality on her people by first of all making them drunk (Revelation 17:2), just like her predecessor.

Yet modern Babylon will not be excused, just as ancient Babylon was not excused. This defiant act of mixing truth and error, paganism with the worship of God, brought down the wrath of God on ancient Babylon, and Revelation declares that when this final spiritual Babylon comes and mixes truth and error, paganism and the worship of God, it too will bring down the final wrath of God, and spiritual Babylon will fall.

This is why God issues a final call to the world concerning

Babylon. It is part of the three angels' messages of the last days (see chapter 1). Final, spiritual Babylon will be active. God has many people still caught up in this Babylon. Therefore, He calls them to get out (Revelation 18:4).

One may wonder how many Babylons are described in the Bible. There could be several, for anytime we notice the mixing of truth and error together, persecuting those who disagree, and then exalting in ill-gotten riches, you have the presence of Babylon. There are three such scenarios brought out in the books of Daniel and Revelation.

We might refer to them as the three Babylons. Babylon I is Nebuchadnezzar's Babylon, whose fall we have just studied in Daniel 5. Babylon II is described in Daniel 7 and Revelation 13. We will study its fallen condition in a later chapter. Babylon III is described in several places in the book of Revelation. Revelation 13:11-17; 14:8; 17, 18. We will study it in a later section. It is the final Babylon at the end of the world.

Each of the three Babylons builds on the others and helps us better understand the one coming next. Babylon I is ancient history. So is Babylon II, as we shall soon study. The Babylon to concern us is Babylon III, but we cannot be prepared to withstand it unless we fully understand the implications learned from Babylons I and II.

In this chapter, we have discovered that the Bible is predicting a major apostasy in the last days that will attempt to mix truth and error, paganism and Christianity, and then attempt to pawn it all off as the truth of God. If that is true, then every Christian, of necessity, must become a deep student of the Word of God, so that he or she will not be deceived by this final great apostasy.

This is why everything must meet the acid test of the Word of God—the Bible. In the last days, we will not be able to trust preachers or religious leaders, only the Word of God. Begin now to be prepared for that time by testing everything you hear by the anvil of God's Word. Know your Bible for yourself. That is what sustained Daniel in the final test of his life, as seen in chapter 6 of his book.

7

Hope in the Midst of a Crisis

One more story completes the historical portion of the book of Daniel. Remember, these stories illustrate the end-of-time prophecies by using real-life crises from ancient Babylon. The book of Daniel is unified. It gives the same message through story and prophecy—that one must have a deep, abiding relationship with God to withstand the conflicts the enemy of souls brings upon those who believe in God.

Daniel 6 opens after the fall of Babylon. Amazingly, Daniel becomes a key player in the next empire led by Cyrus. One can only speculate on why Cyrus chooses Daniel to be a prime minister, or its equivalent in Persia, as he had been in Babylon. In those days it would be unheard of to take someone who ruled in the conquered nation and put him in charge of the new nation, but that is precisely what happens.

Perhaps it has something to do with the fact that Daniel predicted the fall of Babylon, as told in the previous chapter, and the king was aware of it. Somehow, he feels Daniel can be trusted, so he makes him a key advisor.

Why he did it is not clear, but the fact that he did it is clear. And it makes everyone else jealous. The scheming princes go to work quickly. They must find a way to discredit Daniel. You can understand their hatred of him. He is put over them, yet he is not one of them. They cannot understand it, so they hurry to disgrace him in some way.

They search everywhere. They examine his record books—no mistakes. They check to see if he is keeping two sets of books—no. They check to see whether he pays an honest tax—he did. They simply cannot find a problem with this Daniel. Finally, they come to one conclusion: "We shall not find any charge against this Daniel unless we find it against him concerning the law of his God" (Daniel 6:5).

What a testimony! Can you imagine what an investigation into your life might involve? What would they find? Reporters today are just as ingenious, if not more, than in Daniel's day. If there is a problem, they will find it and expose it with glee. Yet in spite of all the research, the princes turn up nothing except that Daniel serves God.

With no issues to use against Daniel that could stand up in court, they resort to trickery. They will create a law that he will break. So they get their heads together, consider the king's weak point, and come up with an idea. The kingdom is still young. The king needs to make sure of the loyalty of his subjects. He needs to know that they are faithful to him.

They test the idea out on the king, informing him that all his counselors agree on this new policy. All, that is, except Daniel. They do not let the king know that they have neglected to run it past Daniel. Of course not. Daniel would have quickly seen the plot. And if Darius had not been so enamored with their flattery, he would have seen it, too.

The counselors think their plot through well. They begin their presentation with great flattery. Everything is done for the glory of the king (a characteristic of Babylon). The king is feeling good, and then comes the clincher. To ensure that the whole realm will recognize the greatness of the king, the new law declares that no one shall petition anyone else but the king for thirty days. Thus all people will be in loyal submission to the king, and anyone who boycotts this law and dares to petition any human or god will be thrown into the den of lions. The king, caught up in the excitement of self-glorification and deification, quickly grabs the pen and signs it into law—a law that cannot be changed (Daniel 6:6-9).

Soon Daniel hears about the decree. It means he is forbidden to pray, yet this is his custom. Three times every day, he kneels in the window of his apartment, faces Jerusalem, and prays to the God of heaven. Now, to do so will be against the law. I am sure some of his friends urge him to pray in secret for thirty days so no one will know.

To pray in secret would be interpreted as being disloyal to God. Daniel cannot do that. His success with two world empires is due to his deep relationship with the God of heaven. He cannot compromise that relationship at the end of his life, even if it means going to the lions. So, when the time comes, Daniel does what he has always done—he prays in the open window facing Jerusalem.

The issue here may seem to be quite a small issue—praying outwardly. However, the real issue is maintaining a relationship with God. No issue is minor when it comes to having a deep relationship with God. So anything that affects time for my relationship with God can never be a minor issue. Only to those who know God would time for a relationship with God be worth dying for.

The scheming princes watch. It is true that non-Christians do watch Christians to see how they will react under trial. As soon as they observe him praying, they quickly make their way to the king with the information. Of course, the king now sees the folly of the decree, but it is too late. He searches the law, he checks with all the legal experts, but there is no way around the law. It was written too well—there are no loopholes. As much as he wants to rescue Daniel, he is unable to find a way. The king is forced to send this 90-year-old giant of faith to spend a night with the hungry lions.

Daniel knew the consequences, but he had the same faith as the three Hebrews displayed in Daniel's third chapter. He doesn't need a second chance. He would only repeat the offense. Loyalty to God is more important than loyalty to any oppressive law that humankind can invent to destroy one's relationship with God.

Imagine the scene as they lead this 90-year-old man down

to the lions' den. He does not know the outcome, just as the three Hebrews did not know the consequences during the fiery furnace episode. Daniel obviously knew that story, but would God exercise divine power to deliver him after he had already lived such a fruitful life? He does not know, but he trusts God, and he will serve Him no matter what. This is all that matters to him. So he enters the den with peace on his face and hope in the midst of the greatest crisis of his life. Why did he possess such hope? Because of this deep relationship he enjoys with the Almighty.

Daniel is at peace that night, but Darius is in turmoil (Daniel 6:18). When one trusts in God, there is always peace, no matter how tempestuous the waves of life. Even when we experience strong trials, if God is in our lives, we can make it through. God does not promise us that life will be smooth sailing, once we accept Him, but He does promise us that He will be with us during the lions'-den experiences of life. He will go through the trial with us.

The ending of the story is anticlimactic. Morning arrives, and the king is there at dawn. Daniel is alive. He is called out. The lions are still hungry. The scheming counselors are quickly called to account. They must have complained that the lions were not hungry enough. The king sends them in to find out. The lions were very hungry, indeed, as the counselors soon discovered when they became the lions' breakfast. End of story.

The Message of the Lions' Den

This is not just a nice bedtime story to tell our children. This story illustrates the crisis that God's people will face in the end time. The prophecies of Daniel and Revelation reveal a time of crisis for the people of God in the time of the end. When Babylon rules, oppression follows. That will be the path followed to the bitter end.

In Daniel, chapter 3, false worship was commanded, but in chapter 6, true worship is prohibited. Both passages illustrate the crisis of the last days. It will be a time when true worship will be prohibited and false worship will be commanded. Both chapters illustrate the crisis that all the prophecies predict when Babylon III rules the world in the end of time.

In both chapters, God's servants remained true to God. The issue in chapter 3 was obedience to God's law against worshiping images. The issue in chapter 6 involved time for Daniel's relationship with God. Both issues will come together in the last crisis. Thus the issues in the final crisis will be obedience to God's law and time for our relationship with God.

The only way the Hebrews in the time of Daniel remained faithful was their uncompromising desire to be obedient to God. Because of their love for Him, they would not knowingly disobey Him, even if it meant their lives. The reason they could take such an uncompromising stand was that they had built such a strong relationship with God throughout their lives.

Today, as we face the crisis of the last days, we must copy these Hebrews. Our relationship with God must be so deep that we will not compromise our faith, no matter how "small" the issue. Obedience to God in maintaining this relationship is more important than life itself.

Our great need today is for this same deep relationship with God. Relationships take time and are not developed quickly. That is why it is so crucial for Christians, and especially new Christians, to begin to develop a deep, trusting relationship with God. We can't wait until the crisis hits before we develop this relationship—we must start now.

Good relationships are rarely built in the midst of a crisis. They begin in good times, and become accentuated during a crisis. A new Christian begins a walk with Jesus that must continue to grow. The first experiences with Him are marvelous, but this is only the beginning. God wants to make it much deeper.

The wonderful part about this God is His genuine desire to know us through an intense relationship. He is not a distant God—He is a God who is near us. He is a God who really wants to get to know us. He is a God well worth spending quality time with. Jesus declares: "And this is eternal life, that they may know You, the only true God, and Jesus Christ whom You have sent" (John 17:3).

It is eternal life to know God and Jesus. That reality shouts at us. A relationship with this God is more important than anything else. Nothing can compromise my time for a relationship with such a God. This relationship is the most important thing in the world.

Yet any relationship that I develop requires that I spend quality time with the person. That is how all human relationships work. If a husband and wife are going to make it to their golden anniversary, they must spend quality time together.

My wife and I both lead busy lives. Because of my travels, we regularly spend some time apart. Even when I am home, our busy schedules mean we hardly see each other during the day.

Yet we know we need time with each other every day. That means time for the two of us to just chat, even for five minutes, if that is all we can take. However, five minutes a day will quickly lead to disaster, so we have learned that in addition, we need to set aside at least one day a week for quality time together. We know that this special time is essential if our marriage is to survive.

If this is true for human relationships, it is also true for the divine relationship. We must spend quality time with God every day, but in addition, we need to spend a day with Him regularly to feast on His Word and develop that deep relationship that God so desperately wants to have with us.

How do we spend that time? The apostle Paul suggests that we need to study the Bible as part of our relationship time with God. "Be diligent to present yourself approved to God, a worker who does not need to be ashamed, rightly dividing the word of truth" (2 Timothy 2:15).

Part of our relationship time needs to be spent in the Bible, studying it for ourselves, so we know exactly what it says. We need to know how to accurately handle God's Word, so those who are misusing the Bible won't deceive us. This is my best safeguard against Satan's attacks. It is much more difficult to be deceived if I have learned how to properly handle the Word of God.

Reading the Bible is like listening to our friend Jesus speak to us; however, relationships require two-way conversations. We must not only listen to God speak through His Word, we must also take time to talk to God ourselves. He wants to hear from us. That is the nature of God.

Prayer is not reciting the same thing to God all the time. What would your spouse say if every time you opened your mouth to talk, you said the same thing—a memorized repetition? Very few relationships could ever survive such an ordeal. Prayer is part of a relationship; therefore, open up and just share what is going on in your life. Tell God every detail. He wants to hear it. Don't worry about the right words to say; He is not flattered by our vocabulary. Just be yourself. God wants to know the real you.

As you spend time regularly with God in prayer and Bible study, you will hear God speak to you. Remember that He speaks through His Word. Your relationship with God will deepen and grow as you spend quality time together, both daily and weekly.

The crisis that is about to strike the planet demands strong Christians, just as it did in Daniel's day. You can be one of those "towers of strength" that Revelation describes as standing on the sea of glass having gotten the victory over the beast and his image (Revelation 15). The only way to make it in this final crisis is by maintaining a deep relationship with Jesus.

When you accepted Jesus as your Savior, you began to walk with Him. You were saved solely by His grace, not by anything you did. Now you need to develop this deep relationship with the One who has saved you by His grace. Time with God carries no merit, no brownie points; it is just something all Christians love to do because of what Jesus has done for them on the cross. When someone dies for you, you want to know everything about that person. Jesus died for you. Begin now a fresh walk into the wonders of a relationship with Jesus.

8

Hope in the Midst of Apostasy

Apostasy! It doesn't even seem possible. How can a person who has once known the beautiful truth about Jesus and basked in the glories of salvation through Christ alone, turn from such a beautiful truth to the error of salvation by works? Yet it has happened. We all have known people who once rejoiced in the grace of Jesus, but are now consumed with earning their way to heaven. Or worse yet, they have known Christ, but no longer even attempt to serve Him.

As with individuals, so it occurs with churches. Yet this possibility seems even more preposterous. How could a church founded by Jesus lose its way, distort the basic gospel of salvation by grace alone, and create a works-based religion? Yet the sad truth of Christianity is that apostasy has entered the Christian church, and people have been led away from the pure gospel of Christ to the error of religion based on works.

It is so much easier to believe that I can earn my way to heaven than it is to accept the free gift of forgiveness and salvation offered through Jesus. That is why the foundation of all false religion is salvation through works of human achievement. In contrast, the foundation of all true religion is salvation through grace alone. When a church moves from salvation by grace to salvation by works, it has gone into apostasy and has ceased to rightly represent the gospel of Christ. It does not matter how long the church has been in existence. Validity is not established by age but by faithfulness to the gospel of free grace.

Not only has it happened, the Bible actually predicted this major Christian apostasy through the prophet Daniel. The stunning revelation of Daniel 7 was meant to offer hope to believers in every age by pointing out that God is aware of the departure of the church from its purity. He told us ahead of time so we could avoid it. Yet millions of sincere Christians have been misled, because they failed to study the Bible for themselves.

In this chapter, we will look at Daniel's prediction of a major apostasy that was to occur in Christianity—an apostasy so great that it would engulf almost the entire Christian world. As we enter this study, we will not be focusing on any particular church, but on a period of general apostasy that occurred in Christianity. We do so, not only to understand the fulfillment of the prophecy, but even more important, in order to be prepared for a similar apostasy that will occur in the end of time.

What we must learn from this study is clear. We must test everything we believe by the Word of God, alone. Just because a preacher teaches it or a church believes it, that does not make it right. Truth can only be ascertained by the Bible. Likewise, since this apostasy has already occurred, we need to test everything we believe today by the Bible, because it is possible that the religion we have inherited could have been tainted in the great apostasy of the church in the past. Just because a belief has been taught for a long time does not make it truth. Always remember: Truth is determined by the Bible and the Bible only.

In chapter 6, we discovered that the Bible speaks of three Babylons: Nebuchadnezzar's Babylon, the Babylonian apostasy of Daniel 7, and the final spiritual Babylon of the last days. In this chapter we will be focusing on Babylon II. In the third section of this book, we will reveal the final Babylon. The only way we can understand and be prepared for Babylon III is to understand the two Babylons that preceded it. We have already noted that the defining characteristic of Babylon is its illicit mixture of truth and error—paganism mixed with

Christianity. The most vivid manifestation of this Babylonian mixture occurred when the church shifted its belief from the gospel of salvation by grace alone to the pagan gospel of salvation by works. Any religious system based on salvation by works has become Babylon.

The Prophecy of Daniel 7

The foundational prophecy of Daniel is that of the great metallic image in chapter 2, formed of gold, silver, brass, iron, and the final mixture of iron and clay. We discovered earlier that the image represents the history of the world from Daniel's day to today, representing the kingdoms of Babylon, Media-Persia, Greece, Rome, and a divided Europe. The prophecy of Daniel 2 is the foundation on which all the other prophecies in Daniel are built. Each succeeding prophecy repeats the sequence of the empires, but adds significant new details.

The helpfulness of this method of interpretation, given us by Daniel himself, is that the prophecy always begins in the prophet's day and proceeds step by step through history. Therefore, historically, there is no guesswork in determining what power is represented, because it must appear in its sequence. To attempt to interpret the prophecy without using Daniel's principle of "repeat and expand" results in futile speculation rather than biblical fulfillment.

Some scholars refer to this as "outline prophecy." It simply means that each prophecy outlines world events from the prophet's day to the end of the world. Each succeeding prophecy builds on the previous ones, repeating the sequence, but continually adding new details and even new powers. The new powers can be identified, because they occur at a certain point in the sequence. We will see that illustrated several times in the prophecy of Daniel 7.

> In the first year of Belshazzar king of Babylon, Daniel had a dream and visions of his head while on his bed. Then he wrote down the dream, telling the main facts. Daniel spoke,

saying, "I saw in my vision by night, and behold, the four winds of heaven were stirring up the Great Sea. And four great beasts came up from the sea, each different from the other." Daniel 7:1-3.

In chapter 1 of this book, we discovered the meaning of some basic biblical symbols. The Bible reveals that seas represent people (Revelation 17:15), beasts represent kingdoms (Daniel 7:23) and a day equals a literal year (Ezekiel 4:6). Daniel 7 opens with conflict in the great sea as differing beasts arise from it. Here is a symbol of the conflict among the nations of Europe as various powers arise to attack the covenant people. So the four beasts represent the four kingdoms that arise out of the teeming populations of Europe to attack the covenant people. Remember, the Bible is not giving us political history, but redemptive history. Therefore, the only powers that are mentioned in prophecy are those that affect the covenant people.

We already know there are four powers: Babylon, Media-Persia, Greece, and Rome. These four are the basic powers described in Daniel 2. They are now to be presented again, utilizing the symbols of ferocious animals. These beasts are obviously not real animals, but animals used symbolically to represent the political powers arrayed against the people of God. Remember that the prophecy always begins in the prophet's time, unless the prophet tells otherwise. So we would expect the first power to represent the kingdom of Babylon: "The first was like a lion, and had eagle's wings. I watched till its wings were plucked off; and it was lifted up from the earth and made to stand on two feet like a man, and a man's heart was given to it" (Daniel 7:4).

Just as in Daniel 2, God chose the choicest of the metals to represent the mighty Babylonian empire, so in chapter 7, He chooses the king of the beasts, the lion, to represent the Babylonian empire—the empire that ruled the world when Daniel received the vision.

And suddenly another beast, a second, like a bear. It was raised up on one side, and had three ribs in its mouth between its teeth. And they said thus to it: "Arise, devour much flesh!" Daniel 7:5.

Daniel 7 is not just regurgitating the Daniel 2 information. The important thing to notice here is the sequence that the chapter is building, with one empire following another. This is essential because of what is to be revealed in some of the empires yet to come. In order to place the events correctly in history, we must keep the sequence in mind. Thus the second beast is a quick reminder that the prophecy is moving away from Babylon to the kingdom of the bear—the Medes and the Persians. The bear raises itself up on one side, indicating the dual nature of the power and the fact that one power was stronger than the other.

However, this is not about the Medes and the Persians. Quickly the prophecy moves on to the representation of Greece, the third beast: "After this I looked, and there was another, like a leopard, which had on its back four wings of a bird. The beast also had four heads, and dominion was given to it" (Daniel 7:6).

A new detail is given about the Grecian empire yet to come. The beast had four heads. Daniel 8 will add more details to this, but note that Alexander the Great, who led the Greeks to victory, died at the early age of 33, having conquered the world. At his death, no one successor was found. Instead, the kingdom was divided among his four generals: Seleucid, Ptolemy, Lysimacchus, and Cassander. Ultimately, they divided into the four Grecian kingdoms of Egypt, Thrace, Macedonia, and Syria. The Bible accurately foretold this very division.

The fourth kingdom, Rome, is represented by a beast that is not likened to any known beast. He appears more like a mythological beast:

After this I saw in the night visions, and behold, a fourth beast, dreadful and terrible, exceedingly strong. It had huge iron teeth; it was devouring, breaking in pieces, and trampling the residue with its feet. It was different from all the beasts that were before it, and it had ten horns. Daniel 7:7.

The Bible clearly links this beast with the iron legs of the Daniel 2 statue, giving it great iron teeth. We cannot miss this litany of the march of the empires: Babylon, Media-Persia, Greece, and now Rome. The great Roman Empire ruled the world from approximately 168 B.C. to A.D. 476, when Germanic tribes invaded the Roman Empire and divided it into what became the nations of Europe.

In Daniel 2, the presence of the ten toes in the image implies that Rome is divided into ten parts. However, Daniel 7 states directly that the beast has ten horns, representing the ten divisions of the Roman Empire in A.D. 476. Notice that the horns are not separate from the beast—they are supported by the beast. The divisions are not new empires, but the recreation of the Roman Empire in a new form—divided, but still Rome.

All of these empires have been restated in the same basic detail in order to clearly place in sequence the new revelation of Daniel 7—the rise of the little horn among the ten divisions of Rome. The focus of Daniel 7 is on this new power, and extensive description is given to us of this power, so we cannot mistake its identity. Notice how Daniel introduces this new power:

> I was considering the horns, and there was another horn, a little one, coming up among them, before whom three of the first horns were plucked out by the roots. And there, in this horn, were eyes like the eyes of a man, and a mouth speaking pompous words. Daniel 7:8.

The little horn is introduced as Daniel observed the ten horns that were already there. He then sees the little one emerging among the ten. We will notice several identifying marks of this power:

1. It rises to power after the breakup of the Roman Empire in A.D. 476. When the little horn assumes power, Rome has already divided.

2. It pulled up three horns. As this "little horn" power grabbed its power base, it eliminated three of the ten divisions. Only seven of the ten survived to form Europe—three disappeared. The power that eliminated the three would be the little-horn power.

3. It had the eyes of a man. There is a man at the head of this power.

4. It had a mouth uttering great boasts. Other parts of the prophecy expand the boasts to include speaking out against the Most High (Daniel 7:25).

5. It will wear down the saints of God (Daniel 7:25). In other words, those who disagree with its boastful claims against God will be persecuted.

6. It will attempt to make alterations in times and in law (Daniel 7:25). This is probably the most horrific act of the little-horn power. An actual attempt will be made to change or make alteration to God's times and law.

7. It will reign for 3½ times (Daniel 7:25).

These seven identifying marks are clearly outlined for us in the two verses that contain the description of the little horn: Daniel 7, verses 8 and 25. Let us expand the understanding of what is meant by blasphemy (speaking out against the Most High) in identifying mark #4 and the "3½ times" in identifying mark #7.

There are three possible interpretations of what is meant by blasphemy. Perhaps all three can describe what the little horn will do. The first was carried out by Belshazzar in Daniel

5 when he mixed the vessels of God with pagan worship. To offer God a mixture of paganism and Christianity would be blasphemous. To be Babylon, the little-horn power would need to mix the two. Thus blasphemy would be this adulterous mixture of truth and error, passed off as truth.

Second, blasphemy is understood through the Jews at the time of Christ, when Jesus was accused of blasphemy. "Why does this Man speak blasphemies like this? Who can forgive sins but God alone?" (Mark 2:7).

Of course, Jesus could forgive sin, so that was not blasphemy for Him, but blasphemy in Bible times was when a human being claimed the power to forgive sins. The little-horn power was to blaspheme God. This interpretation would be accurate if the little horn claimed to forgive sins.

Third, they accused Jesus of blasphemy because He claimed to be equal with God. "The Jews answered Him, saying, 'For a good work we do not stone You, but for blasphemy, and because You, being a Man, make Yourself God'" (John 10:33). Again, Christ *was* God, so the accusation was false; however, it reveals that in Bible times blasphemy was applied to anyone who claimed to be equal with God.

Thus these passages help illuminate what is meant by the pompous, boastful, blasphemous claims accredited to this little horn. To fulfill them, this power would have to mix paganism with Christianity, claim to forgive sins, and claim to be equal with God. No wonder the Bible condemns this power so strongly.

The second area that needs some explanation is the indication in verse 25 that the little-horn power would last for "3½ times." No explanation of this time period is given in the book of Daniel; however, the book of Revelation also mentions this same power, but gives more details as to the meaning of the 3½ times.

Revelation 13:5 indicates that the "beast power" (same as the little-horn power) would be given this power for a total of 42 months. With 30 days in the month, 42 months would equal 1,260 days. Remember that in biblical prophecy, a day is used symbolically for a year, thus making this prophecy 1,260 years.

Revelation 12:6 informs us that the woman flees from this power for exactly 1,260 days. Then, in verse 14, the time is repeated as a time, times, and half a time. These two passages together give irrefutable explanation of the 3½ times. However we look at it, the 3½ times must equal 1,260 days or prophetic years.

Amazingly, the little-horn power lasts for over 1,000 years. Therefore, this power is not one person, but a system that seeks to blaspheme God, change God's law, control kings, and boastfully claim to represent God, and then persecute anyone who disagrees with its claim.

Revelation's Description of the Beast

It would be helpful at this point to notice how Revelation also describes this same power, utilizing the symbolism of the beast rather than the little horn. A comparison of the identifying marks quickly informs us that the same power is being described. A few added details are given in Revelation 13. Notice the identifying marks:

1. It has ten horns and seven heads. Here is the connection with Daniel's beast, with ten horns and three being uprooted (Rev. 13:1).

2. The beast of Revelation 13 is a composite beast made up from Daniel's four beasts: the lion, the bear, the leopard, and the dragon (Rev. 13:2). This reveals its continuity with the powers of the past that have oppressed God's people.

3. The fourth beast, the dragon (Rome), gave this beast its power, its seat, and great authority (verse 2).

4. One of the heads of this beast receives a deadly wound (verse 3).

5. The deadly wound is to be healed (verse 3).

6. The entire world then wonders after this beast (verse 3).

7. People worship the beast. The beast is a religious power that receives worship (verse 4).

8. The beast is blasphemous, just as Daniel's little horn (verses 5, 6).

9. The beast reigns for 42 months or 1,260 days (years)—the exact same time period as Daniel's little horn (verse 5).

10. The beast made war with the saints and overcame them (verse 7).

11. The beast has a number that adds up to 666 (verse 18). Note that the number is not written out, but you have to calculate or add to get it. A common custom in that era was to take a person's name, give numeric value to each letter, through the Roman numeral system, and the total would be the number of a person's name. This text says that if you do this for the beast, it will indeed add up to 666.

Just listing all these identifying marks makes it very clear that the power being described in Revelation 13 as the first beast is the same power being described by the prophet Daniel in chapter 7 as the little horn. So in our attempt to identify this power, we will look at the marks of identification from both Daniel and Revelation.

Who Is the Little Horn?

Even a brief look through these identifying marks makes it very clear who this little-horn power represents. Only one power ever existed that fulfilled every specification of these two prophecies. The power would have to last for 1,260 years, arise to political power at the breakup of the Roman Empire, and blaspheme God by mixing paganism with Christianity, forgiving sins, and claiming to be God on earth. Furthermore, it would have to claim to be able to change God's law, receive its power from the Roman Empire, be a religious apostate that receives worship, and have the number of its name add up to 666.

Only one power fulfills all these marks. That power is none other than the Christian church in its terrible Dark Ages apostasy. It would be very easy here to blame one particular church, because for much of this era there was really only one church, but as Christians we must be careful not to cast stones, for this is the sad heritage of Christianity. It was such a terrible time that historians have dubbed the era as the "Dark Ages." During this awful time, the church lost the simplicity of the gospel and became corrupted by entering the political process. This long period is a time when the church and the state united together to enforce religion.

Even when the Reformation era began in the sixteenth century, the little-horn power continued to dominate both Protestants and Catholics. Both continued to appeal to the state to enforce their doctrines. While Protestants at that time began to see clearly the great biblical truth of salvation by grace alone, they still failed to see that religion cannot be legislated. As a result, the Protestants, like their Catholic neighbors, used the power of the state to enforce obedience to their view of Christianity. As a result, even after the light of the Reformation broke upon the church, Catholics continued to kill Protestants, and, amazingly, many Protestants killed not only Catholics but other Protestants who disagreed with them.

What we must notice here is that Babylon II is a period of religious oppression where church and state were united to force their beliefs on everyone, just as it was in Old Testament Babylon. There were a few, such as the Anabaptists, who refused to use the state to enforce their religion, but they were the exception. The entire period is one of religious oppression.

Thus we must remember when considering the Dark Ages church as the little horn or beast of Revelation 13, that we are not talking about any individual or any present-day church, but about this terrible period of oppression. Therefore, we must study Babylon II so we can be better prepared when Babylon III arises, since the Bible predicts, as we shall discover later, a similar apostasy which will again use the state to enforce its religion. Yet Babylon III will be even more extensive than Babylon II, and even more repressive. So much more, that God has to end it with the second coming of Jesus.

We should also remember that throughout the Dark Ages, there were many sincere Christians who were attempting to serve God as best they knew during this time of overwhelming apostasy. We must be careful not to judge them, since we have not walked in their shoes. The religious system of the times let them down and led them into this apostasy. The people were easily duped, because they did not have access to the Word. Today we have access to the Bible, but it remains unread, which opens us up to the same deception that befell the Christians of the Dark Ages.

Dark Ages Church Fulfills Daniel's Specifications

We will examine the Dark Ages church as the fulfillment of prophecy by first looking at Daniel's marks and then at Revelation's marks. We will discover that the church accurately meets all the specifications indicated.

1. It arose among the ten divisions of the Roman Empire. As the Roman Empire disintegrated into the ten divisions, one power became the unifying power among the tribes. That power was the church. As a result, it soon began to assume political power. No other power arose at this time. The church is the only power that came into political power at this predicted time.

2. It uprooted three of the ten divisions. There were three powers that opposed the Church as it assumed this political state: the Heruli, Vandals, and Ostrogoths. The church then released its armies to vanquish those powers and succeeded in conquering them; therefore, it is the only power responsible for the elimination of the three horns.

3. It was to have the eyes of a man. There indeed was a man at the head of the church that ended up possessing absolute power.

4. It was to become a blasphemous power. In order to accentuate its political power, the church began to ascribe to itself power that formerly had been reserved for God only. It indeed began to mix paganism with Christianity, as Cardinal John Henry Newman declared:

We are told in various ways by Eusebius, that Constantine, in order to recommend the new religion to the heathen, transferred into it the outward ornaments to which they have been accustomed in their own….The use of temples, and these dedicated to particular saints, and ornamented on occasions with branches of trees, incense, lamps and candles; votive offerings on recovery from illness, holy water; asylums; holy days and seasons, use of calendars, processions, blessings on the fields; sacerdotal vestments, the tonsure, images at a later date…are all of pagan origin, and sanctified by their adoption into the Church.—John Henry Cardinal Newman, *An Essay on the Development of Christian Doctrine,* Longmans, Green & Company, London: 1920, p. 373.

The list could go on, but it should be clear that the church from its earliest days began to introduce paganism into its beliefs. Remember, this adulterous mixture of paganism with the worship of God is what brought down the wrath of God on ancient Babylon. It was indeed blasphemous.

Another definition of blasphemy was for a human being to claim the power to forgive sins. Notice that the church of the Dark Ages, when attempting to accentuate its awesome power, actually began to make this bold claim that it could forgive sins. A book used to train priests contains these blasphemous statements:

> And God himself is obliged to abide by the judgment of his priest and either not to pardon or to pardon, according as they refuse to give absolution, provided the penitent is capable of it.—*Dignity and Duties of the Priest*, by Liguori, p. 27.

> Were the Redeemer to descend into a church, and sit in a confessional to administer the sacrament of penance and a priest to sit in a confessional, Jesus would say over each penitent: "Ego te absolvo", and the penitents of each would be equally absolved.—*Ibid*, p. 34.

> The priest holds the place of the Saviour himself, when, by saying "Ego te absolvo" he absolves from sin.—*Ibid.*

In these idolatrous statements, priests did not simply claim to go to God for forgiveness on behalf of the believer, but, so awesome did they feign their power to be, that these priests of the Dark Ages actually thought that God Himself had to abide by their judgment and that they themselves actually forgave people's sins.

The Bible indicated that the final issue on blasphemy would be the church claiming to take the place of God. Did it make this claim? Just look at these unbelievable statements from the Dark Ages church.

> Hence priests are called the parents of Jesus Christ, such

is the title that St. Bernard gives them, for they are the active cause by which he is made to exist really in the consecrated Host.—*Ibid,* p. 32.

Thus the priest may, in a certain manner be called the creator of his Creator, since by saying the words of consecration, he creates as it were, Jesus in the sacrament.—*Ibid.*

All names which in the Scripture are applied to Christ, by virtue of which it is established that he is over the church, all the same names are applied to the Pope.—*On the Authority of Councils,* 1619, ed, book 2, ch. 17.

We hold upon this earth the place of God Almighty.—*The Great Encyclical Letters of Leo, XIII,* p. 304.

Thou art the shepherd, thou art the physician, thou art the director, thou art the husbandman; finally, thou art another god on earth.—From the oration of Christopher Marcellus in the 4th session of the Fifth Lateran Council in 1512, addressing the pope. Labbe and Gossard, *History of Councils,* vol. 14, col. 109.

Such statements need no commentary. It is clear that the Dark Ages church fulfilled every specification of blasphemy as defined by scripture.

1. It made war with the saints. The Dark Ages church was indeed a persecuting church. The entire period was one of constant persecution for those who failed to agree with the church. The conservative estimate is that over 50 million people were killed for their faith by the church during the Dark Ages period. Remember, it was not just Catholics who killed Protestants or dissenters—even Protestants returned the favor and killed Catholics and other Protestants. The characteristic of the entire period

is one of totalitarianism. Even the Pope himself has apologized for what the church did during this terrible era.

2. It would think to alter God's times and laws. We will look at this mark of identification in more detail later. Be assured that the church even attempted this bold move.

3. It was to reign for 1,260 years. The "3½ times" that equaled 1,260 years began in A.D. 538 when the last of the three opposing powers was defeated and the church assumed full political power. It ended exactly 1,260 years later in 1798 when Berthier, the French general, under Napoleon, entered the Vatican, captured the Pope and ended the political power of the church. The period of time was fulfilled to the very year, exactly as foretold in both Daniel and Revelation. The church did not end—it only lost its political power. That was what the prophecy predicted.

Marks of Identification in Revelation

As we have seen, John's writings in Revelation list many identical marks when describing this power. We will notice each one, but will comment only on those not covered in Daniel.

1. The beast had seven heads and ten horns. Notice the connection with Daniel's beast. John is telling us that this is the same power as Daniel's little horn. The ten horns on seven heads indicate the elimination of the three opposing tribes and the domination of the church over the remaining seven tribes.

2. It is a composite beast made up of Daniel's four beasts: the lion, bear, leopard, and dragon. Again, John

unmistakably wants us to see the connection to the Daniel 7 description. The first beast of Revelation 13 is simply a continuation of the beasts that have oppressed God's people through the ages.

3. It received its power, seat, and authority from the dragon—the Roman Empire. Note the historian's account of where the Dark Ages church received its power, seat, and authority:

> The mighty Catholic Church was little more than the Roman Empire baptized. Rome was transformed as well as converted. The very capital of the old Empire became the capital of the Christian Empire. The office of Pontifex Maximus was continued in that of the Pope. Even the Roman language has remained the official language of the Roman Catholic Church down through the ages. Christianity could not grow up through Roman civilization and paganism, however, without in turn being coloured and influenced by the rites, festivities, and ceremonies of old polytheism. Christianity not only conquered Rome, but Rome conquered Christianity. It is not a matter of great surprise, therefore, to find that from the first to the fourth century the Church had undergone many changes.— Alexander Clarence Flick, *The Rise of the Medieval Church,* 1959, pp. 148, 149.

> The Roman Church in this way privily pushed itself into the place of the Roman World-Empire, of which it is the actual continuation; the empire has not perished, but has only undergone a transformation. ... That is no mere "clever remark", but the recognition of the true state of the matter historically, and the most appropriate and fruitful way of describing the character of this Church. It still governs the nations...It is a political creation, and as imposing as a World-Empire, because the continua-

tion of the Roman Empire. The Pope, who calls himself "King" and "Pontifex Maximus", is Caesar's successor. — Adolf Harnack, *What Is Christianity?* pp. 269, 270.

4. The beast was to receive a deadly wound. This is a reference to the elimination of political power at the end of the 1,260-year prophecy in 1798.

5. The deadly wound was to be healed. This political power is to be restored. When it is, it will become Babylon III.

6. The entire world would wonder after the beast. The healing of the wound—the reestablishment of political power by the church—is one of the great signs of the end of the world. The whole world will accept this renewed political power of the church.

7. People would worship the beast. This religious power would be receptive of the worship of people. This fulfillment is very clear. The church indeed was a religious power and allowed people to worship it during the Dark Ages.

8. Revelation indicated strongly that it would be a blasphemous power. We have already noted how accurately this was fulfilled.

9. It would last 42 months, or 1,260 years. This is the Dark Ages period of 538 to 1798, when the church ruled the world politically and religiously.

10. It would persecute those who disagreed with its claims. We have already noticed the persecuting actions of the church throughout the Dark Ages.

11. The number of its name would add up to 666.
Several names could add up to this total. This is not the key indicator. It is one among many. The beast obviously must meet this one as well. One of the titles ascribed to the church during this period was the Latin title: *Vicarius Filii Dei*, meaning "vicar of the son of God"—one who takes the place of God. It was one of the most-often-used titles. Taking the numeric value of each letter indeed adds up to 666.

Having examined all these identifying marks from the books of Daniel and Revelation, it is clear that the church of the Dark Ages is Daniel's little horn and the beast of Revelation 13.

What does this mean? It means that Christianity has some skeletons in its closet. It is easy to bury them and ignore history. But God warned us about this great apostasy so we would not be deceived by it. He would have us examine it today so that we will learn the lesson of history. History repeats itself. The Bible indicates that what happened in the Dark Ages is going to happen again as Babylon III raises its ugly head at the end of time. It will be a greater deception than Babylon II. The Bible indicates it will have three parts to it: the beast, the dragon, and the false prophet. Note that the beast, the church of the Dark Ages, is listed as being resurrected to form a part of the final Babylon.

Yet the final Babylon is only one third composed of the Dark Ages church. Two new powers join it to create this final Babylon. We will study them later.

This has been an awesome, even disturbing revelation. If it has distressed you, do not feel discouraged—it was distressing to Daniel as well. "As for me, Daniel, my thoughts greatly troubled me, and my countenance changed; but I kept the matter in my heart" (Daniel 7:28).

It was disturbing to Daniel. It should be disturbing to us. Religious deceptions are the worst kind, because they cut out our spiritual roots. That is why we cannot rely on any religious institution to save us. We must trust Christ alone for salvation and study the Bible for ourselves.

As the church got entangled in political power, it turned from the pure gospel of Christ which proclaims that people are saved only by the grace of God, and in its stead the Dark Ages church created a system of salvation by human works and merits. Forced, legalized religion always leans toward the support of salvation through human works. That is why the Church of Jesus must stay clear of political entanglements and the attempt to force people to conform to its standards through legal action. When obedience is mandatory, it does not spring from a heart saved by grace but instead becomes a legislated obedience, which ultimately ends up in salvation by human works. Keep up your guard against any attempt by the church to gain control of the state in order to force religion upon us. Our religion must be pure, coming to us straight from the holy Word of God, alone.

9

Hope Foretold

Hope is the ultimate desire of all humankind. No matter how terrible the tragedies of life, as long as we can catch a glimmer of hope, we can survive life's worst encounters. God has provided ultimate hope for His sin-ladened people—the death of Jesus on the cross as our Substitute.

For the Christian, that hope has been realized, since we live this side of Calvary. For the person living before Jesus came to earth, the hope was that someday God would provide the ultimate sacrifice for humankind's redemption. It was not a realized hope—it was an anticipated hope.

Yet God has always wanted His people to have hope. That's why God continually provided pictorial glimpses of the hope of Calvary throughout the Old Testament era, chiefly in the form of the Old Testament sanctuary service. In this chapter, we wish to explore this Old Testament visual prefigurement of the gospel. Not only will it help us better understand the ministry of Christ, it will also enable us to understand the next great prophecy of the book of Daniel.

The Exodus had just occurred. The opening of the Red Sea had warmed the hearts of the Israelites, letting them know that God was with them. They had even seen God descending on Mt. Sinai as He presented Moses with the ten great commandments. The foundation of ancient Israel was the great moral law, the Ten Commandments, proclaimed in thunder-tones upon Mt. Sinai.

If this were the only representation of God witnessed by

the Israelites, it would have been a discouraged group of people there on the Sinai Peninsula. As great as God's law was, they were incapable of rendering perfect obedience to it. How, then, could they survive in the presence of such a holy God? Interestingly, God takes just a few short verses to expand on His law, but He takes fifteen chapters—Exodus 25-40—to describe the plan of salvation whereby God saved Israel when they broke His law.

The Old Testament has far more to say about redemption in the book of Exodus than it has to say about law. Yet the law was there. It was the great standard by which the Israelites were to be judged. In addition, God provided the sanctuary service to show them that redemption only occurs through the sacrifice of an innocent other. In these fifteen chapters mentioned above are detailed instructions for the making of the earthly sanctuary—the place where the Israelites were to receive the forgiveness of sins.

The ancient sanctuary was the literal dwelling place of God on earth. "And let them make Me a sanctuary, that I may dwell among them" (Exodus 25:8). Again, catch the picture of God: a God who desires to dwell among His people, not distant, but ever-present. The construction of this earthly dwelling place for God was clearly described in these fifteen chapters. Moses was shown a pattern in the heavens—a miniature representation of the sanctuary he was to construct according to the particular pattern that God had given him (Exodus 25:9, 40).

This sanctuary that God revealed to Moses seems to be a representation of an original—the sanctuary in heaven. The New Testament illuminates this point:

> Now this is the main point of the things we are saying: We have such a High Priest, who is seated at the right hand of the throne of the Majesty in the heavens, a Minister of the sanctuary and of the true tabernacle which the Lord erected, and not man. For every high priest is appointed to offer both gifts and sacrifices. Therefore it is necessary that this One also have something to offer. For if He were on earth, He

would not be a priest, since there are priests who offer the gifts according to the law; who serve the copy and shadow of the heavenly things, as Moses was divinely instructed when he was about to make the tabernacle. For He said, "See that you make all things according to the pattern shown you on the mountain." Hebrews 8:1-5.

Amazingly, the New Testament informs us that the sanctuary Moses made in the wilderness was not the original, but a copy of a greater and more perfect sanctuary that existed in heaven. The earthly sanctuary had human priests and high priests, but in the heavenly sanctuary, we are told that Jesus is the minister of the sanctuary. There is a sanctuary in heaven itself, and Jesus is our minister. Thus the early sanctuary is given to us to help us better understand the ministry of Jesus Christ. The Old Testament sanctuary service was designed by God to help the Israelites understand in pictorial form the cost of sin: the death of Jesus Christ.

The slaying of the lamb in the Old Testament did not save the people. The lamb was simply a representation of the sacrifice of Jesus. He is the Lamb of God. Old Testament people were not saved by their law keeping but by the precious blood of Jesus. There is no other name by which we can be saved except the name of Jesus. God does not have multiple plans of salvation; there is only one, and it is salvation through grace alone—saved by the blood of Jesus, the Lamb of God.

Throughout the New Testament, sanctuary imagery is used to explain the ministry of Jesus. In fact, one cannot correctly understand the ministry of Jesus apart from the sanctuary service that prefigured it. "Seeing then that we have a great High Priest who has passed through the heavens, Jesus the Son of God, let us hold fast our confession" (Hebrews 4:14).

The work performed by the high priest in the Old Testament is now being performed by Jesus Himself. He is our High Priest. Whereas in the Old Testament, there were priests and high priests, so in the New Testament Jesus has become our High Priest. In fact, the apostle Paul declares Jesus to be the only mediator between God and man (1 Timothy 2:5). A mediator is a "go-between." There is only one who acts on our behalf, and that is Jesus. No one stands between the sinner and God except Jesus. Dear friend, you do not need any human intercessor. You have been given the right to have direct access to the Living God through Jesus Christ. That is why in the New Testament, every one who believes in Jesus is viewed as a priest. The New Testament does not have a priesthood—it *is* a priesthood (Rev. 1:5, 6; 5:9,10; 1 Peter 2:9).

All who have accepted Jesus as their personal Savior have entered the priesthood, where He is the High Priest, and no one else is in between. You don't have to pray through anyone to get to Jesus—you can talk to Him directly. You have your own personal hotline directly to the King of the Universe.

The Design of the Old Testament Sanctuary

The Old Testament sanctuary was divided into three sections. First, there was the outer court, or courtyard. This was the place where the lamb was slain on the altar of sacrifice after the person's sins had been confessed over it. The priest then took the blood from the sacrifice and entered the second section of the sanctuary—the Holy Place—where he sprinkled the blood on the altar of incense, located at the opening to the third section of the sanctuary—the Most Holy Place. In this final section was a large chest, containing the Ten Commandments, with a lid on it called the mercy seat. (See chart, page 135.)

Every day, the priest performed the work in the outer court and Holy Place. Sins were confessed, animals were slain, and blood was sprinkled on the altar of incense. However, once a year, on the Day of Atonement, the high priest entered the Most Holy Place—the third part of the sanctuary. Leviticus 16 describes the awesome ceremony of this day.

First, two goats were chosen, one for the Lord, the other for Azazel (Leviticus 16:7, 8). The Lord's goat was slain, and the blood was taken to the Most Holy Place instead of the Holy

Place, where the priest sprinkled it on the mercy seat (Leviticus. 16:15). The purpose here was to make atonement for the Holy Place, because all the sins of Israel had been transferred there through the blood on the altar of incense (Leviticus. 16:16, 17).

Only after the Holy Place had been cleansed through the Lord's goat was Azazel's goat brought to the priest (*Azazel* was a Hebrew name for the devil). The priest came out of the sanctuary, bearing all the sins symbolically sent in ahead of time. He then confessed those sins over the live goat and sent Satan's goat into the wilderness (Leviticus 16:20-23).

Note that the second goat is never slain—it is not a representation of Jesus. What is happening here? Through the sacrifice of Jesus, Israel's sins—and ours—have been taken from us and sent into the sanctuary, and God has assumed the responsibility for our sins.

Yet God is not responsible for sin—Satan is. Thus there must come a time when God, through a work of judgment, reveals that Satan is really responsible for sin. Satan has charged that God is responsible, but this third phase of the sanctuary reveals clearly that Satan, not God, is ultimately the one who caused sin.

Note that God has three ways He deals with sin: through the work of sacrifice in the outer court; through the work of interceding, by applying the blood in the Holy Place; and finally by a work of judgment in the Most Holy Place, where God is fully vindicated of Satan's charges.

Christ Fulfills the Old Testament Sanctuary

The three phases of ministry described in the Old Testament sanctuary prefigured the three phases of the ministry of Christ described in the New Testament. This whole Jewish system was given to the Israelites to help them understand that salvation is attained only through the shedding of blood—the blood of Jesus.

Phase one of the sanctuary, with its confession of sins and slaying of the lamb, pointed to Jesus as the Lamb of God who takes away the sin of the whole world. Every time the priest killed the lamb, it showed faith in Jesus, who would someday die for all sins. "But now, once at the end of the ages, He has appeared to put away sin by the sacrifice of Himself" (Hebrews 9:26). Phase one of the sanctuary represented phase one in the ministry of Jesus—the sacrifice of Himself for our sins.

Yet in the Old Testament service, the sacrifice of the lamb was not the end of dealing with sin. The blood was taken into the Holy Place and sprinkled before the altar of incense, symbolically transferring the sin from the sinner to the sanctuary through the lamb. Thus Christ, having paid the price of our redemption, must then move into the second phase of the heavenly ministry, applying the benefits of His death to each sinner. "For Christ has not entered the holy places made with hands, which are copies of the true, but into heaven itself, now to appear in the presence of God for us" (Hebrews 9:24).

Phase two in the ministry of Christ represents His work of intercession in the heavenly sanctuary. Just as the earthly sanctuary assumed the responsibility for the people's sins through the sprinkling of the blood before the altar of incense, so Christ presents His perfect blood offering for the sinner. Through Christ's work of intercession, the heavenly sanctuary has assumed the responsibility for my sins. I need never meet them again. God has taken them from me forever through the sacrifice of Jesus.

These two parts to Christ's redemptive activity for the human race were clearly outlined for us by the apostle Paul in Romans 5:10: "For if when we were enemies we were reconciled to God through the death of His Son, much more, having been reconciled, we shall be saved by His life."

We have been reconciled to God through the death of Jesus, but having been reconciled, we are then saved by the intercession of His perfect life. Jesus not only died a perfect death—He lived a perfect life. He offers to place in the record books of heaven His perfect life in place of my sinful life, so that when the record books are examined, my sins do not appear there, but in their place stands the perfect life of Jesus. This work of intercession began when Jesus ascended to heaven and continues to this very day.

The third phase of the Old Testament sanctuary service revealed that there would come a time when those sins assumed by the sanctuary would be forever removed, thus showing that Satan is responsible for them, not God. This, as noted, would necessitate a work of final judgment. Just as Christ died, rose again, and ascended to heaven to intercede for us, so there will come a time when He will perform the third phase of His ministry—the work of final judgment.

Jesus Himself spoke about these three phases to His ministry of reconciliation.

> And when He has come, He will convict the world of sin, and of righteousness, and of judgment: of sin, because they do not believe in Me; of righteousness, because I go to My Father and you see Me no more; of judgment, because the ruler of this world is judged. John 16:8-11.

Three phases to the ministry of Jesus: sin, righteousness, and judgment—all of which are clearly taught in the threefold ministry of the earthly sanctuary. The outer court deals with sin through the sacrifice of Jesus; the Holy Place deals with righteousness through the intercession of the perfect life of Jesus; and the Most Holy Place deals with judgment because the prince of this world (Satan) is judged, having been shown to be responsible for sin.

We have been clearly informed concerning the beginning of each of the three phases to the ministry of Christ. Phase one occurred once and for all at the cross. Phase two began at the ascension of Jesus and continues to the end of time. Our question is, when does this final phase of the sanctuary ministry, the work of final judgment, begin?

It would only be reasonable to assume that judgment must occur before the end of the world, since at the end, Satan, the object of this judgment, is destroyed. At the end of the Old

Testament service, the goat is released into the wilderness. Revelation 20 indicates that Satan is bound to the wilderness at the second coming of Christ for one thousand years. The Old Testament day of atonement service also indicates that someone who confessed a sin that day could have the sin sent into the sanctuary and removed while the priest was in the Most Holy Place. Thus grace was available to the sinner while phase three of the sanctuary continued.

These facts reveal that this judgment must be a pre-advent judgment—a judgment occurring before the second coming of Christ. When does such a judgment occur? Our next prophecy in Daniel 8 and 9 gives us the exact timing for the beginning of this final phase of the ministry of Jesus—the time for the beginning of the final judgment.

The Judgment Begins

We will examine the details of the prophecy in the next chapter, but notice especially Daniel 8:14: "He said to me, 'For 2,300 evenings and mornings; then the holy place will be properly restored'" (NASB). Other translations interpret it: "then shall the sanctuary be cleansed." Both renditions—"cleansed" and "restored"—are possible here. The 2,300 evenings and mornings, or days, represent the morning and evening sacrifices that defiled the earthly sanctuary. That is why it needed to be restored or cleansed. What phase of the sanctuary cleansed or restored the Holy Place? Obviously, it was the work of the Most Holy Place. This is the phase of the sanctuary that symbolized Christ's final ministry of judgment. Therefore, this prophecy is providing us with the beginning date for the third phase of the ministry of Christ—the work of final judgment.

No interpretation of the 2,300 days is given in the eighth chapter of Daniel. Instead, the chapter ends with Daniel understanding everything in the prophecy except the time period of 2,300 days. Remembering that in Bible prophecy a literal day symbolizes a year, this prophecy—the longest in the Bible—stretches on for 2,300 years.

Chapter 9 opens with Daniel still searching for an understanding of the 2,300 days that eluded him in chapter 8. He searches the prophetic books, especially Jeremiah's prediction of the 70-year captivity, hoping to understand this prophetic time period. Daniel 9:3-19 shows Daniel praying, confessing his sin, the sin of his people, and pleading with God to give him understanding of this time prophecy that was not explained.

How quickly God answers. Before Daniel finishes his prayer, the angel Gabriel appears with the explanation:

> Now while I was speaking, praying, and confessing my sin and the sin of my people Israel, and presenting my supplication before the Lord my God for the holy mountain of my God, yes, while I was speaking in prayer, the man Gabriel, whom I had seen in the vision at the beginning, being caused to fly swiftly, reached me about the time of the evening offering. And he informed me, and talked with me, and said, "O Daniel, I have now come forth to give you skill to understand. At the beginning of your supplications the command went out, and I have come to tell you, for you are greatly beloved; therefore consider the matter, and understand the vision." Daniel 9:20-23.

Quickly, Gabriel comes in answer to Daniel's prayer for understanding. Remember, the only thing in the previous vision that Daniel did not understand was the time period of 2,300 days. No other vision has been given since the 2,300 days were foretold, and the first thing the angel says deals with time. All of which unquestionably links the interpretation of the 2,300 days to the next few verses.

> Seventy weeks are determined for your people and for your holy city, to finish the transgression, to make an end of sins, to make reconciliation for iniquity, to bring in everlasting righteousness, to seal up vision and prophecy, and to anoint the Most Holy. Know therefore and understand, that

from the going forth of the command to restore and build Jerusalem until Messiah the Prince, there shall be seven weeks and sixty-two weeks; the street shall be built again, and the wall, even in troublesome times. And after the sixty-two weeks Messiah shall be cut off, but not for Himself; and the people of the prince who is to come shall destroy the city and the sanctuary. The end of it shall be with a flood, and till the end of the war desolations are determined. Then he shall confirm a covenant with many for one week; but in the middle of the week He shall bring an end to sacrifice and offering. Daniel 9:24-27.

You will recognize this as the same prophecy we studied in chapter 2 of this book. This is the tremendous prophecy that predicted the year for the baptism and crucifixion of Jesus. (Please review this study in chapter 2.) What is fascinating here is that the text actually tells us that this 70-week prophecy is cut off from the larger 2,300-day prophecy. In verse 23, the angel tells Daniel to consider the vision (2,300 days); then immediately declares that 70 weeks of the 2,300 are determined for the holy people. (See chart, page 136.)

If you cut off or remove the first seventy weeks or 490 years from the prophecy, you arrive at the year A.D. 34, the year the Jewish leadership sealed their rejection of the Messiah by stoning Stephen, the first Christian martyr (Acts 7). Subtracting 490 years from the 2,300 years leaves 1,810 years after A.D. 34 to the ending of the 2,300-year prophecy. Adding 1,810 to A.D. 34, we arrive at the year 1844 for the ending of the 2,300-day prophecy and the beginning of the third phase of the ministry of Christ in the heavenly sanctuary—the final work of judgment.

What an awesome hour we are living in! This final phase of the ministry of Christ has already begun. Time indeed is running out for Planet Earth. In the next chapter, we will explore the ramifications of this tremendous revelation from the heart of the book of Daniel.

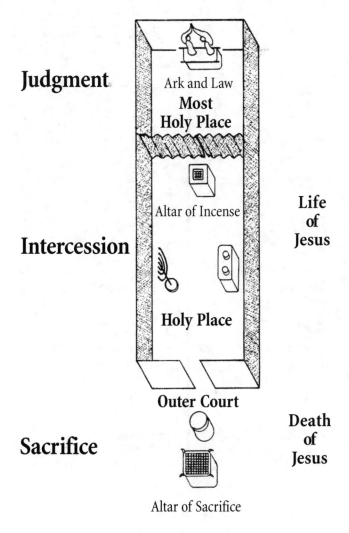

Judgment

Intercession

Sacrifice

Ark and Law
**Most
Holy Place**

Altar of Incense

Holy Place

Life
of
Jesus

Outer Court

Death
of
Jesus

Altar of Sacrifice

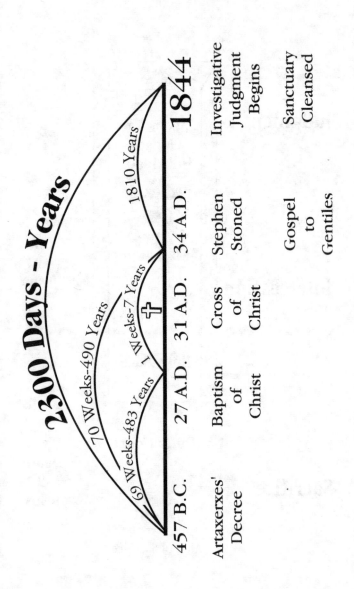

2300 Days - Years

457 B.C.   27 A.D.   31 A.D.   34 A.D.   1844

Artaxerxes'   Baptism   Cross   Stephen   Investigative
Decree   of   of   Stoned   Judgment
               Christ   Christ   Begins

                                    Gospel   Sanctuary
                                    to   Cleansed
                                    Gentiles

69 Weeks-483 Years
70 Weeks-490 Years
1 Weeks-7 Years
1810 Years

10

Hope in the Judgment

Going to court is not my favorite activity. I remember having to go to court for a traffic violation. I dreaded the day. I was nervous, because I did not know the outcome. Would the judge find me guilty? What fine would he levy on me? Receiving judgment is never an object of great and happy anticipation. It is usually one of fearful apprehension.

Yet God's judgment is not to be feared. In fact, the Bible ascribes the greatest praise to God because He has convened the judgment. Judgment in scripture is good news. In fact, it is part of the good news of the gospel. There is nothing frightening about God's judgment. Listen to what God says about judgment:

> Alleluia! Salvation and glory and honor and power belong to the Lord our God! For true and righteous are His judgments, because He has judged the great harlot who corrupted the earth with her fornication. Revelation 19:1, 2.

Why is judgment such good news? Because God has been vindicated against Satan's charges. The judgment has been decided in God's favor. So it is with the judgment of the saints—it is a judgment in favor of the saints. That is why all heaven erupts in a grand ascription of praise to God over the judgment.

The Old Testament sanctuary revealed three phases in the ministry of Christ, symbolized by the three parts of the ancient Jewish sanctuary: the outer court, Holy Place, and Most Holy Place. This three-part sanctuary represented Christ's work of sacrifice, intercession, and final judgment. Jesus referred to His threefold work in John 16—Christ through the Holy Spirit convinces the world of sin, righteousness, and judgment. (See chart, page 135.)

Christ fulfilled phase one on the cross, engaged in phase two beginning with His ascension to heaven, while phase three began at the end of the 2,300-day prophecy in 1844. (See chart, page 136.)The amazing truth is that we are living today during the final phase of Christ's threefold ministry in heaven. At the end, He will come to take His vindicated people home.

This final phase of judgment is the key message brought to us in the book of Daniel. The focal point of the prophecies of Daniel 7-9 is the great revelation of this pre-advent judgment. The book of Daniel is not primarily about the little horn or all the beasts. They are part of the story, but the ultimate message is that God will decide in favor of His people, in spite of the little horn and all these powers that are attempting to destroy God's people. The good news of the book of Daniel is that God's people are vindicated, even as God is vindicated against Satan's charges. While this message of the judgment is not focused on humanity, it reveals a great deal about our God.

As we examine the final phase of Christ's ministry in this chapter, let us refocus on these three great chapters in the heart of the book of Daniel. Please note the sequence of events as they are given five different times in these chapters.

The first sequence begins in Daniel 7:4, where Babylon is described as the lion beast, followed by Media-Persia as the bear (verse 5). Then the leopard beast—Greece (verse 6) with four heads (four divisions of the Grecian empire)—is quickly followed by the iron-toothed dragon representing Rome. Verse 7. The ten horns on this beast represented the ten divisions of the Roman Empire (verse 7). Then comes the description of the little horn (verse 8), depicting the apostasy of the Christian church in the Dark Ages.

Only one verse describes each power: Babylon, Media-Persia, Greece, Rome, ten divisions, and Dark Ages church. These powers are not the focus of the prophecy. The next event, a judgment scene, occupies six verses. Why? This is the message of the chapter. It is not about beasts—it is about the judgment of God. The rest of the prophecy is given us to help us place this judgment scene in the correct sequence. It is to occur *after* the reign of the little-horn power. Notice Daniel's description of this judgment scene, immediately following the reign of the Dark Ages church:

> I watched till thrones were put in place, and the Ancient of Days was seated; His garment was white as snow, and the hair of His head was like pure wool. His throne was a fiery flame, its wheels a burning fire; a fiery stream issued and came forth from before Him. A thousand thousands ministered to Him; ten thousand times ten thousand stood before Him. The court was seated, and the books were opened. I watched then because of the sound of the pompous words which the horn was speaking; I watched till the beast was slain, and its body destroyed and given to the burning flame. As for the rest of the beasts, they had their dominion taken away, yet their lives were prolonged for a season and a time. I was watching in the night visions, and behold, One like the Son of Man, coming with the clouds of heaven! He came to the Ancient of Days, and they brought Him near before Him. Then to Him was given dominion and glory and a kingdom, that all peoples, nations, and languages should serve Him. His dominion is an everlasting dominion, which shall not pass away, and His kingdom the one which shall not be destroyed. Daniel 7:9-14.

This is the message of chapter 7. There is a judgment coming, in which God is triumphant against all that the little horn does to oppose Him. The point to note is that this judgment scene occurs in the sequence of all the powers that oppose God. It appears at the end of the reign of the little horn. Since the little horn was to reign from 538 to 1798, this pre-advent judgment of Daniel 7 should occur sometime after 1798.

The sequence of the empires is repeated again in verse 17, indicating that the four beasts are four kingdoms. They pass with scant notice, to give us again the focal point of this prophecy in verse 18: "But the saints of the Most High shall receive the kingdom, and possess the kingdom forever, even forever and ever." The outcome of this judgment is already decided—the saints will inherit the kingdom.

In verses 18 and 19, Daniel again reviews the beasts to give us the sequence. In two verses, he traces the fourth beast, Rome, with its ten divisions, and the little horn. Yet the little horn can only prevail against God's saints for its allotted time. Note verses 21 and 22:

> I was watching; and the same horn was making war against the saints, and prevailing against them, until the Ancient of Days came, and a judgment was made in favor of the saints of the Most High, and the time came for the saints to possess the kingdom.

For the third time in this chapter, Daniel has reviewed the sequence of the empires and always ends with the focal point of the message of the book—judgment will come; God will prevail. Note again that it has already been decided in favor of the saints. The outcome of the judgment is never in doubt. Satan's powers may appear to dominate, but God's judgment, the message of this book, will forever settle the issue in favor of God and His saints.

For the fourth time in this chapter, Daniel repeats the sequence, ending in the judgment scene. Daniel 7:23 begins with the fourth beast (Rome). Verse 24 predicts the ten divisions, followed by the rise of the little horn, who prevails for 1,260 years speaking great words against God (verse 25). Then the prophecy refocuses our attention on the main message of the book: In spite of the little horn, there will be a judgment against this power, in favor of God's saints.

But the court shall be seated, and they shall take away his dominion, to consume and destroy it forever. Then the kingdom and dominion, and the greatness of the kingdoms under the whole heaven, shall be given to the people, the saints of the Most High. His kingdom is an everlasting kingdom, and all dominions shall serve and obey Him. Daniel 7:26, 27.

Four times in this chapter, Daniel has moved us through the sequence of empires: Babylon, Media-Persia, Greece, Rome, ten divisions, Dark Ages church. In each of the four renditions, the prophet always spends more time with the main revelation of the judgment that occurs after the reign of the little horn than he does with the rendition of the powers that seek to destroy God's people.

All these powers will pass away, but the judgment forever seals the truth about God. He is victorious. This final pre-advent judgment, beginning in 1844, fully vindicates God and His people against all that Satan and his cohorts have charged against God.

The Message of Daniel 8

For a fifth time in Daniel 8, the prophet outlines the empires in sequence. However, this time he uses different symbols for the empires. It is also a separate prophecy, which is given near the end of the Babylonian empire in the third year of the reign of Belshazzar, king of Babylon. Note the vision:

I saw in the vision, and it so happened while I was looking, that I was in Shushan, the citadel, which is in the province of Elam; and I saw in the vision that I was by the River Ulai. Then I lifted my eyes and saw, and there, standing beside the river, was a ram which had two horns, and the two horns were high; but one was higher than the other, and the higher one came up last. I saw the ram pushing westward, northward, and southward, so that no animal could withstand him; nor was there any that could deliver from his hand, but he did according to his will and became great. Daniel 8:2-4.

The symbol of the ram is used to represent the kings of Media and Persia (verse 20). There is no mistaking the starting point for this prophecy. It is an exception.

Normally, the prophecy starts with the nation in power when the prophecy is given—in this case, Babylon. Instead, this prophecy begins with the next empire—Media-Persia. Why? The timeline in the last part of the prophecy is to begin in Media-Persia. We will look further into that point later.

Again, the focal point is not the beasts. They are merely given to provide the historical context for the main message of the book—the beginning of the judgment. So the prophecy quickly continues with the next power—Greece:

> And as I was considering, suddenly a male goat came from the west, across the surface of the whole earth, without touching the ground; and the goat had a notable horn between his eyes. Then he came to the ram that had two horns, which I had seen standing beside the river, and ran at him with furious power. And I saw him confronting the ram; he was moved with rage against him, attacked the ram, and broke his two horns. There was no power in the ram to withstand him, but he cast him down to the ground and trampled him; and there was no one that could deliver the ram from his hand. Daniel 8:5-7.

There is no mistaking the fact that the he-goat represents the same power as the leopard beast—the Grecian empire. Just in case there is any question, verse 21 names Greece as the power, and the great horn it declares represents the first king of Greece, Alexander the Great.

Further details are given in Daniel 8:8, indicating that the horn would be broken and four horns would arise toward the four winds of heaven. Verse 22 indicates that this is a representation of the four divisions of the Grecian empire that we have already noted in a study of the leopard beast of Daniel 7.

Verse 9 captures for us the rise of the Roman Empire—the same power as the iron-toothed dragon in chapter 7. "And out of one of them came a little horn which grew exceedingly great toward the south, toward the east, and toward the Glorious Land" (Daniel 8:9).

At first reading, it appears that this little-horn power grows out of the Grecian ram, which is not historically true. Rome was a new empire, not coming out of the Grecian power. However, a closer examination reveals that in the language Daniel used, the antecedent for "one of them" is not "horns." but "winds." This accurately indicates the origin of the little horn from one of the four winds of the compass—an accurate description of the Roman Empire. It is this power that verses 23 through 25 declare will stand up against the Prince of princes (Christ). Rome accomplished this when Jesus was nailed to the Roman cross.

In chapter 7, the fourth beast, Rome, is pictured with the ten horns on its head and the little horn arising in their midst. All of this indicated the intimate connection between all three powers. Rome was still Rome, even with the ten divisions and the little horn. Separate powers, but still connected together. In chapter 8, Daniel uses the same symbol of the little horn to represent Rome in its two basic stages: pagan and Christian. They are separate, yet intimately connected. Note as Daniel continues his description of the little horn:

> And it grew up to the host of heaven; and it cast down some of the host and some of the stars to the ground, and trampled them. He even exalted himself as high as the Prince of the host; and by him the daily sacrifices were taken away, and the place of His sanctuary was cast down. Because of transgression, an army was given over to the horn to oppose the daily sacrifices; and he cast truth down to the ground. He did all this and prospered. Daniel 8:10-12.

Note the heavy emphasis on blasphemy by the little horn. Daniel 7 and Revelation 13 pictured the claims of the Dark Ages church as blasphemous because of its bold claim to be equal with God. Notice again in this passage the little horn claims to be equal with the Commander of the host, who is Jesus.

However, the great sin of the little horn is identified in Daniel 8 as what it does to the truth of the sanctuary. The little horn takes away the regular or daily sacrifice and makes the work of the sanctuary a work on earth, casting the truth of the sanctuary to the ground.

In the last chapter, we studied the ancient Jewish sanctuary and noted the depiction of the earthly and the heavenly sanctuaries. Since the heavenly sanctuary is inaugurated at the ascension of Jesus after His death, and since the little horn is operating after the death of Christ, the sanctuary here mentioned must be the heavenly sanctuary. Thus the crime increases: The church has destroyed the work of the regular sacrifice and cast the truth of the sanctuary to the ground, making it a work of earth, rather than a heavenly work.

The regular or daily sacrifice referred to the work of the outer court and Holy Place, which occurred every day, morning and evening. This Old Testament service, we have noted, represented Christ's work of sacrifice and intercession. Here, then, is a prediction that the church in her apostasy would destroy the concept that Christ sacrificed Himself once to save all sinners; and this would confuse people about His work of intercession in the heavenly sanctuary.

How did the church of the Dark Ages accomplish this? Instead of pointing people to the one-time sacrifice of Christ for all mankind, the church instituted the daily sacrifice of the mass. Here, the bread and the wine ceased to be a *symbol* of the body and blood of Jesus, but were declared to be the *actual* body and blood of Christ. Thus, when the priest lifted up the host, he was actually offering Christ in sacrifice, again. As a result, the work of the outer court was destroyed. Instead of pointing people to Christ's single sacrifice for the salvation of all, the people were drawn to the church as the dispenser of grace, as she offered Christ daily in sacrifice.

Instead of pointing people to the heavenly sanctuary to receive forgiveness of sins, people were summoned to an earthly confessional box, where an earthly priest provided forgiveness for sins.

Thus, the work of the outer court (sacrifice) and Holy Place (intercession) were made a work on earth, as the daily or regular sacrifice was cast down. Again, note the emphasis in Daniel 8 on the fact that the sanctuary is cast to the earth. It is this attempted transfer of the work of Christ from the heavenly sanctuary to an earthly sanctuary, when the heavenly sanctuary has already been inaugurated by the death of Christ, that brings down the wrath of God on this little-horn power.

The Ultimate End of the Prophecy

The focus of the prophecy of Daniel 8, however, is not this despicable act of the little horn in making the work of the sanctuary a work on earth. The focus instead is on the fact that this truth of the heavenly sanctuary will be restored and that God and His people will be vindicated. This was the same message given in Daniel 7—the judgment will vindicate God of the charges and implications conveyed by the actions of the little horn.

The immediate question is, How long will God allow this to continue before He is vindicated? Note the question that someone in the vision asks and then answers:

Then I heard a holy one speaking; and another holy one said to that certain one who was speaking, "How long will the vision be, concerning the daily sacrifices and the transgression of desolation, the giving of both the sanctuary and the host to be trampled under foot?" And he said to me, "For two thousand three hundred days; then the sanctuary shall be cleansed." Daniel 8:13, 14.

The question is asked: How long will this vision apply that

began with Media-Persia and continued through Greece, Rome, and the Dark Ages church? How long will God allow His truth to be trampled under foot by these apostate powers? The answer comes quickly—2,300 days. The fact that the prophecy extends from Persia to the Dark Ages church makes clear that these are prophetic days representing literal years.

A literal time period of 2,300 days would be less than seven years, hardly enough time for all these empires to exist. That is why the prophecy begins in Media-Persia rather than Babylon, since the time element starts in the realm of Media-Persia with the decree of Artaxerxes in 457 B.C. and stretches all the way to the end of the reign of the little horn in 1798, on to the ending of this prophecy in 1844.

Daniel 8:14 is parallel to the judgment scene in chapter 7. Whereas Daniel 7 spells out exactly what happens after the reign of the little horn by informing us that the judgment will occur, Daniel 8 instead uses the symbolism of the sanctuary to express the same point.

As we studied the sanctuary in the previous chapter, we discovered that phase three of the sanctuary—the work of the Most Holy Place—depicted the work of the cleansing of the sanctuary or the restoration of the sanctuary to its proper place after the removal of sin. This work symbolized the judgment—the very scene that we would expect to occur here because of the remarkable parallel with Daniel 7.

Now, for the fifth time, Daniel has taken us through the same sequence of the empires, and in each case he concludes with the message of restoration and vindication of God through judgment. Clearly, this is the centerpiece of the message of the entire book of Daniel—a message about the beginning of the judgment in 1844, which is the final phase of the ministry of Christ in dealing with the sin problem.

The Judgment Scene

You may be wondering why God has to have a judgment phase to complete the work of Christ. This is a valid question.

Only as we understand the great controversy that erupted in heaven in the very beginning when Lucifer rebelled against God, does the judgment make sense.

There is more involved in salvation than the redemption of mankind as individuals. The rebellion of earth disrupted the entire heavenly universe. Our universe has observed the great controversy being played out on this planet. Satan's rebellion actually occurred in heaven itself; it is carried forth on this planet only because this is the world that succumbed to Satan's enchanted schemes.

Now God is about to bring an end to the great controversy. Satan is to be destroyed, along with all his followers. God is about to take the redeemed from earth and bring them to heaven.

Imagine the thoughts running through the minds of the unfallen beings and angels of the universe! Could these people bring the disasters of earth to heaven? Would they pollute heaven as they have destroyed the earth with sin? These are real questions. God could just ask them to trust Him, and they probably would, but in order that the unfallen beings of the universe would be completely satisfied with the justice of God, He convenes the judgment. In this way, there will never be a question about what God has done. The pre-advent judgment impacts human beings, but it is primarily about the vindication of God against Satan's charges before the onlooking universe. That is the thrust of what we have read in Daniel 7 and 8 about this judgment.

The heavenly sanctuary has been polluted. This is why it needs to be restored or cleansed, according to Daniel 8:14. What pollutes the heavenly sanctuary? Daniel 8:10-12, in context, informs us that the sin of the little horn in making the work of the sanctuary a work on earth creates a need for the sanctuary to be restored or cleansed. The sanctuary imagery, drawn from Leviticus 16 and the cleansing of the earthly sanctuary on the Day of Atonement, indicates that the sanctuary was tainted by the sins of God's people, for which the sanctuary temporarily assumed responsibility. This was demonstrated by the sprinkling of the blood in the Holy Place, symbolically transferring the sin to the sanctuary.

Thus, two things defile the sanctuary: the sin of the little horn, and the sins of the saints transferred to the sanctuary. The pre-advent judgment, beginning in 1844, must restore the sanctuary in both respects. That is why there are two parts to this final judgment—a positive and a negative aspect.

In the negative phase, the judgment will decide against the little horn. This is one of the major thrusts of both Daniel 7 and 8. God is vindicated against the charges made by this apostate power. How does God accomplish this judgment? By a special message on earth, beginning in 1844, that reveals the truth of the ministry of Christ in the heavenly sanctuary and the fallacy of the little horn in making that ministry a work on earth. That message is given in Revelation 14:6, 7:

> Then I saw another angel flying in the midst of heaven, having the everlasting gospel to preach to those who dwell on the earth—to every nation, tribe, tongue, and people— saying with a loud voice, "Fear God and give glory to Him, for the hour of His judgment has come; and worship Him who made heaven and earth, the sea and springs of water."

Here is this special message that we examined in chapter 1 of this book—the unique three angels' messages of Revelation 14 to be proclaimed to make ready a people for the coming of Jesus. We examined this in great detail in chapter 1, but note here that this special message proclaims "the hour of His judgment has come." When this message is proclaimed, the judgment of the earth will have already begun. Since the pre-advent judgment began in 1844, this is the special message for the time when Christ is engaged in the final act of His heavenly ministry—the pre-advent judgment.

The message to be proclaimed is not just that the judgment has begun. The focus must be on restoring the sanctuary from the damage done by the little horn. How is this restoration message delivered? By preaching the everlasting gospel. Note that the heart of the final message is the preaching of the gospel. The gospel is the good news that Jesus Christ forgives sins through His sacrifice on Calvary and His intercessory work in the heavenly sanctuary.

This is the gospel message, and it strikes at the heart of the sin of the little horn. It points people to Jesus and His heavenly sanctuary ministry rather than to a work accomplished on earth. When the inhabitants of earth hear the gospel and learn that Jesus alone can forgive sins, the little horn loses its power, and God's great truth of the sanctuary restores the message of salvation solely through the blood of Jesus.

The gospel strikes at the heart of the little horn. The gospel is the antithesis of the little horn's system of salvation by human works. God has brought judgment on the little horn by the preaching of the eternal gospel of salvation by grace alone. The result is that the entire universe sees the crime of the little horn, and there is no question about its destruction. Its dominion indeed is taken away (Daniel 7:26). It can be annihilated and destroyed forever.

As the judgment is decided negatively against the little horn, so it is decided positively in favor of the saints. Daniel 7:27 declares that as a result of the destruction of the little horn, the sovereignty, the dominion, and the greatness of all the kingdoms under the whole heaven will be given to the saints of the most high, and the time will come that they will possess the kingdom (Daniel 7:27).

Yes, the good news is that the judgment is decided in favor of the saints. The little horn prevailed "until the Ancient of Days came, and a judgment was made in favor of the saints of the Most High, and the time came for the saints to possess the kingdom" (Daniel 7:22). In the Old Testament sanctuary imagery, the sins were removed from the sanctuary, placed over the live goat, and it was then sent into the wilderness. God through that service was simply telling the story that someday Satan will be seen as the instigator of sins, and God and His people will be fully vindicated from all of Satan's charges.

So God conducts the pre-advent judgment for the sake of

the unfallen beings of the universe. He brings up each redeemed person and reveals how they are totally in Jesus as their Savior and Redeemer. The record books are examined, but no sin remains. All sin has been covered in the blood. The only thing that remains is the perfect life of Jesus. Thus there is no question on the part of anyone in the unfallen universe that the people whom Jesus has redeemed are totally in Christ and therefore safe to be saved.

The pre-advent judgment has thoroughly satisfied the entire universe. No one has any questions about what God has done. Our patient God takes the time to answer every question so that sin will never raise its ugly head in God's universe again. That's why He conducts the judgment. It is not a judgment for God to find out who is to be saved. He already knows that. It is a judgment for the sake of the unfallen universe. It is not even a judgment for the saints to be worried about, for it is a judgment for God to be vindicated.

We do not appear in this judgment. Christ, our attorney, appears in our place. First John 2:1 declares that Jesus is our advocate, or lawyer. The Bible also indicates that Christ is our judge (Romans 2:11; 14:10 and 2 Timothy 4:1).

Now think through this scenario: Jesus is your lawyer, who by law is on your side, yet He is also your judge. Consider the fact that you do not have to go to court at all—just send your lawyer, Jesus, who will also act as your judge. Now you can see why there is no need to be afraid of this judgment. It is "rigged" in your favor! You can't lose! No wonder heaven erupts in such wonderful praise with the news that God has convened the judgment. This time of judgment should be a great time of rejoicing and celebration on Planet Earth. Since 1844, Christ has been engaged in this final act of His ministry. God and His people are being vindicated against Satan's charges. Hallelujah! What a time to be alive! What a time for rejoicing!

Knowing this great truth about the outcome of the judgment should give Christians absolute confidence and assurance regarding their salvation. There is no doubt, because we know the outcome. The only way we could be filled with doubt is if we have not accepted Jesus as our Savior, Lord, and Lawyer. Then judgment becomes fearful, because Jesus cannot plead any case not entrusted to Him. For that reason, our only goal today is to make certain that we have engaged Christ as our Lawyer by accepting Him as our Savior and Lord.

This great truth of the pre-advent judgment has been revealed to us to give us assurance of salvation. If we have accepted Jesus, there can be no doubt that we are going to heaven and that we possess the gift of eternal life right now. Listen to the apostle John as he explains this great assurance of salvation that the Christian has in Christ:

> And this is the testimony: that God has given us eternal life, and this life is in His Son. He who has the Son has life; he who does not have the Son of God does not have life. These things I have written to you who believe in the name of the Son of God, that you may know that you have eternal life, and that you may continue to believe in the name of the Son of God. Now this is the confidence that we have in Him, that if we ask anything according to His will, He hears us. 1 John 5:11-14.

This is the marvelous privilege of those who have accepted Jesus as their personal Savior. There is no doubt about their salvation. They know they possess eternal life. It is not a self-made assurance. It is an assurance rooted and grounded in the person of Jesus. You possess this assurance only if you possess Jesus. If you fail to possess Jesus, you no longer have this assurance. John's testimony is abundantly clear: to possess the Son is to possess eternal life. When you possess the Son, Jesus is your lawyer in the judgment, so you now have the absolute assurance that when your name comes up in judgment, you are counted blameless. It is not you, but Jesus, your Substitute, who is being judged.

This is the marvelous truth of the book of Daniel. God convenes judgment. God is vindicated through this judgment, beginning in 1844. His people are vindicated with Him. As a result, they will possess the kingdom. The little-horn power will be destroyed, and God's people will triumph at last. This is the tremendous assurance of the children of God.

No wonder Christians are so happy. No wonder they live without guilt. "There is therefore now no condemnation to those who are in Christ Jesus" (Romans 8:1). Freed from condemnation, secure in Jesus, assured of salvation—what more could we ask for? What a privilege and a joy to be a Christian! If you have not yet accepted this wonderful Jesus as your Savior, why not do so right now and discover the peace, joy, and assurance that comes when one is totally submitted to Jesus Christ? Do it right now as you close the last page of this chapter.

SECTION II

The Unchanging God Provides Us With Hope

The biblical God is an unchanging God. "For I am the Lord, I do not change" (Malachi. 3:6). Even the writer to the Hebrews assures us that Jesus does not change. "Jesus Christ is the same yesterday, today, and forever" (Hebrews 13:8). Imagine trusting a God who kept changing His mind! No wonder the Christian has such hope. The One in whom we trust is an unchangeable God.

The steadfastness of God is the foundation for security in the life of the believer. We can be certain that when God declares something, He stands by His word and will not change His mind in the future. God can be trusted. This is especially true regarding salvation. The gospel of Jesus Christ does not change. That is why the biblical writers refer to it as the "everlasting gospel" (Revelation 14:6, KJV). It is just that—everlasting. It does not change, even as God does not change.

Some have suggested that God has multiple plans of salvation that He uses at different times in history. If that were true, God would not be unchangeable. Fortunately, the scripture is clear—there is only one plan of salvation. From Genesis to Revelation, that plan is always salvation by grace alone, solely through the blood of Jesus shed on Calvary. That is why the Bible declares: "Nor is there salvation in any other, for there is no other name under heaven given among men by which we must be saved" (Acts 4:12).

As we have previously studied, the little horn made the bold assertion that it can change God's law. The unchangeableness of God, so prominently revealed through the biblical record, makes the claim of the little horn of Daniel 7:25 even more unimaginable. Daniel 7:25 declares that this little horn would "intend to change times and law" (Daniel 7:25). Other translations render the passage that he would "think to change times and laws" (KJV). This amazing prediction actually foretells that the church, during its Dark Ages apostasy, would even attempt to change the very law of God, and especially the part that deals with time.

It seems incredible. How could any religious system attempt to change the law of the very God they serve? This could only be accomplished by a system that thinks itself equal to or above God Himself. As we have seen, that was the boastful claim of the church in its hour of deepest apostasy—it actually began to think that it was above God. Imagine believing that it would be possible for the infinite God of the universe to be under the control of the creatures He had made! Certainly there is no limit to self-deception!

The text is also explicit. It does not declare that the church could *accomplish* this feat—it would only *think* it had brought about the change. It would intend to do it, but as far as God was concerned, it would never be successful. So even though the church should boast about changing God's law, the Bible is clear that this is self-deception. No one can change God's law. He is always the same. We can trust Him and have the assurance that He is the same God who spoke in Bible times.

Can You Change God's Law?

When God gave the Ten Commandments as the great moral standard of the universe, it was certain that these grand moral precepts would last forever, for they are the very foundation of the government of heaven. Yet amazingly, in the twenty-first century, there are those who actually question the validity of these ten great precepts given by God Himself. What is even more surprising is that some have suggested that they are no longer binding on modern society.

It seems incredible. Abolish the Ten Commandments? It

would be heart rending to hear this advocated by the secular world, but the amazing thing is that today certain religious leaders are the most prominent advocates of abandoning the Ten Commandments as the foundation of society. They may call it the "new morality," but as Billy Graham once said: "It is simply the old immorality." In his regular newspaper column, Billy Graham once wrote:

> The Ten Commandments—all of them—are just as valid today as they were when God gave them to His people thousands of years ago. God does not change, and neither does His basic moral standard.—Billy Graham Evangelistic Association, P.O. Box 779, Minneapolis, MN, 55440.

Yet, all preachers are not as honest with scripture as Billy Graham. The result is that many have dared to stand in the pulpits of the land and declare that God's immortal code is no longer binding on modern society. They advocate what they call "situation ethics." There are no absolutes, they say. They declare that behavior is always determined by the situation. Arbitrary laws to bind us in every situation are unnecessary. This belief removes the standard for morality. No wonder we have a crime epidemic in the world today! When there is no absolute moral standard of right, people become a law unto themselves. The ultimate result is anarchy.

D. L Moody, the great evangelist of the nineteenth century, once declared:

> Now men may cavil as much as they like about other parts of the Bible, but I have never met an honest man that found fault with the ten commandments.—D. L. Moody, *Weighed and Wanting, Addresses on the Ten Commandments* (Chicago: Fleming H. Revell Company, 1898), pp. 10-17.

Yet Moody could not make such a statement in the twenty-first century, because critics of the Ten Commandments abound today.

The problem is that certain obligations of God's ten eternal rules are no longer palatable to modern society. We do not like all the "thou shalt not's." In an effort to bypass them, preachers have found a way around these absolutes. Thus they suggest that the law of God has been abolished, changed, superseded, or done away with. How can preachers dare to make such wild suggestions? These claims are made only through twisting scripture. Some then proceed to inform us that since we have been saved by grace, we no longer need to keep God's law.

It would appear to these people that law and grace are opposed to each other, yet in reality, you cannot have one without the other. Grace is needed only when there is a broken law. To abolish the law is also to abolish grace. Law and grace are heaven's Siamese twins—they are inseparable. The gift of grace produces in us a willingness to obey God that is greater than if we had not received this gift.

Again, it needs to be clear—keeping the law will never save us. Grace is the only basis of salvation. But one who is saved by grace desires to obey God, not to earn salvation, but because of an overwhelming love for Jesus. Grace, if anything, puts us under greater obligation to God.

Suppose my friend and I are driving down the highway, exceeding the speed limit. A police car quickly pulls us over, and the officer writes me a ticket for exceeding the speed limit. My friend is very generous. He takes the ticket and says that he will pay it for me. Since I am low on cash, I am very grateful to my friend. To show him how grateful I am, I get back on the road and go even faster this time. When my friend tells me to slow down, I declare that I don't have to obey the speed limit any longer, because he has already paid my fine. Ridiculous, you say? Yes. Just so it would be if God forgave us and we used His forgiveness as an excuse to continue in sin. The apostle Paul made it very clear: "What shall we say then? Shall we continue in sin that grace may abound? Certainly not! How shall we who died to sin live any longer in it?" (Romans 6:1, 2). Grace is clearly no excuse to continue sinning. Having received the grace of God in our life puts us under greater obligation to show our love to God by obeying the Ten Commandments. We don't keep the law to be saved, but out of love for the One who has saved us in spite of our sins. We will still sin, and Jesus will still forgive us, but no Christian would ever dare to deliberately disobey God. How could we deliberately hurt the One who has saved us by His grace?

Law and Grace

Law and grace are inseparable. The presence of law demands grace, and the presence of grace reveals there was a law that was violated. There is only one plan of salvation—by grace alone. Since sin first reared its ugly head in the Garden of Eden, until the second coming of Christ, God will always save people by grace alone.

Yet some have cast doubt on the unchangeableness of God by declaring that God has used several different schemes to save humanity throughout history. One of the most popular views states that in Old Testament times, God saved people through the law, but that in the New Testament era, He saves them only by grace. Thus we end up with a changing God—a God who tries a plan of salvation on the human race for thousands of years and then declares it doesn't really work, so He invents a new plan at the cross. Therefore, we no longer need to keep God's law since we are living in the domain of grace.

The basic problem here is that it destroys the unchangeableness of the God who declares: "For I am the Lord, I do not change" (Malachi 3:6). Imagine arriving in heaven and meeting Moses. You walk up to Moses and start talking. You ask Moses how he got to heaven, and he tells you it was because he kept the law. You respond: "I lived after the cross, Moses, so I didn't have to keep the law—I got here by grace." Can you imagine two groups in heaven: one that got there by their own efforts, and the other by the grace of God? No, friend, everyone who enters heaven will do so because of the blood of the Lamb. There is no other way to heaven than through Jesus

Christ. Salvation is always by grace alone, whether we live in Old Testament or New Testament times.

In the Old Testament, humanity was saved by faith in the Christ who was to come. In the New Testament, we are saved by our faith in the Christ who has come. Yet it is only Jesus who saves us. When the Old Testament sinner needed redemption, he did not perform works to clear his sin—he brought a lamb and slew it, for this symbolized the death of Jesus.

In both testaments, law keeping is never presented as a means to salvation, but only as the loving response of a regenerated people who love God for what He has done for them. Even the giving of the Ten Commandments to Israel clearly reveals that they are to be a vehicle of grace and not obligation. God did not give the Ten Commandments to Israel while they were in Egypt, but only after He had redeemed them purely by His grace, baptized them in the Red Sea, and delivered them from Egyptian bondage. Only after redemption does God give the Ten Commandments. The Ten Commandments are never given to a people in bondage—they are given solely to a redeemed people. Redemption always precedes obedience.

Even the Ten Commandments themselves reveal this connection between redemption and obedience:

> And God spoke all these words, saying: "I am the Lord your God, who brought you out of the land of Egypt, out of the house of bondage. You shall have no other gods before Me." Exodus 20:1-3.

Most people who quote the Ten Commandments begin with verse 3—the actual first commandment. They skip over the preamble. Yet if we recite only law, it is misrepresenting what God said. Law keeping is only given to a people whom God has redeemed by His grace. The Ten Commandments in context are given only in the aftermath of redemption. We are redeemed apart from law, but the law is given as a guide to help redeemed people learn how to live for God.

Law and Grace in the New Testament

In the Old Testament, humankind was saved only by grace and then given the Ten Commandments as a guide to live for God. Obedience was never a means to salvation, but only a result of a saving relationship already received. They did not earn salvation by what they did—they received it solely as a free gift of God. Does this relationship of law and grace change in the New Testament? Does the New Testament believer still obey out of love and not obligation? Does he or she obey as a result of salvation—or as a means of salvation?

By the time Jesus arrived on Planet Earth, Old Testament religion had become so corrupted that God's beautiful plan of salvation was distorted into one of legal obligation. The people put great emphasis on obedience to gain heaven and lost sight of the beautiful truth of salvation by grace alone. This was a corruption of Jewish religion and never a part of the scriptures. Much of the New Testament was written to help early Christianity return to a grace orientation of religion instead of the pharisaic righteousness of many first-century Jews.

As Jesus and the New Testament writers attempt to return religion to grace, do they talk about the same balance found in the Old Testament between grace and law? Do they still expect people to be obedient as a result of being saved by grace, or does this change? Let's examine what the New Testament declares concerning law.

As Jesus began teaching about a new righteousness—a righteousness that came through faith in Him—some began to question whether Jesus was suggesting that the law was no longer applicable. Note how Jesus upholds the eternalness of the law of God:

> Do not think that I came to destroy the Law or the Prophets. I did not come to destroy but to fulfill. For assuredly, I say to you, till heaven and earth pass away, one jot or one tittle will by no means pass from the law till all is fulfilled.

Whoever therefore breaks one of the least of these commandments, and teaches men so, shall be called least in the kingdom of heaven; but whoever does and teaches them, he shall be called great in the kingdom of heaven. Matthew 5:17-19.

One thing is clear: Jesus did not change the relationship between law and grace. The law is still there. In fact, as long as heaven and earth continue, He declares that the smallest commandment will not be altered. He even intimates what Daniel predicted—that someone would come and attempt to annul one of the least of the commandments. Clearly, Jesus abides by the perpetuity of the great moral standard, indicating that even the smallest of the commandments of God cannot be altered in any way. Yet the little horn thinks it can change the law.

If there is one writer in the New Testament era that people have tried to misuse regarding the law, it is the apostle Paul. Paul was an adamant anti-legalist. He battled those in the church who sought to bring the legalism of pharisaic Judaism into Christianity. Much of what Paul wrote was written against the misuse of law. Paul was contending with those who were making obedience to the law a means of salvation. Therefore Paul declares in Romans 10:4: "For Christ is the end of the law for righteousness to everyone who believes." The law cannot save. It is not a source of righteousness. Only Jesus is.

Yet some have taken Paul's counsel on misusing the law to attain righteousness and used it to suggest that one does not need to keep God's law at all once they have been saved by grace. They even charged this against Paul himself. Paul reacted vehemently to such charges. "Do we then make void the law through faith? Certainly not! On the contrary, we establish the law" (Romans 3:31). Faith in Jesus establishes the need for the law; it does not nullify the law. Paul is very clear: We are saved by grace and keep the law as a result of receiving Jesus. It is never a means to salvation—it is always a result of salvation.

The apostle John, writing near the end of the first century, had to battle those who had gone to extremes even in early Christianity and were declaring that one need not keep the law anymore. Note John, the apostle of love, arguing for an obedient Christianity:

> He who says, "I know Him," and does not keep His commandments, is a liar, and the truth is not in him. But whoever keeps His word, truly the love of God is perfected in him. By this we know that we are in Him. He who says he abides in Him ought himself also to walk just as He walked. 1 John 2:4-6.

If you know Jesus, you will be obedient. Again, note that John places obedience in proper perspective: It is the result of salvation, not the means of salvation. The New Testament writers, without exception, attempted to return Christianity to the same premise as biblical Judaism: People are saved by grace and are obedient out of love. When we make the profession of belonging to Jesus to be saved, and then deliberately disobey, we show that our profession is false. If we have been saved by grace, we will be obedient. These are strong words, but John is concerned that profession match character. There is no such thing as one professing to be saved and deliberately disobeying God. When one is saved, obedience will follow as a result of a loving relationship with Jesus.

This is the same picture that the Old Testament draws. Only "heart obedience" is acceptable to God. "But this is the covenant that I will make with the house of Israel after those days, says the Lord: I will put My law in their minds, and write it on their hearts; and I will be their God, and they shall be My people" (Jeremiah 31:33). The heart of Old Testament religion was heart obedience rather than legal obedience.

When I was a child, a friend of mine and I would occasionally get into trouble. We found a way to justify our actions. Before we did anything we thought might be wrong, we would recite the Ten Commandments. If the commandments did not precisely name what we were about to do, we concluded it was all right. That is legal obedience. When we have heart obedience, we don't have to consult an outside law. When we accept God, He writes the law on our hearts. Therefore we desire to obey God, not because the law says so, but because Jesus has written that law on our heart and we want to obey not just the letter, but also the very spirit of the law.

Paul and Jeremiah agree. Law-keeping stems from a relationship with Christ rather than from a legal obligation. Both Old and New Testaments tell the same story about the relationship of law and grace. The last book of the Bible gives further indication that law and grace belong together: "Here is the patience of the saints; here are those who keep the commandments of God and the faith of Jesus" (Revelation 14:12). Note that even in Revelation, the last-day saints are identified by the fact that they have this proper relationship between law and grace. They are saved through their faith in Jesus, and they keep the commandments of God as a result of that relationship. Throughout the Bible, there is one description of salvation—it comes by grace alone; and works—or law-keeping—comes as a result of a saving relationship with Jesus.

Thus, to declare that God's law has been abolished or changed is to deny one of the plainest teachings of scripture. This makes the claim of the little horn even more unbelievable. To attempt to change the unchangeable law of God is an attack on God Himself.

Law and the Character of God

The God of the Bible is a holy God. Sin is out of harmony with the character of God. When one sins, one is departing from the character of God. God is perfect, holy, and righteous. Any deviation from that perfection, holiness, or righteousness is sin. That is why John declares: "Sin is lawlessness" (1 John 3:4). Sin is the opposite of the law, for the law is a transcript of the divine character. The law reveals what God is like, and to sin is to depart from that holy character.

What law defines the character of God? The Ten Commandments. "What shall we say then? Is the law sin? Certainly not! On the contrary, I would not have known sin except through the law. For I would not have known covetousness unless the law had said, 'You shall not covet'" (Romans 7:7). Here Paul states that the law told him what sin was. And this law is the Ten Commandments. Paul even quotes the tenth commandment as an illustration. Here then is another function of the law: It reveals sin to us—it tells us what sin is. The law that reveals sin is the Ten Commandments, and sin is a departure from the holy character of God. Thus the Ten Commandments are a revelation or transcript of God's character. Each one of the Ten Commandments reveals something to us about God. Look at what each commandment declares about God.

The first commandment states that we should have no other gods. It tells us that God is unique. The second commandment forbidding images reveals that God is the only one worthy of worship, for He is a living God. The third commandment protects the name of God, calling upon people to reverence God because He is holy. The fourth commandment commands us to keep the Sabbath. It reveals that God is a God of relationships—that He is one who wishes to spend time with His people.

The fifth commandment honors the family and indicates that God respects the family unit that He created. The sixth commandment forbidding killing indicates that God protects all life and that life is sacred. The seventh commandment forbidding adultery pronounces that God is pure, while the eighth commandment declares that God is honest, and the ninth commandment reveals God to be truthful. Finally, the tenth commandment reveals a God who respects other people and their property.

Each of the Ten Commandments reveals something about the character of God. It tells us that this is what the God of the Bible is like—a holy God with an unblemished character. The scripture, however, attempts to summarize the law. Jesus was asked what was the greatest commandment in the law. He responded: "You shall love the Lord your God with all your heart, with all your soul, and with all your mind. This is the first and great commandment. And the second is like it: You shall love your neighbor as yourself" (Matthew 22:37-39).

Jesus declares that all the commandments can be summarized by these two commandments that include the whole law. The first commandment reveals our love to God and summarizes the first four commandments of the Decalogue, whereas the second commandment reveals our love to our neighbor and summarizes the second tablet of the Ten Commandments. The essence of the law is love to God and neighbor.

However, these two commandments are not Jesus' replacement of the Ten Commandments. They are the summary of the ten. In fact, Jesus is not instituting any new commandment here, for He is merely quoting from the heart of Old Testament religion. The most sacred passage for the Jewish people in the entire Old Testament was this passage from Deuteronomy 6:4, 5: "Hear, O Israel: The Lord our God, the Lord is one! You shall love the Lord your God with all your heart, with all your soul, and with all your strength." This passage appears right after the giving of the Ten Commandments in the book of Deuteronomy, chapter 5. Then appears the summary.

Likewise, the second commandment, while not as prominent in the Old Testament period, was still found in the book of Leviticus 19:18: "You shall love your neighbor as yourself." In giving the two great commandments, Jesus recites the Old Testament, revealing that what He is instituting is not new but a recovery of the purity of lost Judaism—a religion of love to God and neighbor that was the heart of Old Testament religion.

Jesus sums up the law as love to God and neighbor. The apostle Paul builds on Jesus' summary by declaring: "Love is the fulfillment of the law" (Romans 3:10). The essence of the law is love. The apostle John declares that "God is love" (1 John 4:8). The essence of the character of God is love, and the essence of the law is love. Therefore the law is a reflection of the character of God. Both reveal who God is. The Ten Commandments, revealing that God is love, are the only part of the scripture that God Himself wrote for us. Most of scripture was written by prophets and apostles, but the Ten Commandments, that reveal the character of God, God Himself wrote with His own finger on two tablets of stone, indicating that this transcript of the divine character was unalterable or unchangeable. You write on stone only that which is permanent. The Ten Commandments are the only revelation of God written in stone. How reassuring it is to know that the character of our God—the character of love—can never be changed.

Into this biblical picture of the enduring nature of the character and the law of God comes the little horn, declaring that it can change the unchangeable. He would "think to change times and laws" (Daniel 7:25, KJV). That holy character of the unchangeable God, the little horn declares it would attempt to alter or change.

To change a precept of the Ten Commandments would be to change the character of God. No wonder Daniel reveals the seriousness of the apostasy of the little horn. It would actually attempt to change the character of God. Any assault on the Ten Commandments is a charge against the character of God.

If the little horn could change the law, then it could change God. If you eliminate the Ten Commandments as no longer relevant today, you are stating that the character of God is no longer relevant today. Any attack on the Ten Commandments is a frontal attack on the very character of God. It cannot go unchallenged.

The little horn's attempt to alter the character of God by changing His law must be challenged. God does not change. Neither does His law, which reveals His character. Thankfully, God does not change. The little horn may attempt to change the law or even think that it has done so, yet God remains the same. He does not change. His law does not change. He is still the same God.

Law and the Sacrifice of Jesus

One purpose of the law is to reveal that we are sinners in need of the grace of Christ in our lives. The law does not save—it only points out my need for salvation. However, if the law were done away with, there would be no sin, since sin is the transgression of the law. If there were no sin, then there would be no need of a Savior. To attempt to abolish the law not only abolishes the character of God but also renders totally unnecessary the sacrifice of Jesus for our sins.

When God was faced with the sin problem, He had two choices. He could change His law (character) to allow sin, which would have destroyed the holy God. The second choice God faced was to send His Son to pay the penalty of the law, which would reveal that God is unchangeable and His standard beyond question. The only way to save humanity and preserve the character of God was for God Himself to pay the penalty of violation of His law or character. Jesus must die for the transgressions of humankind. The Bible declares that "Christ died for our sins" (1 Corinthians 15:3). The very name, *Jesus*, means to save from sins (Matthew 1:21).

The strongest proof that the law has not been changed is the cross of Christ. The fact that Jesus died on the cross, paying the price of our sins, reveals that the character of God has withstood the test. God Himself has paid the penalty of our sins. We do not need to pay that penalty. He has paid it for us. Therefore He has preserved the unchangeableness of His character. On the other hand, if the law has been changed or abrogated, then the death of Jesus on Golgotha's hill is only a farce and has no salvation value. How thankful we should be that the character of God remains in place—it has not been changed. The eternal law of God still stands unmovable, in spite of the attempt of the little horn to change it.

If the law does not save us, what then is the purpose of this law? Romans 3:20 declares: "Therefore by the deeds of the law no flesh will be justified in His sight, for by the law is the knowledge of sin." The law does not save—it only reveals sin.

It tells us that we are sinners. In verse 19, Paul declares that the law causes the whole world to stand guilty before God. The law has revealed that I am a sinner, but the law cannot save me. Only Jesus can.

The law is heaven's mirror, reflecting our need of cleansing and redemption. Just like the mirror that reflects our dirty faces, so the law reveals the heinousness of our sins. But the mirror doesn't cleanse us. It only reveals that we need to become clean. So the law reveals our need of cleansing but cannot cleanse us. Soap and water clean us physically, and the blood of Jesus alone cleanses us spiritually. Then we look back in the mirror, and it reveals that our face is now clean. So we look back in the mirror of God's law, clothed in the perfect righteousness of Jesus Christ, and the law reveals that we are clean—not of ourselves, but in Jesus alone. Paul declares that any law that can produce this great effect of revealing sin and pointing us to our need of salvation in Christ is a good law. "Therefore the law is holy, and the commandment holy and just and good" (Romans 7:12).

The apostle James exalts the law that is a transcript of God's character.

> For whoever shall keep the whole law, and yet stumble in one point, he is guilty of all. For He who said, "Do not commit adultery," also said, "Do not murder." Now if you do not commit adultery, but you do murder, you have become a transgressor of the law. So speak and so do as those who will be judged by the law of liberty. James 2:10-12.

James quotes two of the Ten Commandments and states that if you break one commandment, you are guilty of breaking them all. That seems like a very strong assertion until you think about it. The person who breaks one commandment is a transgressor of the law—a sinner. To be saved, he or she needs Jesus. A person who breaks all ten of the commandments is likewise a sinner in need of cleansing. To be saved, that person too needs Jesus. The point James is making is that any sin demands a Savior. It is not a matter of how many or how few sins we have committed—it is a picture of a God who is perfect, and any deviation from His character unfits us for the presence of God. Therefore, no matter how small the sin, we still cannot save ourselves. We need the cleansing blood of Jesus.

What then is the response of the Christian to the truth about God's law? If the blood of Jesus alone has saved us, we will want to study carefully God's law, so that we better understand His character. As we spend time reflecting on God's law (character), we will discover more of our life that needs the cleansing blood of Jesus. That is why the Christian loves God's law. He wants every part of his life covered in the blood of Jesus. He wants the power of Jesus operating in His life, providing him with the strength to live a life in harmony with the character of God.

Can the little horn change God's law? Obviously, it is impossible. It can't be done. Yet the church in its apostasy attempted to alter God's law. In the next chapter, we will examine how the little horn actually attempted to change God's law and times. Right now, we can have hope, because we have seen that in spite of what the little horn has attempted to do, God remains unchangeable. This immovable, unchanging God is at the foundation of the hope that we possess. It is a hope born in the crucible of a God who is the same yesterday, today, and forever. May God give you the freedom to totally trust Him—this God who does not change.

12

Hope in a Relationship With an Unchanging God

We rest assured in our hope, because we have a God who is unalterable and unchangeable. One of the most significant charges levied against the little-horn power by God in Daniel 7:25 is its attack on His character, in suggesting that His law or character can be changed. In this chapter, we wish to explore an area of God's law that most people think has been changed. However, we have seen the Bible declare that not the smallest part of the commandments can be changed, because to do so would be to change the character of God, and He is a God who does not change.

What is a Christian? Jesus declared that a Christian is one who follows Him (Matthew 4:19). That is the essence of what it means to be a Christian. A Christian is one who lives in a trusting relationship with Jesus Christ. A Christian is one who follows Jesus all the way.

Christianity is not a way of life—it is not a set of dogmas and rules. Christianity is a relationship with a person, and not just any person—it is a relationship with the One who has paid the price of our redemption on Calvary. It is a relationship with the One who has saved us, not by what we have done, but by what He has done on Calvary. Christianity is Jesus—and Jesus is Christianity.

A Christian in love with Jesus desires to study the life of Jesus—to know how to follow this One who did so much for humanity. But we will discover that the little horn wishes to change the commandment—the one designed to help us establish a strong relationship with Jesus. He wants to alter the time for our connection with God. But the God of relationships does not change. He remains committed to this connection with His people, no matter what the little horn does.

When we accept Jesus as our Savior and Lord, He enters our life, and He lives out His life in us through His power and strength. Even our loving response to God's salvation—the works that we perform—is accomplished only through the power of God and not human effort. Jesus works through us. Our struggle is to allow Him to have full control of our lives rather than attempting to live life on our own.

When we accept Jesus, He substitutes His perfect life for our sinful life. As a result, the record books of heaven reveal a divine transfer—Jesus' perfect life in place of our polluted life. At the end of His life, Jesus declared that He had kept His Father's commandments perfectly (John 15:10). He admonishes His followers to do the same. Jesus wants us to allow Him to work out His perfect righteousness in our lives.

Christ's followers will always be distinguished by commandment keeping. A person redeemed by the blood of Jesus would never think of doing anything contrary to Jesus. How could a person, redeemed by the blood of the Lamb, time and time again deliberately transgress the commandments of God?

Yes, the person may slip and fall, and God forgives, but the person does not deliberately and defiantly transgress God's commandments. When we love Jesus, we automatically want to obey Him and keep His commandments, because we love Him.

Jesus grew up in Nazareth. As a young man, He helped out in the family business. He was a carpenter like His earthly father Joseph. The Bible declares that Jesus lived in subjection to His parents, even though He was the Son of God. Jesus honored His father and mother because of God's respect for families. However, on Saturday morning, you never found Jesus in the carpenter's shop—He was in the synagogue or church of His day. Why did Jesus set the example by resting on Saturday, while today, nearly the entire Christian world worships on Sunday?

The Bible declares: "So He came to Nazareth, where He had been brought up. And as His custom was, He went into the synagogue on the Sabbath day, and stood up to read" (Luke 4:16). Jesus' custom was to go to the synagogue every Sabbath. He is the founder of Christianity, and Christianity is following Jesus. Isn't it strange that nearly the entire Christian world goes to church on a day different from the founder of Christianity? Truly, if Christianity is following Jesus, then we should do as He did. Why did Jesus have such a custom? It was because, as we have already noted, He kept His Father's commandments perfectly. One of those ten immortal principles that God wrote with His own finger—one of those principles that reflect the character of God and cannot be changed without changing God's character—is the fourth commandment.

> Remember the Sabbath day, to keep it holy. Six days you shall labor and do all your work, but the seventh day is the Sabbath of the Lord your God. In it you shall do no work: you, nor your son, nor your daughter, nor your male servant, nor your female servant, nor your cattle, nor your stranger who is within your gates. For in six days the Lord made the heavens and the earth, the sea, and all that is in them, and rested the seventh day. Therefore the Lord blessed the Sabbath day and hallowed it. Exodus 20:8-11.

Here in the heart of the Ten Commandments is a commandment detailing with great specificity that God made the Sabbath—a day for humankind to celebrate God's creation rest. God has set aside a special day for Him and His creatures to enjoy a relationship together.

Most of the commandments begin with "Thou shalt not," but the Sabbath and the commandment on the home do not. Interestingly, these are the two commandments that originate in the Garden of Eden—Sabbath and marriage. All the commandments that deal with life after sin entered are commanded in the negative, but the two commandments from

Eden are specified from a positive perspective.

God begins the Sabbath commandment with the word *Remember*. This indicates that the Sabbath was not introduced when God gave the law on Sinai. You cannot remember something you have never heard of before. Later on in the commandment, God directs us to the Sabbath's origin in the Garden of Eden. When God gave the Ten Commandments on Sinai, He was codifying it for the Jewish people that He had just redeemed to Himself.

This redeeming God now tells them that He wants to spend one day each week in a relationship with His redeemed people. Of course, they were already keeping the Sabbath before God announced it again on Sinai. Exodus 16 details the story of the manna and how it fell on every day but Sabbath, and a double portion fell on Friday that kept over Sabbath. That is one reason God said "Remember."

Another reason God used *Remember* in this commandment is to indicate that it is of special importance. When I teach classes, occasionally I will tell my students to remember something. They immediately know this item is of vital importance. Remembering indicates the importance of an issue. The fact that God chose to begin this commandment with the word *Remember* would indicate that God considered the Sabbath of great importance.

A third reason God said to remember the Sabbath may be that God looked down the stream of human history and saw that this was the one commandment that most people would have a tendency to forget. Isn't it strange that the one commandment God said to remember is the one that most people today suggest we forget? Evidently God's priorities are different than ours.

The Purpose of the Sabbath

Nine of the Ten Commandments are readily accepted by humanity. They are all recognized as great moral standards. Most people keep them, whether they are Christians or not.

They are the foundation of a moral society. However, there is no reason for society to keep the Sabbath. The only reason is because God asked us to.

The Sabbath thus becomes a test of our complete trust in Christ. It is actually the key commandment that makes it possible to keep the other nine commandments. It is the one commandment that deals with setting aside time for our relationship with God.

Only through a deep relationship with God are you enabled to keep the other nine commandments. In the heart of the Ten Commandments, God gave us one commandment that deals with our relationship with Him. The commandments cannot be kept without having a relationship with Jesus. The Sabbath is the one commandment that intimates grace in the midst of law.

Why did God command the Sabbath? Look at what the commandment tells us. We are to stop all human work and spend the day with the One who made us. The whole purpose of the Sabbath is for God and His children to spend a day together building a relationship. God is the God of relationships. The fact that He has given us the Sabbath indicates that He is not a distant God—He is the God who wishes to get close to His people.

We need to spend time with God every day. A daily relationship with Jesus is vitally important for our Christian growth. Yet God declares that He wants a deeper relationship than the few minutes we spend with Him daily. In order to develop this deep, abiding relationship, God declares that once a week we need to spend a whole day together. We may think we can get by on thirty minutes a day, but God says He needs more than that. We need a whole twenty-four hours once a week to develop the kind of relationship with God that will make us into mature followers of Jesus Christ. If we declare that we don't need that much time, we announce to God that we know ourselves better than He does. God made us, and it is He who tells us we need this amount of time to build the relationship.

Relationships take time. They cannot be hurried. You cannot have a good relationship with your spouse unless you take time together regularly. If that is so for a human relationship, it is even more crucial for the divine relationship. This is the one commandment in ten that deals with our relationship with God. It is the one commandment that requires us to spend quality time with God.

This is not a commandment for the non-Christian. It is a commandment for those who have entered into a relationship with Jesus. If I were not a Christian, why would I want to spend a day with Jesus? Yet when Jesus is our Savior, we love to spend time with Him. No one enjoys spending time with people we don't know, but all of us enjoy the time we spend with our friends. And Jesus is our best friend. This is why Sabbath is the happiest time of the week for the followers of Jesus.

On Sabbath, I can put aside all my weekly cares. I don't have to worry about the job, paying the bills, or hearing about the latest crises in the world. Instead, I get to put all that aside and spend the time enriching my relationship with Jesus.

Some people think that Sabbath is a time to rest. Sabbath does provide rest, but a different kind of rest. It is not just physical rest. It is a resting from everyday work so that we can enjoy a time with Jesus and deepen our relationship. If we spend all Sabbath sleeping and catching up on our rest so we can go back to work refreshed, we have not kept the Sabbath.

God is not looking for people to just do nothing on His day. The whole purpose of the day is for humans and God to spend time together and deepen their relationship. If we do not use these sacred hours to enhance our relationship with Jesus, we are not keeping the Sabbath.

Now we begin to see why the Bible views the crime of the little horn against the times and the law as being of such great offense to God. The little horn has attacked the one commandment that deals with the time for a relationship with God. In attacking the Sabbath and changing the Sabbath, the little horn has attacked the God of relationships.

Which Day Is the Day for the Relationship With Jesus?

The commandment declares that God has assigned one day each week for God to get together with His people. God our Creator has set the appointment time. To change the appointment would be an insult to God. It would be like my spouse telling me that we are going to meet together for dinner on Monday night at our favorite little restaurant, but I don't show up, since I don't think it's really important which night we go out. Instead, I go out by myself on Tuesday night, keying in on the "going out," but completely missing the "meeting together." If I did that too often, we wouldn't be married long! God can meet with us anytime, but He, our Creator, has specified when this special time will be, and He tells us "Six days shalt thou labor, and do all thy work: But the seventh day is the sabbath of the Lord thy God" (Exodus 20:9, 10 KJV).

God has spoken. He does not change. His words are unalterable. He did not tell us that any day would do—He specified the seventh day as the day for this special time to build a relationship. The seventh day is Saturday, not Sunday. From ancient times, the weekly cycle has begun on Sunday and ended on Saturday.

In fact, the seven-day week itself has no reason for existence as a vehicle of time. We celebrate years because of the earth rotating around the sun. We celebrate months because of the lunar cycle, and we celebrate days because of the earth rotating. Yet there is no astronomical reason to celebrate a week except that God commanded it.

This weekly cycle is ingrained in the human experience. Our bodies seem to be in a seven-day rhythm. Attempts at a longer week, such as the ten-day week, have always failed, because God has seemingly placed within us a need to rest every seven days. Our calendar today has the same weekly cycle that existed in the time of Christ. In fact, since the time of

Jesus, there has been only one major change in the calendar. That year was 1582. Scholars discovered that they had kept too many leap years, which had altered the calendar from the solar system. To bring the calendar back into line, they dropped ten days from the calendar. One day it was Thursday, October 4, and the next day was Friday, October 15.

The change did not affect the weekly cycle, only the numbering of the days of the week. That is why we can have absolute confidence that the day we call Saturday today is the same day that Jesus called Sabbath. There is absolutely no question about the validity of which day is the biblical Sabbath. Even those who keep Sunday admit that the Bible Sabbath was Saturday.

The Jewish people have kept a separate calendar from the rest of society down through the ages. God made clear which was the seventh day, in the manna experience. For forty years, it was ingrained in them which day was Sabbath. When one examines the Jewish calendar, one quickly discovers that Sabbath is Saturday.

In fact, in over 100 languages, the word for *Saturday* has as its root meaning, "Sabbath," indicating the universal knowledge that the day we call Saturday was one time known universally as Sabbath. For example, in Spanish, Saturday is *sabbado*. In Russian it is *subbota*. In Italian, it is *sabbato*. At one time, nearly the entire world acknowledged Saturday as the Sabbath day.

The Bible itself makes clear which day is the Sabbath. In Mark 15:24, Jesus is hanging on the cross. It is Friday afternoon. All Christians acknowledge that Jesus died on Good Friday. Notice how the Bible refers to this day: "Now when evening had come, because it was the Preparation Day, that is, the day before the Sabbath" (Mark 15:42). The day of the crucifixion was the day before the Sabbath.

As soon as Jesus died, His body was removed from the cross and placed in Joseph's new tomb. The women hastened to prepare His body. "Then they returned and prepared spices and fragrant oils. And they rested on the Sabbath according to the commandment" (Luke 23:56). Here we discover that the Sabbath was the day after Jesus died. When sunset came on Friday, the Sabbath began, and the women rested according to the commandment.

"Now when the Sabbath was past, Mary Magdalene, Mary the mother of James, and Salome bought spices, that they might come and anoint Him. Very early in the morning, on the first day of the week, they came to the tomb when the sun had risen" (Mark 16:1, 2). Here it is stated that the Sabbath was past when Jesus was resurrected on the first day of the week. Easter Sunday is declared to be the day after the Sabbath.

Note that the biblical Sabbath is the day between Good Friday and Easter Sunday. There is only one day between those two days, and that is Saturday. The evidence is overwhelming from the New Testament. The seventh-day Sabbath is Saturday, not Sunday. Nowhere in scripture is the day of the resurrection ever specified as the Sabbath. The Sabbath is always Saturday.

Is the Sabbath for the Jews?

Some have attempted to avoid honoring God's unchangeable Sabbath by suggesting that the Sabbath is just for the Jews. If that is true, then so are all the other Ten Commandments.

Are only Jews not supposed to steal and murder? In the Bible, the Jews kept the Sabbath, and it is also recorded that they served God. They were the only representatives in the whole earth who worshiped the true God. So obviously, they would keep the Sabbath.

Remember the purpose of this special day—it is a time to build a relationship with God. If the Sabbath is only for Jews, then only Jews could develop a deep relationship with God. But God is the God of all the earth. He wants a relationship with all His creatures. This is why Sabbath is for all humans.

"And He said to them, 'The Sabbath was made for man,

and not man for the Sabbath'" (Mark 2:27). Jesus declared the Sabbath to be an institution for humankind—not a Jewish institution. Jesus informs us that the Sabbath is "made." It was created, not for the Jews, but for the entire human race. The Sabbath is God's great gift to humanity. It is His great gift of love, demonstrating God's desire to have a deep relationship with all people.

Note that Jesus does not refer us back to Sinai for the origin of the Sabbath but to creation. He does not declare the Sabbath to be "given," but to be "made" for humans. It is a creation institution. If the origin of the Sabbath is creation, then it is of universal application. That is why most Sunday keepers will not admit the Sabbath stems from creation. Yet Jesus declares creation to be the origin of the Sabbath.

Even the Ten Commandments themselves clearly identify the Sabbath as coming from creation week. "For in six days the Lord made the heavens and the earth, the sea, and all that is in them, and rested the seventh day. Therefore the Lord blessed the Sabbath day and hallowed it" (Exodus 20:11). It is undeniable from scripture: The Sabbath originated at creation when God rested on the seventh day after finishing His creative work on the sixth day.

Even the creation account itself declares the Sabbath to originate in creation:

> Thus the heavens and the earth, and all the host of them, were finished. And on the seventh day God ended His work which He had done, and He rested on the seventh day from all His work which He had done. Then God blessed the seventh day and sanctified it, because in it He rested from all His work which God had created and made. Genesis 2:1-3.

Jesus, the Ten Commandments, and the creation story itself, ratify the origin of the Sabbath. All tell us that the Sabbath originated in the perfect paradise of Eden before sin ever entered the human experience. If the Sabbath originated in Eden before sin, then the cross could not affect it when Jesus dealt with sin. This is why the Sabbath is clearly presented in scripture as a universal human experience instead of a Jewish experience.

Imagine Adam and Eve on that first Friday afternoon. As God comes down in the cool of the evening to greet His newly created human pair, He tells them that when the sun sets that night, His Sabbath will begin. I can imagine Adam asking God about the Sabbath. Can you imagine God telling him not to worry about the Sabbath because it was for the Jews? The fact that the Sabbath was given to Adam and Eve thousands of years before any Jew walked the planet reveals that the Sabbath was intended for universal application.

Why God Gave the Sabbath to Humankind

On that first Sabbath, Adam and Eve are invited to enter the Sabbath rest, but they had not yet worked. They did not need physical rest. However, God made their first full day on the planet the Sabbath. Why? Because the Sabbath is not about human rest—it is about entering God's rest. The Sabbath in the Bible is never referred to as "our Sabbath," but always as "the Sabbath of the Lord your God." We are invited to enter into the presence of the God of the universe.

Here is a tremendous picture of the God of the Bible. He desires to have a relationship with the creatures He has made. He is so anxious for that relationship that He sets aside the first day Adam and Eve are alive as a day to cultivate an acquaintance with the One who made them. Even the origins of the Sabbath show the relational aspect of this day that God has given us. When we examine the purpose of the Sabbath as demonstrated in the Bible, it is clear that God gave this day for humans to have time for a relationship with God. It is inconceivable that any Christian would ignore God's Sabbath, since to take that position would basically be rejecting the opportunity for a deep relationship with God. The Sabbath is all about a relationship with God.

Will Any Day Do?

Can we choose whichever day we wish to keep as the Sabbath? Only if we created the world. And we did not. God did. And He tells us that He chose the seventh day. He did not say we could choose any one of the seven. He specified *the seventh day*. How can humans dare to consider a substitute for what God has decreed? To do so would be to put ourselves in the place of God.

Sometimes, people have told me that they realize that my Sabbath is Saturday but that they keep Tuesday because they work Wednesday through Monday each week and have Tuesdays off. Yet Sabbath is not about a day off. If the Sabbath celebrated my rest, then I could easily choose whatever day I wished—just work six days and rest the seventh. However, the Sabbath is not about my rest—it is about God's rest. He invites us to cease our own work and enter His rest on this day by spending it with Him. It is not a sign of our rest, but God's, and God rested on the seventh day—Saturday.

To indicate the importance of the Sabbath, God did three things to the Sabbath at creation as He initiated this wonderful day for a relationship with God. Genesis 2:2, 3 declares that, first, God *blessed* the day. Then God *rested* on the day. And, finally, God *sanctified* the day. God put His blessing into this specific time. He sanctified it. The word *sanctify* means to set aside for a holy purpose. And God demonstrated His intentions by resting Himself on this day. Here is the infinite God of the universe entering into human time in order to communicate and develop a relationship with His people.

If the entire world rested on a day, it would not make that day the Sabbath. No human enactment can overturn what God has already established. What makes a day the Sabbath is the fact that God rested, sanctified, and blessed this specific day—the seventh day. No other day will do—no other day has been given the blessing the Bible declares God gave to the Sabbath at creation.

Today, however, almost the entire Christian world rests on Sunday, the first day of the week. Very few Christians honor God's Sabbath on Saturday, the seventh day of the week. It appears that somehow this day that God gave as the Sabbath was changed. But who changed it? Certainly not God, for He declares that He is the Lord who doesn't change even the smallest part of His law. If God did not change the Sabbath, who did?

Could it be that the little-horn power is the one that mandated and authorized the change? Daniel 7:25 seems to suggest that the little horn, the church of the Dark Ages, would attempt to change something to do with time and the law. The only part of the law dealing with time is the Sabbath commandment. It appears that someone other than God changed the day. The next chapter will unfold the amazing story of the change of the Sabbath.

This is a book about hope. This chapter is about hope through a relationship with an unchanging God. When we keep God's sacred Sabbath, we develop a much deeper relationship with Jesus. The result of that relationship is that we get to know God and His Son Jesus Christ. The hope is not in the relationship—the hope is in the unchanging God behind the relationship. This is why the Sabbath is so important in the life of the Christian, for it is the day to spend getting to know the King of the universe.

13

Hope When the Little Horn Tries to Change God's Law

Changing God's law is unthinkable and impossible, as the Bible has adequately demonstrated. Yet the scriptures predict that the little horn—the Dark Ages church of apostate Christianity—would actually attempt to change the law and the times. In examining the Ten Commandments—the eternal, changeless law of God—we discovered the Sabbath. It indicates that God wishes to have a deep relationship with each of the people He has created, so He has set aside the seventh day each week for God and humanity to spend time together getting better acquainted.

The only way we can live for God is through a living relationship with this God. That is why the Sabbath is so important. It is also the reason the devil wishes to distort the Sabbath blessing—the enemy of souls does not want God's people to develop this deep relationship with Him. The devil distorted the Sabbath in the time of Christ by making it a legalistic nightmare. He distorts it today by confusing the world on which day God has specified. The result is that most people do not spend any day building a relationship with God.

Yet God's Word is clear. The seventh-day, Saturday, is specified by God as the Sabbath. It is God's Sabbath, not ours, but He has invited us to enter into His rest and enjoy this special time with Him.

Lacking any biblical evidence to indicate that one should keep Sunday as a New Testament Sabbath, people have attempted to cast reflection on the Sabbath by attributing it to legalism. Yet the Sabbath, as God gave it, is the opposite of legalism. To say that the Sabbath is legalistic is to say that having a relationship with Jesus is legalistic. There is absolutely nothing legalistic about the Sabbath as God gave it.

On the other hand, the Jews in the time of Christ had distorted the Sabbath by placing all kinds of legalistic burdens on the day that God never intended. For example, the leaders decreed that one could travel only a short distance from one's house on the Sabbath. So if a Jew needed to travel on the Sabbath a distance longer than that prescribed, he would take a possession and put it away from his home. He then could declare that his home extended as far as his possession was located. Thus he could circumvent the law. Jewish leaders would spend endless hours discussing whether one should eat an egg that a hen laid on the Sabbath day.

Jesus came and removed all these human-created restrictions that caused people to lose sight of the Sabbath blessing. In fact, Jesus spent more time dealing with the Sabbath than any other issue. Jesus never questioned the legitimacy of the seventh day. What He questioned was how people kept the Sabbath. Jesus sought to restore the Sabbath to what God intended—a day of blessing designed for God and His people to spend time together. Jesus healed the sick and did all kinds of miracles on the Sabbath to reveal how God brings restoration through the Sabbath blessing. It would seem strange that Jesus would spend all this time helping His disciples to see the beauty of the Sabbath experience, only to change it or eliminate it after He died on the cross.

The Sabbath is mentioned more than sixty times in the New Testament. That means the Sabbath is referred to more often than any of the Ten Commandments in the New Testament, yet there is not one mention of any change in the day for the relationship with God. In fact, one can search the entire New Testament for any indication that there is a change in the day of worship. None will be found, for the Bible fails to give us any change. Certainly, if such a momentous event as changing the Ten Commandments were made, there would be plenty of evidence in the New Testament to support it.

Circumcision nearly split the New Testament church. Whole books of the New Testament were written over the issue of circumcision. Yet no mention is ever made of any controversy over the Sabbath. If the early church had attempted to change the day, our Bibles would be much thicker, for it would contain evidence of the conflict—but there is none. The Sabbath was never in question in the biblical era.

If we base our faith on the Bible only, then we cannot accept Sunday as the Sabbath, since it is never mentioned as Sabbath in the Bible. Only the seventh day is ever referred to as the Sabbath.

Recognizing the dilemma that faces many Christians who keep Sunday with no biblical evidence, well meaning individuals have sought to find some reason to justify their disobedience of this clear commandment of the God who does not change. One of the most popular is that it doesn't make any difference what day you keep as long as you keep one in seven. However, God never said one in seven—He said the seventh day. It is not ours to decide, for God has already made the decision.

One text, often misused to claim that the day we keep doesn't make any difference, is Romans 14:1-6:

> Receive one who is weak in the faith, but not to disputes over doubtful things. For one believes he may eat all things, but he who is weak eats only vegetables. Let not him who eats despise him who does not eat, and let not him who does not eat judge him who eats; for God has received him. Who are you to judge another's servant? To his own master he stands or falls. Indeed, he will be made to stand, for God is able to make him stand. One person esteems one day above another; another esteems every day alike. Let each be fully convinced in his own mind. He who observes the day, observes it to the Lord; and he who does not observe the day, to the Lord he does not observe it. He who eats, eats to the Lord, for he gives God thanks; and he who does not eat, to the Lord he does not eat, and gives God thanks.

Pulling this text out of context, individuals will quote only verse 5 about one person regarding the day and the others not. However, the text does not appear in isolation. It has a definite context. One cannot manipulate the Bible to say whatever is desired by pulling a text out of its immediate context, so let's examine the background of this test.

There are several issues involved in the passage. In the first part of the passage, the issue seems to be about some people who will eat anything and others who only eat vegetables. One of the questions the early church dealt with was the issue of meats that had been offered to idols. Should they eat them? Some did without question. Others, because they did not know the origin of the meat, would eat only vegetables. Paul's counsel is, don't judge each other on such issues.

The last part of the section talks about people eating on one day and others not eating on the day but keeping it to the Lord. Eating or not eating indicates the passage is dealing with fast days, and Paul is telling the early Christians it makes no difference what day you keep as a fast day, or even if you keep any day as a fast day. Fasting on specific days was not an issue, and they were told not to judge each other over what day they kept as a fast day. The issue in esteeming one day above another is over fast days, not Sabbath days. The Sabbath is not mentioned anywhere remotely near this text. To take a text like this out of context and apply it to the concept that it doesn't make any difference what day you keep as the Sabbath is just a deceptive interpretation. When this vague reference is used to support this interpretation, it becomes clear that the evidence for this concept is so weak that it can only be supported through texts taken out of context. This is something a Bible-believing person cannot tolerate.

The other misused text is Colossians 2:13-17:

> And when you were dead in your transgressions and the uncircumcision of your flesh, He made you alive together with Him, having forgiven us all our transgressions, having canceled out the certificate of debt consisting of

decrees against us and which was hostile to us; and He has taken it out of the way, having nailed it to the cross. When He had disarmed the rulers and authorities, He made a public display of them, having triumphed over them through Him. Therefore let no one act as your judge in regard to food or drink or in respect to a festival or a new moon or a Sabbath day—things which are a mere shadow of what is to come; but the substance belongs to Christ. (NASB)

First of all, Paul is assuring the Colossians of the forgiveness of their sins. Some have suggested that this text indicates that the Ten Commandments have been nailed to the cross. What is nailed to the cross is not the law that condemns us, but the charges that the devil has made against us. It is the "certificate of debt"—the debt we owe because we have sinned. Jesus nailed my sin debt to the tree of Calvary. This is what is nailed to the cross.

Therefore no one is to judge others in the future about observing all the ceremonies of the ceremonial law of sacrifice and ritual. The issue in this text is similar to the one in Romans 14—it is the issue of judging. Christians are not to judge each other. Paul then lists several areas in which we are not to judge each other: food or drink (probably the food and drink offerings of the Old Testament system), festivals, and new moons. All of these are part of the Old Testament ceremonial system. He then adds "sabbath days." The Sabbath day was never a part of the ceremonial system—it was always a part of the moral law of Ten Commandments.

However, in the Old Testament system, there were two kinds of sabbaths: ceremonial sabbaths and the seventh-day Sabbath. Ceremonial sabbaths were days like Passover, the Feast of Tabernacles, the Feast of Trumpets, the Day of Atonement, and others. Israel was required to rest as they would on the seventh-day Sabbath and come together in solemn assembly. (Leviticus 23:27-32 is a reference to the Day of Atonement as a ceremonial Sabbath.) These ceremonial sabbaths were always in addition to the seventh-day Sabbath of creation. The ceremonial sabbaths pointed forward to the cross. For example, Passover was one of these ceremonial sabbaths that pointed forward to the blood of Calvary. The lamb of Passover was not the reality, it only prefigured the reality of Calvary—it was the shadow of the cross.

However, the seventh-day Sabbath never pointed to the cross. It always pointed backward to creation. The ceremonial sabbaths were given to a redeemed people who had sinned. They were never introduced until humanity sinned. However, the seventh-day Sabbath originated before sin entered the world. Therefore the cross did not affect the seventh-day Sabbath.

Which sabbath is being referred to in Colossians 2:16? Verse 17 declares that it is the ones that are the shadow of the reality to come—Christ. Only the ceremonial sabbaths were shadows of the cross, never the seventh-day Sabbath. So Paul declares that we should not judge each other over whether to keep all these ceremonial sabbaths that have now been fulfilled in Christ. Yet, even the seventh-day Sabbath could be included here, if it is made to be a legalistic tool instead of the day of delight that God designed. Certainly, the Sabbath as the Jews kept it in the time of Christ had lost its joy and delight and had become a shadow. Yet the Sabbath as God originally gave it is to be the opposite of a shadow—it is to be this great day of celebration with God.

The Change of the Sabbath

The scripture record ends with no indication of any controversy over the Sabbath. There is only this one very slight reference in Colossians 2 that primarily refers to the ceremonial feast days—hardly convincing evidence of a change in Sabbaths. Yet the change was coming. It began in the second century and was fully implemented by the eighth century. It took nearly seven hundred years to accomplish the change. It did not happen overnight. It was a gradual shift, but one that can be accurately traced through the pages of history.

The first indication of Sunday keeping actually occurs about one hundred years after the death of Christ. Hadrian, the Roman Emperor, began a terrible persecution of the Jews. Since Christianity was viewed by many in the Roman Empire as a Jewish sect, and because Christians had many of the same practices as the Jews, such as keeping Sabbath, the Roman Christians, hoping to avoid persecution, wanted to differentiate themselves from the Jews. Therefore, in Rome the suggestion was made that Christians, in addition to the Sabbath, meet together on the first day of the week. This was never meant to be a substitute for the Sabbath, only an additional meeting time. Interestingly, the reason given for choosing Sunday was not the resurrection but the fact that God created light on that day. Evidently even these early Christians recognized the connection of Sabbath with creation. Years later, the resurrection on Sunday was accepted as an additional reason for keeping this day. This new idea of meeting on Sunday in addition to keeping Sabbath occurred only in Rome. The rest of Christianity continued to keep the seventh-day Sabbath.

Several years later, a conflict arose in the church over Easter observance. The earliest Christians never kept any day in honor of the resurrection. Sometime in the second or third century, the practice of keeping one day a year in honor of the resurrection was introduced. No one viewed it as a replacement of the biblical Sabbath—just a celebration of the risen Christ. No one could condemn such a practice.

Different practices of observing Easter began to arise. Most Christians kept the exact day of the resurrection—according to the Jewish calendar, Nisan 16. As a result, the observance of Easter floated through the week from year to year, just like Christmas does today. The Roman Christians wanted stability. They argued for the first Sunday after the first full moon after the vernal equinox. It also happened to be the same day as the pagan festival of new life. Ultimately, Rome won the argument, and the time of Easter has remained unchanged since that time. Rome appears as the chief advocate of the moves for the elevation of Sunday in place of the Lord's Sabbath. Again, even the observance of one Sunday a year was innocent enough. It never was intended to take the place of the Lord's Sabbath. It was always in addition to the Sabbath.

By the third and fourth centuries, the practice of observing both Saturday and Sunday each week was happening in much of the Christian world. In fact, the observance of both days continued for some time, indicating the fact that the seventh-day Sabbath was observed for nearly five hundred years after Christ by most of the Christian church. The following statements from prominent church leaders of this time indicate the practice of keeping Sabbath and Sunday was nearly universal.

> In some places no day is omitted on which the Communion is not offered: in some only on the Sabbath and the Lord's day (Sunday), and in some only on the Lord's day.—Augustine (died A.D. 430), *Letter 54 to Januarius,* chapter 2, in *MPL,* vol. 33, col. 200.

> There are no public services among them in the day except on Saturday and Sunday, when they meet together at the third hour for the purposes of holy communion.—John Cassain (died A.D. 440), *Institutes III,* book 3, ch. 2, trans. in *NPNF* 2nd series, vol. II, p. 213.

> With what kind of eyes do you see the Lord's Day (Sunday), you who dishonor the Sabbath? Do you not know that these days are sisters?—Gregory of Nyssa (A.D. 331-396), *De Castigotione* ("On Reproof") in *MPG,* vol. 46, col. 309. Greek.

This slow change of the Sabbath was accelerated by making the Sabbath a fast day, while Sunday became a feast day. It is understandable then that in later years, it became easier to drop the Sabbath. By not allowing people to eat on Sabbath, the church leaders turned Sabbath into a burdensome day, as it had become to the Jews in Christ's day. Meanwhile, they turned Sunday into a great day of feasting instead of the Sabbath. The Sabbath should have been a day of joy and celebration. Thus, as suggestions came to drop Sabbath observance and observe Sunday only, the duped multitude easily followed, for they had been programmed to hate the Sabbath.

As a result, Sabbath observance began to disappear, and Sunday was set forth as the special day. Once again, this change was pressed hard by Rome, while the rest of Christianity resisted.

> The people of Constantinople, and almost everywhere, assemble together on the Sabbath, as well as on the first day of the week, which is never observed in Rome, or at Alexandria.—Sozomen (died A.D. 440), *Ecclesiastical. History,* VII, ch. 19.

> Although almost all churches throughout the world celebrate the sacred mysteries on the Sabbath (Saturday) of every week, yet the Christians of Alexandria and Rome, on account of some ancient tradition, have ceased to do this.— Socrates Schutasticus, *Ecclesiastical History*, bk. 5, ch. 22, trans in *NPNF*, 2nd series, vol, 2, p. 132.

> On the Sabbath day we gathered together, not being infected with Judaism, for we do not lay hold of false Sabbaths, but we come on the Sabbath to worship Jesus, the Lord of the Sabbath.—Athanasius, *Homilia de Semente*, sec. 1, in *MPG*, vol. 28, col. 144. Greek.

In the fourth and fifth centuries, history reveals that Sabbath was dropped and Sunday was elevated. Many seemed to oppose the change and claimed that they were not a part of Judaism just because they honored the Sabbath. Again, the changes were initiated in Rome and Alexandria. Over the next several centuries, Roman Christianity became elevated as the prime form of Christianity. As Roman Christianity became the norm, Sunday keeping spread with it.

As late as the seventh century, when Roman Christianity invaded England, it was discovered that Roman Christianity had not touched the English church. One of the areas of dispute between Rome and England was the fact that the English church still kept the Sabbath.

> The Celts used a Latin Bible unlike the Vulgate, and kept the day Saturday as a day of rest with special religious services on Sunday.—A. C. Flick, *The Rise of the Medieval Church*, p. 237.

The Roman position overpowered the English church. The time of the Dark Ages began when Roman Christianity dominated the Roman world. During this time the Sabbath was nearly lost. A few faithful believers continued the practice of keeping holy God's special day, but most forgot all about the command to keep the seventh day holy and instead honored the day the church had decreed—Sunday.

While this was a gradual shift, Rome was the initiator in every move toward keeping Sunday and neglecting the Sabbath. Years later, Rome looked back on this period and proudly proclaimed that it was the one who changed the Sabbath:

> Q: Which is the Sabbath day?
>
> A: Saturday is the Sabbath day.
>
> Q: Why do we observe Sunday instead of Saturday?
>
> A: We observe Sunday instead of Saturday because the Catholic Church transferred the solemnity from Saturday to Sunday.
>
> —Peter Geierman, *The Convert's Catechism of Catholic Doctrine*. 1951.

> Q: How prove you that the Church hath power to command feasts and holy days?
>
> A: By the very act of changing the Sabbath into Sunday which Protestants allow of; and therefore they fondly con-

tradict themselves by keeping Sunday strictly, and breaking most other feasts commanded by the same church."

—Henry Tuberville, *An Abridgement of the Christian Doctrines*, 1833, p. 58.

Apostasy does not occur overnight. It begins gradually when one small principle is compromised. In fact, this change happened very innocently, and those who made the first strides toward Sunday keeping were motivated by good ideals. But those who followed slowly compromised the faith. The ultimate result was that God's Sabbath was lost during the Dark Ages.

What paved the way for this apostasy on the Sabbath? There were strong sociological reasons that this change occurred. These reasons do not justify the substitution, but they help us understand why things happened as they did. First of all, the early centuries had a very strong anti-Jewish sentiment. Since Christianity had so many ties to Judaism, there was a need to separate the two. Changing the Sabbath was one way to do so. However, this anti-Jewish feeling then entered the church, and the church stigmatized those who kept the Sabbath by calling them Jewish. The very fact that the church had to legislate against Sabbath keeping reveals that there were many who were keeping the seventh-day Sabbath.

Christians should not Judaize and be idle on Saturday, but shall work on that day; but the Lord's day they shall especially honor, and, as being Christians, shall, if possible, do no work on that day. If, however, they are found Judaizing, they shall be shut out from Christ.

—Oh. Y. Hefele, *A History of the Councils of the Church,* vol. 2, p. 316.

Second, the leaders of the Christian church, especially at Rome and Alexandria, had been heavily influenced by both Gnostic and Platonic pagan philosophy. The pagan day of worship was Sunday.

Third, one of the greatest influences on the choice of Sunday to replace the Sabbath was Mithraism. Mithraism was an Oriental cult of the sun that arose in the first century and was the greatest rival to Christianity in the Roman Empire. It became extremely popular in the second and third centuries. The central feature of the cult was the worship of the sun on the first day of the week. As the two religions battled for the allegiance of the Roman Empire, Christianity ultimately won, but at the price of incorporating some of the practices of Mithraism into the Christian church. Note the secular historian's view of the origin of Sunday:

> The worshippers of Mithra held Sunday sacred and celebrated the birth of the Sun on the 25th of December.
> —Franz Cumont, *The Mysteries of Mithra,* trans. by Thomas J. McCormack, p. 191.

> Our observance of Sunday as the Lord's day is apparently derived from Mithraism. The argument that has sometimes been used against this claim, namely, that Sunday was chosen because of the resurrection on that day, is not well supported.
> —Gordon J. Laing, *Survivals of Roman Religion*, p. 148.

> As a solar festival, Sunday was the sacred day of Mithra, and it is interesting to notice that since Mithra was addressed as Dominus, "Lord", Sunday must have been the "Lord's Day" long before the Christian times.
> —A. Weigall, *The Paganism in Our Christianity*, p. 145.

The fourth influence on Christianity in its adoption of Sunday was the conversion of Constantine at the beginning of the fourth century. He became the first Roman emperor to become a Christian and quickly sought to bring the empire together under the Christian banner. His motives were probably more political than religious, but Constantine had a profound effect on the Christian church as he sought to wed the

Christian and pagan elements of the Empire. Since he resided in Rome, he came under the strong influence of the Roman church, which at the time was attempting to elevate Sunday keeping above Sabbath keeping. Thus it is not surprising that Constantine passed the first civil Sunday law.

> On the venerable Day of the Sun let the magistrates and people residing in cities rest, and let all workshops be closed.
> —March 7, 321, *Codex Justinianus* lib.3, tit. 12, 3; trans. in Philip Schoff, *History of the Christian Church,* vol. 3, p. 380, note 1.

The Bible declared that the little horn (Dark Ages church) would attempt to change the times and the law. History bears out the naked truth. The church did it and boldly proclaimed that it had done it. Remember, however, that God said it would only *think* to do it. The church could not actually do it, because God doesn't change. The same seventh-day Sabbath of creation is still the day that He has set aside for Christians to spend worshiping Him and developing a deep relationship with Jesus.

For Christians, the Sabbath carries added meaning. It is the great truth that links the Creator and the Redeemer together.

At creation, Jesus our Creator set aside the seventh day as a sign of His finished work of creation. He then invited His people to enter into His rest by ceasing from their work, as He did from His. Yet in spite of spending time developing a relationship with God in Eden, Adam and Eve still sinned. The perfect relationship was marred.

Jesus did not give up on humanity. Our Creator returned to this earth as a human being. In the garb of humanity, He went to a hill called Calvary and died for our sins. He finished His work of redemption on the cross on the sixth day of the week, just as He had finished His work of creation on the same sixth day. Then He went into the tomb and rested again on the same seventh day. In both creation and redemption, Jesus rested as a sign of His finished work on humanity's behalf. Thus God's seventh-day Sabbath becomes God's great memorial of creation and redemption.

No wonder Jesus declared that He is Lord of the Sabbath day (Mark 2:28). The actual term *Lord's day* only appears one time in the Bible (Revelation 1:10). It does not tell us which day the Lord's day is. It would be easy to read back into the text the usage of this phrase today, but that would not be honest. Only the scripture can tell us which day the Lord's day is. Jesus is very clear on it. Mark 2:28 declares that Jesus is Lord of the Sabbath day.

If Jesus is Lord of the Sabbath day, then the day He presides over needs to be an important part of my life. The fact that Jesus is Lord of a specific day indicates that just any day won't do. There is a day that is special to the Lord—the Lord's day. The Bible tells us that day is the seventh day. Because we love Jesus and want Him to be Lord of our life, we keep His seventh-day Sabbath, the great memorial of creation and redemption. We desire to enter Sabbath rest and develop a deep personal relationship with Jesus by spending time with Him every day and keeping holy His seventh-day Sabbath each week. This is done not to gain salvation, but because He has already redeemed us, and we are so thankful for that redemption that we want to spend this time with Him to really get to know our Redeemer.

Even though the little horn has attempted to change the Sabbath from Saturday to Sunday, we have hope, because God is still in control, and He has brought this great Sabbath truth to us so that we can have a deep relationship with God and Jesus. In this relationship alone, we can find hope.

14

Hope in Sabbath Rest

S abbath rest! There is nothing more hopeful than the rest the Sabbath provides. This rest is not primarily physical rest, but spiritual rest—trusting completely in Jesus my Savior. Sabbath rest is a sign of our complete trust in God. It is a signal that we totally trust in the God who desires a relationship with the creatures that He has created. It is a sign that we really know God. Even the Old Testament writers caught this hopeful glimpse of the purpose of the Sabbath as a relationship with God. "Hallow My Sabbaths, and they will be a sign between Me and you, that you may know that I am the Lord your God" (Ezekiel 20:20).

Note that Ezekiel declares God's Sabbath to be a sign that we know the Lord. The Sabbath is the outward indication of a growing, deepening relationship with God. The Sabbath is not insignificant when the scripture labels it a sign—especially the sign of a relationship with God. Nothing brings greater hope to humankind than entering Sabbath rest and developing this deep experience of really knowing God. Nothing is more important as we face the final stages of earth's history than to develop such a relationship with God. That is why the Sabbath carries extra significance for Christians at the end of the age. Here is an institution, given by God, to give us hope as we face the dramatic issues of earth's last days.

It is natural, then, to expect that something God gave as a sign of a relationship with Him would come under the fierce attack of the enemy of souls. As noted in the last chapter, it did. And Satan succeeded in replacing the biblical seventh-day Sabbath with a sabbath of his own creation. Sunday is never seen in the same light as the Sabbath, for Sunday is of human origin, whereas Sabbath is of divine origin.

Satan does not want us to develop a deep relationship with Jesus, so he has counterfeited God's sign of the relationship. The result is that most Christians who observe Sunday no longer keep a whole day to the Lord, but most keep only the hour or so they attend worship. It is hard to keep a day that God has not sanctified.

Of course, keeping the Sabbath is not a way to be saved. Only Jesus can save. The Sabbath is one of those delights that God has given His people to help them live the Christian life. Instead of attempting to live for Christ on our own, He has given us the Sabbath to spend with Him. Having spent the day with Jesus, the result is that we have a deeper relationship with Jesus, which enables us to obey Him, not in our strength, but in the strength of heaven.

Satan obviously does not want us to feel the strength that comes through keeping the Sabbath. This is why he has attacked the Sabbath so vehemently. When a Christian knows the beautiful truth of Sabbath as a relationship-building time with God and then refuses to enter Sabbath rest, that Christian is virtually telling God that a relationship with heaven is not that important.

We have discovered that the argument claiming it makes no difference what day you keep is not valid. It does make a difference, because there is only one day that God has blessed, rested on, and sanctified. He calls it "My Sabbath." The King of the universe has invited us to join Him for His Sabbath.

It is never "my" Sabbath. If it symbolized my rest, then it would not make any difference what day I keep, but the seventh-day Sabbath is a symbol of God's rest, and He, as Creator and Redeemer, has specified the seventh day as His special day.

When the church attempted to change God's Sabbath from Saturday to Sunday, as predicted in Daniel 7:25, it sought to find some biblical reason to justify the change. However, there is no text anywhere in the entire New Testament suggesting a change in the day of worship. Even Cardinal Gibbons of the Roman church acknowledges this:

> You may read the Bible from Genesis to Revelation and you will not find a single line authorizing the sanctification of Sunday. The Scriptures enforce the religious observance of Saturday, a day which we never sanctify.
> —James Cardinal Gibbons, *The Faith of Our Fathers*, p. 111.

Even though the church acknowledged that there was no biblical authority, it still persisted in the change. At first, the reason given was that God created light on the first day, but there was no biblical proof for that argument. Then the fact that Christ rose on the first day was offered as convincing proof that we should now honor Sunday as the new Sabbath of Christianity. However, there was no biblical text to support a change of Sabbaths based on the fact that Christ rose from the dead.

Yet, all acknowledged that Christ indeed arose on the first day, so the argument was quickly developed that we honor Sunday because of the resurrection on that day. Several texts were offered as proof. They were never quoted—just listed as a reference. Most people did not take time to look them up and assumed they contained evidence of the change. All that the texts actually revealed was that Christ rose on the first day; they did not hint at any change in the day of worship.

The Sunday Texts

There are only eight references to the first day of the week in the entire New Testament. We will quickly examine each of them. Most will need little explanation, since they are merely declaring that Christ rose on the first day, but none of them specify that the first day is now God's Sabbath. Here are the first five references:

Now after the Sabbath, as the first day of the week began to dawn, Mary Magdalene and the other Mary came to see the tomb. Matthew 28:1.

Now when the Sabbath was past, Mary Magdalene, Mary the mother of James, and Salome bought spices, that they might come and anoint Him. Very early in the morning, on the first day of the week, they came to the tomb when the sun had risen. Mark 16:1, 2.

Now when He rose early on the first day of the week, He appeared first to Mary Magdalene, out of whom He had cast seven demons. Mark 16:9.

Then they returned and prepared spices and fragrant oils. And they rested on the Sabbath according to the commandment. Now on the first day of the week, very early in the morning, they, and certain other women with them, came to the tomb bringing the spices which they had prepared. Luke 23:56 - 24:1.

So there they laid Jesus, because of the Jews' Preparation Day, for the tomb was nearby. Now on the first day of the week Mary Magdalene went to the tomb early, while it was still dark, and saw that the stone had been taken away from the tomb. John 19:42 - 20:1.

Just a quick reading of these five passages informs us that these texts reveal nothing about a change in the Sabbath. Each passage is simply telling us that Jesus rose on the first day of the week. Each of the four gospel writers is proclaiming the same story. There is no mistake—Jesus rose on the first day.

Someone might wonder why each gospel writer emphasized the resurrection being on the first day. There was a reason. Jesus had predicted that He would rise on the third day. Since He died on Friday, the third day was Sunday. Each one of the gospel writers wanted to assure their readers that Jesus fulfilled His own prophecy: He rose on the third day, which was the first day of the week. They were not attempting to prove a new Sabbath, but reassuring us that Jesus again was fulfilling prophecy.

There was another possible reason for this emphasis. Jesus was also fulfilling the Old Testament ceremonial sabbaths. Thus He died on Nisan 14 (Jewish calendar). Nisan 14 was the Passover. Jesus was the fulfillment of the Passover Lamb. Nisan 16 (Sunday) was the Jewish feast of first fruits. Jesus was resurrected as the first fruits of them that sleep in the grave. Therefore, He fulfilled the Jewish feast of first fruits by rising on Sunday. This may also have been in the minds of the gospel writers. They wanted us to see Jesus as the Messiah predicted in the Old Testament, so they were very careful to inform us when Jesus fulfilled any Old Testament prophecy.

It is interesting to note that in almost every instance when the first day is mentioned in the gospels, it specifies that the Sabbath was past. It is almost as if God made sure that people could not get confused on which day was the Sabbath. Thus, each gospel writer tells us that Jesus rose on the first day, which was the day after the Sabbath. The Sabbath was already past. Therefore Sunday could not be the Sabbath, since the day of the resurrection, according to the Bible, is the day after the biblical Sabbath. To be honest with scripture, we must admit that there is no foundation for Sunday keeping in the texts quoted.

Three other references to the first day remain in the New Testament. The first is found in John 20:19:

> Then, the same day at evening, being the first day of the week, when the doors were shut where the disciples were assembled, for fear of the Jews, Jesus came and stood in the midst, and said to them, "Peace be with you."

Again, in this passage there is no indication of a change in the Sabbath. It merely assures us that the same day He rose, He came and brought assurance to the disciples that He had indeed been resurrected from the dead. Some have attempted to read into this text that the disciples were there celebrating the resurrection, and Jesus appeared. However, the text tells us that they were assembled behind locked doors for "fear of the Jews." They did not even believe in the resurrection at this point. They were still afraid that the same thing that had happened to Jesus would happen to them, so they gathered together behind a locked door. To these unbelieving disciples, Jesus suddenly appeared with the glorious hope of His resurrection. Nothing in this passage gives the slightest indication of a change in the day of worship.

> Now concerning the collection for the saints, as I have given orders to the churches of Galatia, so you must do also: On the first day of the week let each one of you lay something aside, storing up as he may prosper, that there be no collections when I come. 1 Cor. 16:1, 2.

In this passage, Paul directs the Corinthians to participate in a special collection for the saints in Jerusalem. Palestine was having a famine. The believers there needed food. Paul was going to stop by Corinth on his way to Jerusalem. He wrote them ahead of time to get the collection of food ready before he came, so he would not have to wait for them to gather the food when he arrived, since the needs of the brethren were urgent and Paul did not want to take a long time waiting for the Corinthians to gather their offerings.

When a person gave to famine relief in the first century, he or she did not give money. The people to whom they were giving could not buy food, so the Christians needed to take food to them. So it is very logical to assume that this offering was food. Interestingly, they were to gather this offering on the first day of the week. They were not to turn it in at church—they were to save it at home. If the members were giving money, they would obviously just give it at church, as most of us would today, but Paul tells them to put it aside and save it till he got there. This would make sense if it were a food offering.

In this passage, Paul is not requiring an offering at church, but requesting that on the first day of the week they go into their fields and put aside some food for this special offering. Why does he mention the first day of the week? Paul's letter would have been read to the believers on Sabbath when they assembled for worship. The next day was the first day, and Paul wants them to do this before they forget, so he tells them to set it aside on the first day of the week.

The very fact that the believers are being commanded to go out into the fields on Sunday and gather food for this offering indicates that Sunday was regarded as a normal working day in the first-century church. Rather than support Sunday keeping, this passage actually declares it to be one of the six common working days. Thus there is no indication of any change in Sabbath here—only that the early church still kept the same seventh-day Sabbath and regarded Sunday as a regular day of work. There is only one passage left that even mentions the first day of the week.

> Now on the first day of the week, when the disciples came together to break bread, Paul, ready to depart the next day, spoke to them and continued his message until midnight. There were many lamps in the upper room where they were gathered together. And in a window sat a certain young man named Eutychus, who was sinking into a deep sleep. He was overcome by sleep; and as Paul continued speaking, he fell down from the third story and was taken up dead. But Paul went down, fell on him, and embracing him said, "Do not trouble yourselves, for his life is in him." Now when he had come up, had broken bread and eaten, and talked a long while, even till daybreak, he departed. And they brought the young man in alive, and they were not a little comforted. Acts 20:7-12.

This is the only passage in the New Testament where there is a meeting occurring on the first day of the week. Some have jumped on this passage as an indication that this was the usual custom of the early church. However, one notices very quickly that this was a highly unusual meeting. It only got recorded because Eutychus fell out the window and died and was resurrected. Otherwise, we would never even know about it. So if this is the only scripture passage to indicate we should observe Sunday, we are skating on very thin ice.

Furthermore, we note that the meeting occurred in the evening and was an all-night meeting. If we are to base our meeting together on this passage, we would need to meet for worship all night long, but no Sunday-keeping church does that. There is another factor here. This meeting really did not occur on our Sunday. The text declares that the meeting took place on the evening part of the first day of the week. In biblical times, days began at sunset rather than midnight. When the sun set on Saturday night, the evening part of the first day of the week began, so this meeting occurred on our Saturday night. That is why some modern translations, such as the New English Bible, translate the passage: "On Saturday night." Many scholars, most of whom are Sunday keepers, being honest with the text, recognize that the meeting occurred on Saturday night.

On Sunday morning, Paul travels to the next location. If Paul were keeping Sunday, he would have stayed for Sunday morning worship. However, Paul gave no special significance to Sunday, so he left to his next location. He had spent the Sabbath with them and realized that he might never see them again, as he was headed to Jerusalem. He was anxious to impart all the knowledge he could, so he spent the whole night talking. Even Paul put people to sleep with his preaching that night, and poor Eutychus ended up falling down three stories, dying, and being resurrected. What a powerful meeting that Saturday night was!

That's it. There are no other texts that even mention the first day of the week. None of the texts we reviewed contain the slightest indication that there has been a change in the day of worship. The overwhelming evidence of the New Testament is that there has been no change in the day of worship. If we accept the Bible as the sole authority, then we must keep

God's seventh-day Sabbath. Those who keep it are in good company, because the founder of Christianity kept it too. Remember, Christianity is following Jesus, and Jesus never did worship on Sunday. If you follow Jesus, you must keep the same day He kept, and that is Saturday.

Someone might wonder what is wrong with keeping Sunday in honor of the resurrection. Nothing is wrong, as long as you don't miss keeping God's Sabbath. It becomes wrong when I substitute a commandment of man for a commandment of God. The plain truth, however, is that God has already provided a memorial of the events of Easter weekend—baptism.

> Or do you not know that as many of us as were baptized into Christ Jesus were baptized into His death? Therefore we were buried with Him through baptism into death, that just as Christ was raised from the dead by the glory of the Father, even so we also should walk in newness of life. For if we have been united together in the likeness of His death, certainly we also shall be in the likeness of His resurrection, knowing this, that our old man was crucified with Him, that the body of sin might be done away with, that we should no longer be slaves of sin. Romans 6:3-6.

Just as Christ died, was buried, and rose again, so we too are to die to sin, bury the old way of life in the watery grave of baptism, and then rise to newness of life in Christ Jesus. This is God's memorial of the events of Easter weekend. Every time someone is baptized, the church is reminded anew of the events of that glorious weekend. Nowhere are we commanded to keep a day—we are only commanded to practice baptism as a reminder of the death, burial, and resurrection of Jesus.

The Sabbath in the Early Church

We have discovered that there is no indication of the early church keeping Sunday, the first day of the week, as the Sabbath. The Bible is totally silent on any change in the day of worship. However, is there any indication that the early church still practiced Sabbath keeping in the New Testament period? Here, the evidence abounds.

It begins with the women immediately after the crucifixion. "And they rested on the Sabbath according to the commandment" (Luke 23:56). Luke, a companion of Paul, writing many years after the cross, thought it significant to record that the women who followed Jesus knew no change in the Sabbath, so rested on the Sabbath after Jesus died. Matthew, likewise writing many years after Calvary, records that Jesus told His followers to pray that they would not have to flee Jerusalem in winter or on Sabbath (Matthew 24:20). Jerusalem was destroyed in A.D. 70, and Christians, following the counsel of Christ, fled the city and saved their lives. Evidently, Jesus was still intending that His church keep the Sabbath forty years after the cross.

The book of Acts records the practices of the early church. Time and time again, Luke indicates that the early church and early church leaders met together for worship on the Sabbath day. Acts 13:13, 14 records that "Paul and his party ... came to Antioch in Pisidia, and went into the synagogue on the Sabbath day and sat down." Evidently, Paul and his team still honored the Sabbath.

Some may feel that Paul only went to the synagogue because he was trying to reach the Jews, but in verse 42, Luke records what happened when Paul left the synagogue: "So when the Jews went out of the synagogue, the Gentiles begged that these words might be preached to them the next Sabbath" (Acts 13:42). The people wanted more information, but they asked to wait till next Sabbath. Why not meet on Sunday if Paul was also keeping Sunday? Evidently, they recognized that Paul kept only the Sabbath. We then read, "On the next Sabbath almost the whole city came together to hear the word of God" (Acts 13:44). Most people in Antioch were Gentiles, and the pagans of that day honored Sunday, not the Sabbath, like the Jews. The fact that the Bible records that nearly the whole city came together would clearly indicate that Sabbath was the chosen day for Christians to meet and preach the gospel.

When Paul arrived at Philippi, there was no Jewish synagogue. Yet Paul and his company still honored the Sabbath.

"And on the Sabbath day we went out of the city to the riverside, where prayer was customarily made; and we sat down and spoke to the women who met there" (Acts 16:13).

No synagogue, yet still Paul honored the Sabbath.

At Thessalonica, there was a synagogue of the Jews, so Paul went. Acts 17:1-4 records that going to church on Sabbath was Paul's custom (verse 2). Imagine that—Paul had the same custom as Jesus. We certainly cannot go wrong following Jesus and Paul. For three Sabbaths, Paul preached to the Jews and saw many come to Christ. Not only did this preaching on the Sabbath reach Jews but also many Greeks.

Paul stayed at Corinth for a year and a half (Acts 18:11). During that entire time, Luke records that Paul preached every Sabbath (verse 4). This is seventy-eight weeks of Sabbath keeping! If he were going to make a change, certainly Paul would have switched over to Sunday during the year and a half in which he established the church. Yet there is no mention of any switch—only records showing that Paul preached every Sabbath.

Actually, there are eighty-four Sabbaths kept by the apostle Paul recorded in the book of Acts, alone. Yet in that same book, there is not one mention of a single Sunday kept by the early church. The biblical evidence is actually overwhelming. The universal day of worship in the early church was the same as it has always been—the seventh day. They kept it simply because they followed Jesus, the Lord of the Sabbath.

The book of Hebrews discusses total trust in Jesus. The writer struggles to find an example of what it means to fully enter God's rest of total trust in the person of Christ. Finally, an illustration comes to his mind—the seventh-day Sabbath. This is the clear example of what it means to trust fully in Christ and develop a saving relationship with Him.

For He has spoken in a certain place of the seventh day in this way: "And God rested on the seventh day from all His works"; and again in this place: "They shall not enter My rest." Since therefore it remains that some must enter it, and those to whom it was first preached did not enter because of disobedience, again He designates a certain day, saying in David, "Today," after such a long time, as it has been said: "Today, if you will hear His voice, Do not harden your hearts." For if Joshua had given them rest, then He would not afterward have spoken of another day. There remains therefore a rest for the people of God. For he who has entered His rest has himself also ceased from his works as God did from His. Let us therefore be diligent to enter that rest, lest anyone fall according to the same example of disobedience. Hebrews 4:4-11.

No more fitting example of what it means to trust fully in Christ can be given than the seventh-day Sabbath. When we keep Sabbath, we no longer trust in our own works.

We cease from them as God did from His in the beginning. We enter His rest—a rest of complete trust in the person of Christ. We develop a relationship with Him. That is why the writer to the Hebrews then commands us to enter that same rest and tells us clearly that there still remains a Sabbath rest for the people of God (verse 9).

What Do We Do?

Perhaps the evidence in the preceding three chapters of this book has overwhelmed you. As you examine the evidence, it is very clear that the seventh-day, Saturday, is the biblical Sabbath commanded by God in the unchangeable Ten Commandments, ratified by Jesus while on the earth, and kept by His early New Testament church. You wonder what to do with this information. Is everyone who doesn't keep the Sabbath lost?

Of course not! God only holds us accountable for what we know. "Therefore, to him who knows to do good and does not do it, to him it is sin" (James 4:17). Relatives, friends, and family who have not known this beautiful truth are not accountable, but praise the Lord, you now know it. And the Bible indicates you are accountable for what you know. Yet this is something wonderful to be accountable for—it is a delight to know the truth of the Sabbath. It is life changing! Happiness, hope, and peace are the results of following God's Sabbath. But are you lost if you don't keep it?

Let us remind ourselves that Sabbath-keeping does not save us. Only Jesus can save us through His death on the cross. However, saved people want to be obedient because they have been saved. It is impossible for one who has been redeemed by the blood of Jesus to go forth deliberately and break the commandments of God. We want to obey, because we love Jesus. Obedience becomes the prime evidence that Jesus is living in our heart. We may slip and fall, but we will not deliberately go contrary to what Jesus says, because we love Jesus. It is not a question of being saved or lost—it is a question of whether or not we really love Jesus.

Some of the greatest indictments that Jesus levied against the Jewish leadership of the first century were regarding their substitution of human traditions for the commandments of God. Listen to these piercing words of Jesus recorded by Mark:

> And in vain they worship Me, teaching as doctrines the commandments of men. . . . He said to them, "All too well you reject the commandment of God, that you may keep your tradition . . . making the word of God of no effect through your tradition which you have handed down. And many such things you do." Mark 7:7, 9, 13.

These are strong words with which Jesus indicts the Jewish leadership of His day. What crime called for such denouncements? The leaders had substituted needless traditions for what God had commanded. Nothing seems to stir the heart of Jesus more than putting human traditions in place of the commandments of God. Jesus is not condemning tradition.

There is nothing wrong with traditions. They become wrong and under the condemnation of God when they are used in place of a clear command of God.

Sunday keeping is a human tradition. Sabbath keeping is a God-commanded experience. Jesus declares that we worship God in vain when we substitute human tradition for the Word of God. Sabbath keeping is not merely an option for the Christian who loves Jesus. No true Christian can ever allow any day commanded by human beings to take the place of the day commanded by Jesus and God the Father.

In these final days of human history, God is calling out a people who will worship according to the commandment of God and not human tradition. He is calling for a people to keep His Sabbath—the great memorial of creation and redemption. Why? Because in earth's final hour, there is a tremendous need for a group of people who will enter into a deep relationship with the risen Lord, and relationship building is what Sabbath keeping is all about.

If you have not yet begun to keep God's seventh-day Sabbath, then why not begin right now? When the sun sets next Friday night, gather your family together for sundown worship, or if you are alone, open your Bible and begin the day with God. Make the seventh day special in your life. Discover the joy and the delight to be found in keeping the Sabbath. It is not an obligation—it is an honor and a privilege to join God for this special day to build a deeper relationship with Him. May your experience with Jesus deepen as you begin this new journey of Sabbath-keeping.

15

Heaven Is Our Hope

Of all the hopes we have examined thus far, the hope of heaven is without a doubt the greatest hope we have. Heaven envisions the time when all the brokenness of earth has been removed, and humanity is fully restored to the place God originally planned for us to be. Heaven is not about harps and clouds—it is about the restoration of broken relationships.

That is why the Sabbath that we examined in the last few chapters is so important. Sabbath rest is simply a foretaste of heaven. If we do not enjoy Sabbath, we will not enjoy heaven. Sabbath is a day to build our relationship with Jesus and get to know our Redeemer on a much deeper level. It could be very boring to spend a day with someone who is unfamiliar to us. That is why Sabbath keeping means nothing to those who have not received Jesus as Savior. But for those who know Jesus, spending the whole day with our best friend on Sabbath is the climax of the week.

If Sabbath has become that kind of delight and joy for you, then you are prepared for heaven. If Sabbath is a burden for you, heaven will be too. When Adam and Eve sinned, their relationship with God was broken. Since then, humanity has been living in the time of this broken relationship. We gain only a few glimpses of what the restored relationship will be like. Sabbath is one of them. Yet in heaven, the broken relationship will be fully restored, and God and His humanity will once again connect as they did in the Garden of Eden. Eden lost will have become Eden restored.

Heaven is a place of hope for the Christian, because the broken relationship between God and humanity—and all the bruised relationships of earth as well—will be made right. The greatest hope, the greatest joy of heaven, will be spending an eternity with our Redeemer. Nothing can supersede the blessedness of an eternity with the One who loved us so much that He died for us.

This heavenly hope is not just "pie in the sky." It is a real and joyful hope that God has given to all who believe in Him. Yet such wild and fanciful ideas exist about the state of the redeemed that we must clearly examine the biblical teaching on heaven. Satan does not want people to discover the realities of the heavenly hope, so he has invented a counterfeit hope that few are willing to give their lives for. However, the real heaven, as described by scripture, is so wondrous, so glorious, that I am willing to fully give my life to Jesus so that I might enjoy this eternity with Him.

The book of Daniel ends on the triumphant note that Daniel will inherit this eternity with God. This faithful servant of God who had developed a deep relationship with His Lord is given the blessed assurance that he, along with all the redeemed, will someday spend eternity with this relational God. Humanity may pass through some rough times before inheriting eternity, but God reassures us that He will be with us in these final climatic hours of earth's history, and the hope of heaven is to be constantly kept before us as we face these trials. Note as Daniel concludes his book:

> At that time Michael shall stand up, the great prince who stands watch over the sons of your people; and there shall be a time of trouble, such as never was since there was a nation, even to that time. And at that time your people shall be delivered, every one who is found written in the book. Daniel 12:1.

Daniel's vision of the last days is one of great conflict for the people of God. He calls it the worst time of trouble the world has ever faced. Yet the focus of what Daniel tells us is not trouble—it is deliverance. There will be distressing times, but God's people are facing it with hope in their hearts, because they know the ultimate outcome of the conflict. God's people will be delivered in the midst of this final, great time of trouble. No matter how evil the world gets, God provides us with the hope of supernatural deliverance.

This deliverance is not human but divine. It is at this time that Daniel declares there will be a glorious resurrection: "And many of those who sleep in the dust of the earth shall awake, some to everlasting life, some to shame and everlasting contempt" (Daniel 12:2).

A day of resurrection is coming. Those who have died will be resurrected. This is not fanciful thinking—this is realistic hope. And the result of this resurrection, for the righteous, is that they will shine like the stars forever and ever (Daniel 12:3).

Along with these tremendous prophecies given to Daniel, he receives the promise to which all the prophecies really point—an eternity with His God. Daniel may not have understood all that had been revealed in this little book, but one thing was clear to him: Resurrection is coming.

Daniel will not be alone in that resurrection. Those who have developed a living relationship with God will join him on that grand resurrection morning. In the meantime, Daniel is told to seal up his little book of twelve chapters. And he is told it will remain sealed till the time of the end (Daniel 12:4). But a glimmer of hope is given him. At the end time, people will run to and fro throughout the world, and knowledge of the book of Daniel will be greatly increased (verse 4). Therefore, the hope of heaven would have to wait until the time of the end (Daniel 12:9). He was not to expect to see the fruition of this hope in his lifetime, but make no mistake, Daniel is told that he will be there, along with all the redeemed, at the end time.

What was to happen to Daniel between the giving of the promise of resurrection and the realization of the hope of an eternity with his Redeemer? Daniel 12:13 provides Daniel with the assurance: "But you, go your way till the end; for you shall rest, and will arise to your inheritance at the end of the days." What a promise! Daniel was not to worry about future events. He was to continue his life, trusting in his Savior. When his life ended, he would rest in the grave, but that would not be the end for Daniel. At the last day, he would rise with all the righteous to receive his allotted portion at the end of the world.

Even though he would rest in the grave till the end of the world, he would rest in the assurance of an eternity with God, then stand in his lot and be resurrected with all God's people. Resurrection hope! That is how the book of Daniel ends. Christ has not yet been resurrected, but Daniel is still told that his hope is in the resurrection at the last day. The book of Daniel foretells so much of human conflict and rebellion against God, yet take note of how the book ends. It is a triumphant conclusion. Troubles may arise, but God will resurrect all who trust in Him at the last day. Loved ones may die and enter rest, but God has given us the hope of resurrection in earth's final hour.

This hope of resurrection resonates throughout the scripture. Daniel is not the only biblical proponent of the bodily resurrection. This belief was so different from the old pagan hope that filled the Old Testament world. The pagan hope centered on the spirit's journey to the netherworld after death. The Egyptians prepared their dead extensively for this journey. They even buried their servants with them, mummified them, and provided them with treasure and food for the journey to the spirit world. But into this pagan environment come the Bible writers, declaring that one does not need this elaborate preparation of the body for the afterlife, for God Himself will resurrect us from the dead. We shall be real people once again. We shall not be semi-material spirits, floating on clouds throughout all eternity. This is why Bible writers in both testaments attest to the enduring hope of the literal, physical resurrection. This is our unmistakable hope as Christians.

Most scholars suggest that the book of Job was the first Bible book written. Even in this first book, Job declares his hope in the resurrection after death.

> For I know that my Redeemer lives, and He shall stand at last on the earth; and after my skin is destroyed, this I know, that in my flesh I shall see God, whom I shall see for myself, and my eyes shall behold, and not another. Job 19:25-27.

Even though his body would be destroyed, yet Job had the same assurance Daniel was later given—that he would see God in his flesh. It would not be a spirit existence—it would be a literal, bodily existence. Death may destroy the body, but God will restore it in the resurrection. The hope of the resurrection enabled Job to withstand all the attacks that Satan thrust upon him in his earthly life. That same resurrection hope sustains the Christian in the twenty-first century.

When Jesus was on earth, his friend Lazarus died. Jesus quickly arrives at the home of the deceased. He is there to comfort the bereaved and provide them with a living hope. He quickly tells Martha: "Your brother will rise again" (John 11:23). Note that Jesus gives Martha the hope of the resurrection. She was well aware of it, for she declared that she knew that her brother would rise again at the last day (verse 24). Yet Jesus is about to give them a foretaste of what the resurrection will be like at the last day, for He declares that "I am the resurrection and the life. He who believes in Me, though he may die, he shall live. And whoever lives and believes in Me shall never die" (verses 25, 26). There again is this marvelous resurrection hope. If we believe in Jesus, we do not die, we only sleep, for He will come and wake us up to eternal life.

The apostle Paul was a great conveyer of the blessed hope of the resurrection. His epistles resonate with this hope. In four classic passages, Paul provides us with this ultimate hope of Jesus and the Old Testament.

> But if there is no resurrection of the dead, then Christ is

not risen. And if Christ is not risen, then our preaching is empty and your faith is also empty. . . . And if Christ is not risen, your faith is futile; you are still in your sins! 1 Cor. 15:13, 14, 17.

Behold, I tell you a mystery: We shall not all sleep, but we shall all be changed—in a moment, in the twinkling of an eye, at the last trumpet. For the trumpet will sound, and the dead will be raised incorruptible, and we shall be changed. 1 Cor. 15:51, 52.

For the Lord Himself will descend from heaven with a shout, with the voice of an archangel, and with the trumpet of God. And the dead in Christ will rise first. Then we who are alive and remain shall be caught up together with them in the clouds to meet the Lord in the air. And thus we shall always be with the Lord. Therefore comfort one another with these words. 1 Thess. 4:16-18.

For I am already being poured out as a drink offering, and the time of my departure is at hand. I have fought the good fight, I have finished the race, I have kept the faith. Finally, there is laid up for me the crown of righteousness, which the Lord, the righteous Judge, will give to me on that Day, and not to me only but also to all who have loved His appearing. 2 Tim. 4:6-8.

In passage after passage, Paul reaffirms the same hope that flowed through the veins of the prophet Daniel. Paul may fall asleep in death, but like Daniel, he is given the assurance that at the last day—the day of the resurrection—he, along with all the righteous, will receive the crown of eternal life. This is the tremendous hope that resonates throughout the entire Bible.

The hope of the Christian is in a real, literal resurrection at the last day. That is why the second coming of Jesus looms so brightly on the horizon for born-again believers. When Jesus comes, they receive the consummation of all their hopes. Jesus comes, and the dead are resurrected.

Notice that in each of these passages, the resurrection always occurs at the last day, just as Daniel had declared in Daniel 12:1, 2. It is a hope not yet realized, but nevertheless, it is still the greatest hope that stirs the blood of God's people. Death so often appears to be the end of it all, but Jesus has promised that death does not finalize human existence. Jesus has won the victory over death and the grave. Because He rose, we have the assurance that He will return and resurrect us at the final hour. No wonder Christians are a people of hope.

The Reality of the Resurrection Hope

The old pagan notion of life after death was so unreal: spirits groping for a touch of immortality. Yet the very words used to describe the biblical hope all denote the reality of the resurrection hope. Spirits don't inherit life after death—real, resurrected people do. It is a promise we all receive together. Along with Daniel and Paul, we will all meet Jesus at the same moment on the resurrection morning.

Even the words Jesus used to describe life after the resurrection denote reality. Matthew 25:34 refers to this new world as a kingdom. It is not some semi-material existence somewhere. It is real. The word *kingdom* denotes reality. In John 14:1-3, Jesus declares that He is going to heaven to prepare a place for us there. Note, again, that it is a literal place. Then He will return to take us to that place that He has prepared. The resurrected saints are taken on the greatest space journey the world has ever experienced.

Heaven is not some kind of spook country. Scripture declares it to be full of reality. It is not a place to sit on a cloud and strum on a harp for all eternity. Who in their right mind would enjoy that? The devil wants you to think of heaven as a boring place, but God declares it to be a real place. It is the most exciting place to be in the entire universe. Boring? Never! Heaven is a place of excitement and joy.

The heaven that God offers is not a spooky, spirit existence. God's redeemed have real bodies. Paul declares that our resurrected bodies will be like Christ's glorified body (Philippians 3:21). What was Christ's glorified, resurrected body like? Luke describes it for us:

> Now as they said these things, Jesus Himself stood in the midst of them, and said to them, "Peace to you." But they were terrified and frightened, and supposed they had seen a spirit. And He said to them, "Why are you troubled? And why do doubts arise in your hearts? Behold My hands and My feet, that it is I Myself. Handle Me and see, for a spirit does not have flesh and bones as you see I have." When He had said this, He showed them His hands and His feet. But while they still did not believe for joy, and marveled, He said to them, "Have you any food here?" So they gave Him a piece of a broiled fish and some honeycomb. And He took it and ate in their presence. Luke 24:36-43.

After the resurrection, Jesus did His best to convince the disciples that He was not a spirit. His body was real. They could touch Him—He could eat. This resurrection appearance forever dispelled any doubts about the literalness of the resurrected body.

And Paul declares that our resurrected bodies will be like Christ's. Wow! What an amazing God to provide us with such a realistic hope.

The only difference between our bodies now and our bodies then will be that they will no longer be subject to death, disease, and sin. Otherwise, they will be just as real as they are now.

This is why Paul declared that at the last day the mortal body puts on immortality and the perishable body puts on the imperishable (1 Corinthians 15:51-54). All the pain, difficulties, and sorrow of this humanity are left in the grave. God's people are resurrected to the joy of eternal youth.

What Will People Do in Heaven?

Picture real people, inhabiting a real world, doing real things. This is the biblical depiction of heaven. The glories of the new world are so wonderful they cannot even be imagined in our feeble human existence. Our loving God, however, wishes to convey to us that which we cannot even begin to imagine. To this end, He has put into human language a glimpse of what heaven will be like. Even though these glimpses are inadequate to describe the realities behind the descriptions, they do give us a concrete picture of the reality of heaven.

In Isaiah 65:17, 21, 22, the prophet is given a vision of the reality of the activities of God's people. He declares they will do real things: They will build houses and live in them; they will plant and eat the fruit. Just as Adam and Eve enjoyed the fruit of the Garden of Eden, so God's redeemed will forever enjoy the fruit of the earth made new. Isaiah's description informs us that heaven will be a busy place. It is not a place of inactivity. It is not a place for loafing, but enjoyable activity.

There will be time to explore the entire universe and learn all about God's creation. There will be no time restrictions, no deadlines, and no stress. Satan's picture of heaven is so bland that no one would ever want to go, but the Bible's picture is so real that all who visualize it will be eager to enjoy this marvelous experience.

God's heaven is beautiful. Isaiah 35:1, 2 declares that the desert will bloom like a rose garden. It is almost as if God takes the blandest and most boring place on earth—a desert—and turns it into a rose garden. If that is what the desert will look like, then we cannot even begin to imagine what the rest is going to be like. Think of the most beautiful sights on earth: Yosemite, the Grand Canyon, Lake Louise, and the Alps. All of these reveal traces of the original paradise created by God for humankind. All are fully restored in the heaven of God's creation. What was lost in Eden is restored in the new earth.

Heaven will be a peaceful place. There will be no terrorists to fly planes into buildings. There will be no fear, no bloodshed, and no war. God takes the most ferocious animal on earth—the lion—and pictures that lion lying down beside a lamb, the most gentle of creatures (Isaiah 65:25). God is simply painting us a word picture of heaven as a peaceful place where even the animals are at home with each other. No one destroys, for sin has been eliminated. The human race, so long unable to get along with each other, now exists in perfect harmony and peace with no racial or ethnic tension. At last, humanity learns to live together.

Heaven will be a happy place. There will be no more death or pain (Revelation 21:4). God takes those human experiences that bring us the greatest heartache in the present earth and tells us that they simply will not exist anymore. Imagine a place with no death and no pain. This is the reality of God's promise. Even our tears will be wiped away. Everything that brings sorrow is removed. No more separation from loved ones— we will be forever united with them. Can you imagine what those family reunions will be like?

Heaven will be a healthy home. Not only is there no death, there is no sickness (Isaiah 33:24). Imagine a place where there is no need for physicians or hospitals. All medical professions are unnecessary in heaven. These professionals will need to be retrained for a world where sickness does not exist.

Not only is there no disease, but all who were deformed in this world are fully restored in God's grand new world (Isaiah 35:5, 6). Imagine the blind seeing, the deaf hearing, and the crippled running. That is God's picture of the reality of a world without sin. Ponce de Leon never found the fountain of youth, but God gives it to His people in the new earth: eternal youth— not as a figment of the imagination—but as a reality.

Heaven will be a glorious place. The New Jerusalem is declared the capital of God's new world, and it is a glorious place (Revelation 21:11). It is so far beyond our wildest dreams that we can't even begin to imagine what it will be like. God tries to help us in Revelation 21 by describing what it would look like to the wild-eyed people of the first century who were used to dwelling in walled cities. Read the description for yourself in Revelation 21:12-18:

> Also she had a great and high wall with twelve gates, and twelve angels at the gates, and names written on them, which are the names of the twelve tribes of the children of Israel: three gates on the east, three gates on the north, three gates on the south, and three gates on the west. Now the wall of the city had twelve foundations, and on them were the names of the twelve apostles of the Lamb. And he who talked with me had a gold reed to measure the city, its gates, and its wall. The city is laid out as a square; its length is as great as its breadth. And he measured the city with the reed: twelve thousand furlongs. Its length, breadth, and height are equal. Then he measured its wall: one hundred and forty-four cubits, according to the measure of a man, that is, of an angel. The construction of its wall was of jasper; and the city was pure gold, like clear glass.

Even in the twenty-first century, it is difficult to imagine a city of this magnitude. To the people of the first century who first heard this, it must have truly been beyond their wildest imaginations. Imagine 1,500 miles around the city—375 miles on each side. That would make the city about the size of the states of Kansas and Nebraska combined. Then add to that all the precious gems that make up the wall, the streets, and the city itself.

What is so amazing is that there is no crime in this city, where gold is as common as asphalt. No one will be digging up gold bricks in the middle of the night. No one will be throwing cigarette butts in the golden gutters. What a fantastic picture Revelation portrays of the heavenly city! There is no earthly comparison. It is beyond imagination. It is wild and exciting, but above all else, it is real. This is our inheritance.

Yet all this beauty and gold is not what excites God's people the most. What causes them to rejoice and be glad is that heaven is God's home. God dwells there. They will see Jesus. That, dear reader, is the most exciting part of being in heaven. Revelation describes for us this heavenly reality:

> Now I saw a new heaven and a new earth, for the first heaven and the first earth had passed away. Also there was no more sea. Then I, John, saw the holy city, New Jerusalem, coming down out of heaven from God, prepared as a bride adorned for her husband. And I heard a loud voice from heaven saying, "Behold, the tabernacle of God is with men, and He will dwell with them, and they shall be His people. God Himself will be with them and be their God. And God will wipe away every tear from their eyes; there shall be no more death, nor sorrow, nor crying. There shall be no more pain, for the former things have passed away." Then He who sat on the throne said, "Behold, I make all things new." And He said to me, "Write, for these words are true and faithful." Revelation 21:1-5.

> And he showed me a pure river of water of life, clear as crystal, proceeding from the throne of God and of the Lamb. In the middle of its street, and on either side of the river, was the tree of life, which bore twelve fruits, each tree yielding its fruit every month. The leaves of the tree were for the healing of the nations. And there shall be no more curse, but the throne of God and of the Lamb shall be in it, and His servants shall serve Him. They shall see His face, and His name shall be on their foreheads. There shall be no night there: They need no lamp nor light of the sun, for the Lord God gives them light. And they shall reign forever and ever. Revelation 22:1-5.

This description is beyond comment. This is simply how God has described for us the beautiful home of His redeemed. But don't miss the best news of all. Heaven is God's home. He will dwell among us. The separation caused by sin is now forever removed, and once again, the God of relationships can enjoy the fellowship of the people He has redeemed. That is what makes heaven, heaven. It is not the streets of gold, the gates of pearl, or all the other beautiful descriptions of heaven, but the fact that our friend Jesus is going to be there, and we will see Him. That is the greatest reason for wanting to go to heaven.

Only those who want to see Him will be there. They have developed such a close relationship with Jesus that they cannot bear to miss heaven, not because of the glories, but because they love Jesus so much that they could not bear to be separated from the presence of the One who has redeemed them by His grace. Heaven without Jesus would simply be hell, even if the same physical realities were there. Heaven is being with Jesus. That is why the Christian today has heaven on sin-polluted earth. When Jesus is in the heart, we already have the joys of heaven. We are with Jesus, and heaven is all about being with Jesus.

Who Will Go?

Who gets to inhabit this glorious place? Only those who have Jesus in the heart. It is that simple. Heaven would be miserable for any who don't know Jesus. That is why they are excluded. God wants us to be happy, and if we would not be happy in heaven with Jesus, then there is no need to be there. Psalm 24 describes the glorious entry of the redeemed into heaven:

> Who may ascend into the hill of the Lord? Or who may stand in His holy place? He who has clean hands and a pure heart, who has not lifted up his soul to an idol, nor sworn deceitfully. Psalm 24:3, 4.

There is only one way to glory. It is the way of forgiveness through a dying Christ, and the way of a new heart and power to live through a living Christ. Only those who have grown to love Him here on earth, accepted Him here, and are allowing Him to change their lives here, will be with Him there.

Jesus invites us all to meet Him there. The last invitation of scripture bids us come.

> And the Spirit and the bride say, "Come!" And let him who hears say, "Come!" And let him who thirsts come. Whoever desires, let him take the water of life freely. Revelation 22:17.

It is an open invitation. It is available to all who accept it. You don't have to make yourself right first—you must come to Jesus just as you are and turn your life completely over to Him. He never forces anyone to come. All who enter do so freely.

At the conclusion of World War I, the soldiers were marched to the Arch of Triumph in France. As they entered the arch area, the question was shouted out to them. "By what right do you come to the arch of victory?" From the lips of 20,000 soldiers came forth the heart-throbbing chorus: "We come by the blood-red banner of Verdun."

Likewise, when the Lord of heaven and earth sweeps through the gates of the New Jerusalem with the redeemed of all ages the question is asked: "By what right do you enter here?" And the answer returns in bold refrain: "We come by the blood-red banner of Calvary." There is no other way to come than this. Will you lift its banner now by an act of deliberate choice? God never compels us. He just invites. Will you respond?

16

Hope When Death Occurs

A world without sin, death, or pain is extremely ap-peal ing to inhabitants of a world wrapped in dis-ease, cor ruption, and loss. This is why the hope described in the previous chapter is so powerful. It is the consumma- tion of all humanity's dreams. It is what keeps us going when life becomes so difficult. Satan has tried his best to distort this glorious Christian hope of eternity. In this chapter, we will explore Satan's deception regarding death and contrast it with the reassuring hope of the resurrec- tion presented in the previous chapter.

There is nothing more devastating to the human experi- ence than the death of a loved one or even the anticipation of our own demise. This is why hope beyond the grave is the most basic religious hope. Yet it is not really a hope—it is a living reality, and it will be realized when loved ones are res- urrected.

Daniel anticipated the resurrection at the last day, as did the apostle Paul. As seen in the previous chapter, the biblical writers all declared that resurrection would occur at the last day, and in the interim, those who die in Christ would sleep the sleep of death, awaiting the call of the Lifegiver on the res- urrection morning.

In contrast to the biblical hope of the resurrection, Satan has suggested that when people die, they are reincarnated as another person or advance to become angels. In some cases, Satan even impersonates the dead in order to deceive people regarding the Christian's hope in the resurrection. Since Satan has also suggested that people go straight to heaven or hell at death, it is easy to project that living people can somehow communicate with those who have died.

Communication with so-called spirits was strongly opposed in ancient Israel. In Old Testament times, people were even sentenced to death for attempting to communicate with those who had died. In fact, the prophet Isaiah proclaimed that attempted communication with the dead was in direct contradiction to communication with God:

> And when they say to you, "Seek those who are mediums and wizards, who whisper and mutter," should not a people seek their God? Should they seek the dead on behalf of the living? To the law and to the testimony! If they do not speak according to this word, it is because there is no light in them. Isaiah 8:19, 20.

Isaiah is very clear. True knowledge is found in the Word of God (the law and testimony), not in spirit mediums or séances. To seek knowledge from the "spirit world" is to flirt with the devil himself. Yet people report loved ones reappearing before them in spiritualistic séances. Who are these reported spirits from the nether world? Are they departed loved ones? Or are they a clever counterfeit of the devil himself? The prophet Isaiah has made it clear: Any knowledge coming out of the spirit world is knowledge from the father of lies—there is no light there, only the darkness of Satan.

However, these spirits, pretending to be our dead relatives, look like the person, talk like the person, and know information that only the dead person would know. Who are these pretenders of the dead? Revelation declares: "For they are spirits of demons, performing signs, which go out to the kings of the earth and of the whole world, to gather them to the battle of that great day of God Almighty" (Revelation 16:14). Revelation declares that the appearance of demons, impersonating the dead, is one of the signs of the end. This phenomenon is to be especially rampant just before the battle of Armageddon, described in Revelation 16. The proliferation of the ideas of eastern mysticism, reincarnation, and even spirit communication abound in our world today. Television and movies are exploiting the ideas of spirit communication, preparing humanity for Satan's ultimate hoax of demonic spirit communication in the last days.

Christian Reaction to Satan's Deception

Christians can no longer remain silent in the face of the onslaught of Satan's spiritualistic deceptions in these last days. Revelation indicates that one of the final great deceptions will be in the area of spiritualistic manifestations. It is time to arise and oppose this vicious attack of the adversary—an attack that is aimed at the very foundation of the Christian gospel.

The cornerstone of spiritualism is the belief that when a person dies, they go immediately to heaven or hell. Since people have consciousness immediately after death, they can communicate with those who are left on earth. This delusion stands in sharp contrast to the hope portrayed in scripture of a real resurrection at the last day and a belief that those who have died in Jesus are resting in their graves until the resurrection morning. It stands in total opposition to Daniel and Paul, who were told they would not receive the hope apart from all believers in the last day.

There are four great central truths to the Christian faith: the judgment, the resurrection, the second coming, and the cross. These four great pillars of Christianity are what make it unique. Yet Satan's teaching of immediate life after death virtually destroys every one of these core teachings of the Christian faith.

No Need of Final Judgment

Earlier, we examined the prophecy of Daniel 8 and 9, proclaiming the great truth of the pre-advent judgment beginning in 1844. It is a judgment in which God reveals to the entire universe those who will be saved. Imagine how inconsistent it would be to have a judgment at the end of the world if the saints were already in heaven. If a person went to heaven at death, there would be absolutely no need of a judgment allowing God to reveal to the unfallen beings of the universe who the saved would be. Everyone in the universe would already know the outcome, since the saved would have been in heaven years before the judgment occurred.

The entire biblical picture of a final judgment is rendered unnecessary by the introduction of the teaching of immediate life after death. There is no judgment immediately after death. The main thrust of the prophecy of Daniel was the grand revelation of the pre-advent judgment beginning, not when one dies, but at the end of the 2300 days in 1844.

No Need of the Resurrection

The previous chapter illuminated the great hope of the resurrection as the core Christian hope. The apostle Paul clarifies this hope in 1 Corinthians 15:13, 14, 17, 18:

> But if there is no resurrection of the dead, then Christ is not risen. And if Christ is not risen, then our preaching is empty and your faith is also empty. And if Christ is not risen, your faith is futile; you are still in your sins! Then also those who have fallen asleep in Christ have perished.

No teaching is more central to the Christian's hope than that of the resurrection.

It is a uniquely Christian hope. No other religion teaches the bodily resurrection. All pagan religions taught the immortality of the soul. Life after death was some kind of spirit existence. Only biblical religion held out this real hope of the resurrection at the last day, in which the body would be literally raised from the grave.

Paul even indicates in this passage that if there is no resurrection, then those who have died (fallen asleep) in Christ have perished. In other words, without resurrection there would be no future life after death. The only way to life after death is through the resurrection, according to the apostle Paul. Yet if people went to heaven as soon as they died, there would be no need of a resurrection to bring them back to life. They would have life without resurrection—an impossibility, according to the apostle Paul.

Through the introduction of the pagan notion of people going to heaven as spirits immediately after death, Satan has totally undermined one of the most basic of Christian doctrines—the hope of the literal resurrection at the last day. This false teaching is aimed at the central pillars of the Christian faith. It can no longer be tolerated in Christian circles.

No Need of the Second Coming

Closely associated with the hope of the resurrection is the dynamic hope of the second coming of Jesus. The hope that Jesus would return the second time resonates throughout the New Testament. Jesus himself provided us with this hope in those immortal words that John records:

> Let not your heart be troubled; you believe in God, believe also in Me. In My Father's house are many mansions; if it were not so, I would have told you. I go to prepare a place for you. And if I go and prepare a place for you, I will come again and receive you to Myself; that where I am, there you may be also. John 14:1-3.

Jesus left the earth, went to heaven, prepares a place for us there, and then returns to get us and take us to the place He has prepared. Nothing could be clearer: The purpose of the second coming is to take the redeemed to heaven—to the place prepared for them. They are not there now, but He will come again and take them there.

If a person went to heaven upon death, there would be absolutely no need for Jesus to return to take the redeemed to a place they were already occupying. This devious teaching of going to heaven immediately after death eliminates any need for the basic Christian hope of the second coming of Jesus.

No Need of the Cross

Those who have accepted this delusion have suggested that human beings are made up of two parts: a mortal and an immortal. They contend that the immortal goes to heaven at death but that the mortal goes into the grave, to be resurrected and rejoined at the second coming. Thus, between death and resurrection, people are merely spirits floating through heaven, not gaining reality until the second coming.

Is this elaborate scheme scriptural? Does the Bible teach that humanity is composed of two parts: mortal and immortal? In other words, do humans have an immortal soul—a soul incapable of dying? Do humans posses immortality or eternal life naturally, or is immortality a gift given by God, through His Son Jesus? "For the wages of sin is death, but the gift of God is eternal life in Christ Jesus our Lord" (Romans 6:23). If a person is immortal by nature, born with an immortal soul, then that person already has the gift of God before God ever gave it. Thus there is no need for the cross. Why would Jesus have to die on the cross to give people everlasting life if they already possessed it when they were born? This doctrine strikes at the very heart of Christianity, rendering useless the act of Jesus dying on the cross. But note that scripture is clear about what Jesus accomplished on Calvary's hill.

"But has now been revealed by the appearing of our Savior Jesus Christ, who has abolished death and brought life and immortality to light through the gospel" (2 Tim. 1:10).

"For God so loved the world that He gave His only begotten Son, that whoever believes in Him should not perish but have everlasting life" (John 3:16).

Jesus died to give us eternal life—immortality. It was not something we were born with—we did not possess it by nature. For humans to receive immortality, Jesus had to die on the cross. The cross is the centerpiece of redemption. Yet if we all were born with an immortal soul, there would be absolutely no need for Jesus to die on Calvary to give us that which we already possessed—eternal life.

Christianity Eliminated

If this doctrine of natural immortality is allowed to gain control of Christianity, Christianity could be destroyed. This fabrication that a person goes straight to heaven or hell at death because they possess an immortal soul strikes at the very core of the Christian faith. If accepted, there is then no need of the judgment, the resurrection, the second coming, or the cross.

If you eliminate these great truths, you have virtually destroyed the Christian faith. There is no teaching that Satan could have introduced to undermine basic Christianity as thoroughly as the teaching that a person goes to heaven or hell at death. It is a false teaching aimed straight at the heart of the Christian gospel and, if believed, renders Christianity no different than all the pagan religions of the past.

The Immortality of the Soul

All pagan religions taught the immortality of the soul. The Bible is the only literature of the ancient world that never mentions the immortality of the soul. You will find the phrase "immortal soul" rampant in the mythological literature of Egypt, Persia, Greece, and Rome, but totally absent in the Bible.

In fact, the adjective *immortal* only appears one time in the entire Bible. The term *immortality* appears elsewhere, but the adjective, describing something that is immortal, appears only one time: "Now to the King eternal, immortal, invisible, to God who alone is wise, be honor and glory forever and ever. Amen" (1 Tim. 1:17).

The only thing described as immortal in scripture is God. He is the sole possessor of immortality. It is a characteristic of divinity. Referring to God, Paul continues in 1 Tim. 6:15, 16:

Which He will manifest in His own time, He who is the blessed and only Potentate, the King of kings and Lord of lords, who alone has immortality, dwelling in unapproachable light, whom no man has seen or can see, to whom be honor and everlasting power. Amen.

Not only does the Bible declare that immortality is a characteristic of God, it unequivocally declares that God is the sole possessor of immortality. In view of such strong statements, no human being should ever dare to claim to have an immortal soul. To do so would be for a human to claim to have a characteristic that scripture declares to be the sole possession of God. Any human that claims to have something that belongs only to God is blaspheming God.

Of course, that is Satan's aim. He wishes to be like God. He wants the human race to think that it possesses an element that is the exclusive domain of God. This is why no Christian would ever dare to claim to possess an immortal soul, when the Bible declares that God is the only one who possesses immortality.

Is There a Soul?

While no human can possess an immortal soul, is there still a soul? Yes. God clearly defines what is meant by the soul in the first usage of the term *soul* in the Bible: "And the Lord God formed man of the dust of the ground, and breathed into his nostrils the breath of life; and man became a living soul" (Genesis 2:7, KJV).

The biblical soul that God created consisted of two parts: the dust of the ground (body), and the breath of life. When the two united, it created a living soul, or living being. The soul is not separate from the body; instead, the body is part of the soul. You cannot have a soul apart from the body. The scriptural usage of the term *soul* is the opposite of the pagan religions, where the soul inhabited the body. Instead, the Bible presents humankind as a holistic creature.

Rather than being a separate entity from the body, the soul is presented as the whole person. God breathes into the body created from the dust. The resulting combination of the body united with the spark of life from God creates a living person—a soul. When a person dies, God takes back the breath of life, the body returns to the dust, and the soul ceases to exist (Ecclesiastes 12:7). The soul only exists when the body and breath of life are united.

At the resurrection, God rebreathes into the dead the breath of life. They are recreated and brought forth out of the tomb, because body and breath are again united. This is why Paul is clear that the only way to life after death is through the resurrection. There is no existence apart from the resurrected body.

A light bulb consists of two basic elements: a filament, connected to a power source. When the filament in the bulb is connected to the power source, the light burns freely. Disconnect the filament from the power source, and the light goes out. Reconnect it, and the light once more appears. That is how it is in death. The person is connected to the power source—God. Death occurs when the power is switched off, and then life is resurrected when the power source is turned back on at the second coming of Jesus.

Can this soul die? If it is immortal, it would be incapable of dying. Yet the prophet Ezekiel declares: "The soul who sins shall die" (Ezekiel 18:4). Romans 3:23 asserts that all have sinned. If all souls have sinned, and the soul that sins dies, then there is no such thing as an immortal soul.

The Origin of the Immortal-Soul Doctrine

It is a lie of the devil that when people die, they go immediately to heaven or hell. Such a teaching, so contrary to the very essence of scripture, originated from the father of lies, Satan himself. The devil would have us believe that when a person dies, he or she doesn't really die, but lives on in a better world. Amazingly, this was the first lie he told in the Garden of Eden. It was so successful then that he has been proclaiming it ever since, until practically the entire world has swallowed this serious delusion. Amos Phelps, a Methodist-Congregational minister of the nineteenth century, succinctly describes the history of this delusion:

> The doctrine can be traced through the muddy channels of a corrupted Christianity, a perverted Judaism, a pagan philosophy, and a superstitious idolatry, to the great instigator of mischief in the Garden of Eden. The Protestants borrowed it from the Catholics, the Catholics from the Pharisees, and the Pharisees from the old Serpent, who first preached the doctrine amid the lowly bowels of Paradise to an audience all too willing to hear and heed the new and fascinating theology—"Ye shall not surely die."—Amos Phelps, *Is Man by Nature Immortal?* 1805-1874 (quoted in Leroy Froom's *Conditionalist Faith of Our Fathers*, p. 553).

In fact, the early Christians of the second century felt so strongly about this teaching that they did not even regard a person as a Christian if he or she believed that when you died, you went straight to heaven:

> If you have fallen in with some who are called Christians, but who do not admit this (truth – of the resurrection), and venture to blaspheme the God of Abraham, and the God of Isaac, and the God of Jacob; who say there is no resurrection of the dead and that their souls, when they die, are taken to heaven; do not imagine that they are Christians.—Justin Martyr, *Dialogue with Trypho*, chap. 80 in *ANF*, vol. 1, p. 239. (Died in A.D. 165.)

Why did the early Christians feel so strongly on this subject? Because they saw that this doctrine virtually destroyed the Christian's hope. As we have seen, it undermined the doctrines of the judgment, resurrection, second coming, and the cross. The early Christians could not tolerate a doctrine that undermined its very foundation. Therefore they opposed it, as we must, so that we can hold high the hope of Christianity—a resurrection at the second coming made certain by the death of Christ on the cross providing humans eternal life.

Where Are the Dead?

If there is no existence immediately after death, what happens to people in the interval between death and the resurrection at the second coming of Jesus? Just look at these very clear passages from the Old Testament:

"For the living know that they will die; but the dead know nothing" (Ecclesiastes 9:5).

"Do not put your trust in princes, nor in a son of man, in whom there is no help. His spirit departs, he returns to his earth; in that very day his plans perish" (Psalm 146:3, 4).

"For in death there is no remembrance of Thee: in the grave who shall give Thee thanks?" (Psalm 6:5, KJV).

The Old Testament could not have made it any clearer: The dead do not know anything. There is silence in death. The day a person dies, the thoughts perish. So whatever existence there is after death, there are no thoughts in the person, nor does the person even have any recollection of God.

Why? Because in death, there is silence. Existence occurs only at the resurrection. The testimony of scripture is so clear here that it needs no comment. "The dead do not know anything." That should settle it for any Bible-believing Christian.

The New Testament likewise affirms the Old Testament teaching regarding death. In Acts 2:29, Peter declares that David is dead and buried in his day. And then he adds in verse 34 that David is not yet ascended to heaven. If David was still in the tomb a thousand years after he died, then clearly the New Testament writers are asserting that the dead are asleep and know nothing till Jesus returns.

The Sleep of Death

Throughout the Bible, over one hundred times, death is

referred to as sleep. It is the most common scriptural word for death. It fittingly describes what happens at death. It is not the end for the righteous—only sleep. They will be awakened at the last day. This is how Jesus described death in John 11:11-14, when his friend Lazarus died. He went to awaken him out of sleep.

As we previously noted, Jesus declares Himself to be the resurrection and the life (John 11:25). The hope Jesus used to warm the heart of Mary and Martha is the hope of the resurrection. But they will not have to wait till the last day. He will resurrect Lazarus before their very eyes, giving them a glimpse of what that final resurrection morning will be like.

Throughout the New Testament, the hope of the resurrection is continually held out to Christians. As the Thessalonian believers saw their loved ones dying, they wondered what would happen to them. Paul wrote them these reassuring words:

> For this we say to you by the word of the Lord, that we who are alive and remain until the coming of the Lord will by no means precede those who are asleep. For the Lord Himself will descend from heaven with a shout, with the voice of an archangel, and with the trumpet of God. And the dead in Christ will rise first. Then we who are alive and remain shall be caught up together with them in the clouds to meet the Lord in the air. And thus we shall always be with the Lord. Therefore comfort one another with these words. 1 Thess. 4:15-18.

Here indeed is a marvelous hope with which to comfort each other. The loss of loved ones does not mean despair. There is hope—not in an immortal soul, but a hope—in the resurrection when Jesus returns. Paul further elaborates on this point in 1 Corinthians 15:51-55:

> Behold, I tell you a mystery: We shall not all sleep, but we shall all be changed—in a moment, in the twinkling of an

eye, at the last trumpet. For the trumpet will sound, and the dead will be raised incorruptible, and we shall be changed. For this corruptible must put on incorruption, and this mortal must put on immortality. So when this corruptible has put on incorruption, and this mortal has put on immortality, then shall be brought to pass the saying that is written: "Death is swallowed up in victory. O Death, where is your sting? O Hades, where is your victory?"

The Ultimate Hope

Both biblical testaments ring clear on this ultimate hope— the resurrection of the last days. Death is declared to be a sleep, a momentary rest, from which the righteous will all be awakened. There is no need to be afraid of death, for it is like going to bed at night and waking up in the morning. We do not fear sleep, for we know we shall awaken. Likewise, the Christian does not fear death, for the hope is clear: Those who believe in Jesus will awake from the sleep of death at the resurrection morning.

Death is not something wonderful. The Bible declares it to be an enemy (1 Corinthians 15:26). It is an enemy that shall be destroyed at the last day. The Christian does not fear death, because our Savior has conquered it by rising from Joseph's tomb. Because He rose, we also shall rise again. Death is not something wonderful that translates me to the realm of bliss. It is an enemy to be destroyed. And God further declares that in the new earth, there will be no more death (Revelation 21:4).

Just imagine it is the resurrection morning. You are awakened by the call of the Lifegiver as He calls the sleeping saints to rise from their graves. As you come forth from the grave, you see tombs opening all over the graveyard. You look beside you, and you see your spouse rising with you. Soon you meet that son or daughter, that mother or father. An angel places a baby in a mother's arms. Death has been conquered. Christ has delivered His people. O glorious day! May the reality of this scene soon become your ultimate reality. Yes, there is hope in death—the greatest hope ever given the human race, the hope that the sleep of death will end and God's people will be resurrected to spend this glorious eternity with Him.

17

Hope in the Destruction of the Wicked

For all who have accepted Jesus Christ as the personal Savior of their life, the ultimate hope of the resurrection at Jesus' return is a glorious reality. However, to those who have not accepted Jesus, there is no hope beyond the tomb. What happens to those who have rejected God's wonderful offer of eternal salvation? This ultimate end of the wicked has been described as hell—an ever-burning punishment for the rejecters of God's love. Yet would a God of love actually torture people throughout all eternity?

The ultimate fate of the wicked is an issue that has made more infidels than any other doctrine ever concocted. Many cannot put together a God of love with a God who would consign people to a place of burning for eternity. Yet the question cannot be settled by human wisdom. One must clearly examine scripture to discover what God Himself has revealed about the punishment of the wicked.

When Does Hell Take Place?

According to popular teaching, a wicked person enters hell immediately following death. Of course, as seen in the previous chapter, humankind is unconscious in death and knows nothing until the morning of the resurrection. The Bible has clearly indicated that there is no life after death until the resurrection at the end of the world. Therefore, the population of hell today would still be zero. No one yet has gone to this dreadful place. We don't have to worry that our loved ones who didn't accept Jesus are currently suffering the agonies of hell.

If people went to hell immediately upon death, God would be viewed as grossly unfair and unjust. Cain, who died over six thousand years ago, would have been burning in hell for all those six thousand years, yet a person who died today and went to hell would burn six thousand years less than Cain, simply because the person was born six thousand years later. Any sense of justice would declare that equal crimes demand equal punishment, but this perversion of the Bible actually indicates that God is unjust, because He punishes some people longer than others simply because they were born earlier. That is unfair.

However, the Bible indicates that no one is in hell today. Notice the clear testimony of scripture: "The Lord knoweth how to deliver the godly out of temptations, and to reserve the unjust unto the day of judgment to be punished" (2 Peter 2:9, KJV).

The wicked are held in reserve until the day of judgment. Obviously, this text cannot be misunderstood. They are not currently being punished, but they are reserved until this special day of judgment. But when is this final day of judgment for the wicked? Listen to Jesus:

> As therefore the tares are gathered and burned in the fire; so shall it be in the end of this world. The Son of man shall send forth his angels, and they shall gather out of his kingdom all things that offend, and them which do iniquity; and shall cast them into a furnace of fire: there shall be wailing and gnashing of teeth. Matthew 13:40-42, KJV.

Jesus has settled the question of hell beyond any doubt. No one is in hell today. Hell does occur, but it occurs at the end of the world. The day of judgment is equated by Jesus with the end of the world. Anyone who declares that people go to hell when they die stands in direct contradiction to Jesus Himself.

Where Does Hell Take Place?

Because of Satan's declaration that people go to hell when they die, the devil had to invent a subterranean pit where the devil pokes people in the fires of hell. Such medieval creations do discredit to God and the revelation He has given in scripture. Since the Bible declares hell to occur at the end of the world, hell will transpire right on Planet Earth, not in a subterranean pit somewhere in the heart of the earth. The ringing testimony of scripture again clearly describes hell, the place of burning, occurring right on the surface of the earth.

> But the heavens and the earth which are now preserved by the same word, are reserved for fire until the day of judgment and perdition of ungodly men. But, beloved, do not forget this one thing, that with the Lord one day is as a thousand years, and a thousand years as one day. The Lord is not slack concerning His promise, as some count slackness, but is longsuffering toward us, not willing that any should perish but that all should come to repentance. But the day of the Lord will come as a thief in the night, in which the heavens will pass away with a great noise, and the elements will melt with fervent heat; both the earth and the works that are in it will be burned up. 2 Peter 3:7-10.

Just as God destroyed the world the first time by a worldwide flood, so He will destroy the world the second time by the fires of hell. It is a fire that totally consumes the earth and all that is in it. This is the end of the wicked. It is not some barbeque pit in the center of the earth, but a worldwide destruction by fire at the end of the world.

How Long Does Hell Last?

The duration of hell has probably been one of the most misunderstood teachings in Christianity. Many have misunderstood the Bible on this subject and have suggested that this place of burning will last throughout the eons of eternity—that it will never come to an end. For the sins of seventy years of life, God consigns one to a punishment that will never end. This just doesn't sound like the God who so loved the world that He gave His only Son to die for us.

In fact, such a teaching makes God out to be a tyrant. During World War II, Hitler tortured his victims brutally, but he finally allowed them to die. Yet some would have us believe God to be a worse tyrant than Hitler, for God would continually renew their bodies so they could be endlessly tortured.

The fires of hell would know no end. Wild imaginations have even suggested that the sight of the lost in hell would be a great delight to those enjoying the bliss of heaven. Yet if one thinks about it, if those in heaven could see the wicked in hell, heaven itself would be a miserable place.

The doctrine of an eternally burning hell has been one of Satan's best deceptions. Many have declared that they could not serve a God who would endlessly torture people for the sins of a mere seventy years of life on this planet, no matter how evil they were. All can agree that God must eliminate sin, but to keep sinners alive for eternity would never solve the sin problem. Instead, it would keep it forever before our eyes.

Some have remarked that the doctrine of an eternally burning hell sounds more pagan than Christian, and they are correct. One can actually trace the sad history of how this doctrine entered the church. Its origin is clearly in the pagan mythological world, not in biblical revelation.

The earliest notions of a place of eternal burning arise among the ancient Persians, who suggested that there were two major powers in the universe: good and evil. According to the Persians, both were eternal. The good power could not eliminate the evil power, nor could the evil power destroy the good. Since both were eternal, the good power consigned the evil power to a place of eternal torture and torment.

This is the ancient pagan origin of the modern doctrine of eternal torment. It comes straight from the pagan Persians. It boldly proclaims that God and Satan are equals. (No wonder

Satan enjoys this pagan doctrine.) Its basic philosophy is that God cannot conquer Satan, for Satan is equal to God. But the God of scripture is greater than Satan! He will conquer him and bring him to an utter end. Satan will be no more. The heart of the error in the pagan notion of an eternally burning hell is placing God and evil on equal ground and declaring that God is unable to conquer evil.

Plato, the philosopher of ancient Greece, popularized the idea of the natural immortality of the soul discussed in the previous chapter. He then borrowed from the pagans the notion that good and evil are eternal. Since all souls are immortal, in this theory, God cannot destroy evil souls, so He places them in eternal torment. This Greek notion basically teaches the same thing that the Persians did: God is unable to conquer evil in any form. Again, this is not the biblical God— this is the lowly gods of paganism.

It was in the third century of the Christian era that Tertullian, an early Christian leader, introduced for the first time the dual doctrines of eternal torment and natural immortality into the Christian church. Yet even then, it took another two hundred years to create the medieval pagan notion of an eternally burning hell. It was this pagan teaching of the church during the Middle Ages that kept millions in submission to the authority of the church. If the members did not obey the rules, the church would consign them to the fiery tortures of the damned in hell. Even the secular press recognized the pagan origin of this doctrine:

> In earliest Old Testament times, all the dead—both righteous and wicked—were believed to go to Sheol, a gloomy underworld separated from God... Then in about the second century B.C. under the influence of Greek and Persian philosophy, Pharisaic Judaism began to embrace the idea of the immortal soul and of Hades—the infernal netherworld of Greek mythology—as a place where all would either rewarded or punished... The idea of purgatory—a place separate from hell where sinners unfit for heaven are reha-

bilitated—became part of church teaching in the sixth century. And later, limbo was conceived as a compartment for unbaptized infants who are spared sensory torments, but never see God.

—*U.S. News,* March 25, 1991.

One can easily wonder how it was possible for such a pagan doctrine to infiltrate the Christian church. Yet history does not lie. This doctrine was muddied in the mire of ancient paganism. Its origin is not biblical revelation but pagan infiltration. To substantiate this perversion of God's character, a few biblical texts were pulled out of their context to seemingly lend support to this Satanic doctrine. Actually, there are only four or five such texts that were manipulated, but it was enough to give credence to the teaching. What is amazing is that there are 182 clear texts in scripture declaring that hell will come to an end—and only four or five texts that can be pulled out of context. Certainly the preponderance of evidence declares which belief is true.

Here is one example of a text pulled out of context to declare this perverted doctrine:

> The devil, who deceived them, was cast into the lake of fire and brimstone where the beast and the false prophet are. And they will be tormented day and night forever and ever. Revelation 20:10.

It is this phrase *forever and ever* that has been distorted. The Greek word translated "forever" in this passage is a word meaning "age-lasting." The Greek dictionary defines the word *forever* as "a space of time, as a lifetime, a generation"—(G. Abbott Smith, *A Greek Lexicon of the New Testament).* The basic meaning of the word used here is, "as long as life shall last." The usage of this phrase in Revelation 20:10 only indicates that the people will burn as long as they are alive—it does not mean without end.

When one examines other passages in the Bible where the

word is used, this same relative meaning is clearly indicated. In Exodus 21:6, KJV, a slave is declared to serve the master "forever." Of course, when the slave died, he ceased to serve his master. It only meant as long as he lived. In 1 Samuel 1:22 and 28, Hannah declares that Samuel has been given to the Lord forever, but in verse 28, she declares that forever means as long as he shall live.

In Jonah 2:6, Jonah is declared to be in the belly of the big fish forever, yet it was really only three days and nights. Clearly, from these and other examples in the Bible, it does not use the word *forever* to mean unending but more accurately, "as long as one lives."

Of course, our modern usage of the word is similar. When a person declares that it took them forever to get home from work because of the traffic, the person does not mean they will be traveling throughout eternity. To insist that Revelation 20:10 must indicate that the wicked burn throughout eternity is inconsistent with the rest of the Bible's usage of the word and with what the Bible declares concerning the punishment of the wicked in other passages.

It is even impossible, in the context of Revelation 20, to indicate that the punishment is never ending. Revelation 20:10 declares that the wicked will be tormented forever and ever. In fact, verses 11-15 indicate that the wicked will be consigned to this lake of fire, where they will be tormented forever. However, the next verse, Revelation 21:1, boldly declares: "Now I saw a new heaven and a new earth, for the first heaven and the first earth had passed away" (Revelation 21:1). The first earth, where the wicked were being destroyed, is now declared to pass away. Thus it is absolutely impossible to interpret "forever" in this passage as never ending, for just six verses later, the Bible pointedly declares that the first earth will cease to be.

The Punishment of the Wicked

The punishment of the wicked is not burning in hell. Romans 6:23 offers two choices for humankind: "For the wages of sin is death, but the gift of God is eternal life in Christ Jesus our Lord" (Romans 6:23).

The choice is not between burning in hell and living in heaven. The clear biblical choice is between life and death. The punishment for sin is not endless suffering in hell, but instead, it is death. Hellfire is not the punishment—death is. The fire is only the means God uses to bring about the punishment, which is death.

If a wicked person lived throughout the endless ages of eternity in hell, that person would never receive the wages of sin—death—but amazingly, would be receiving the gift of God, eternal life. Granted, it would not be a pleasant life, but it still would be life. Yet the scripture is clear—the punishment for sin is death.

Only those who accept Jesus receive everlasting life.

> And this is the testimony: that God has given us eternal life, and this life is in His Son. He who has the Son has life; he who does not have the Son of God does not have life. 1 John 5:11, 12.

Life is available only in the Son. The possession of the Son provides life. Failure to possess the Son results in the absence of life. The devil would have you believe there is some other way to eternal life, other than through the Son of God. Yet scripture is crystal clear. Life is available only to those who accept Jesus. There is no eternal life—in heaven or in hell—for those who do not receive Jesus as their Savior. The alternative to accepting Jesus is eternal death, not a life in hell.

In the Old Testament sacrificial system, the lamb symbolically bore the penalty for sin. That penalty was death, not torture of endless suffering. Likewise, on Calvary, Christ paid for my sin by suffering the second death. He did not endure endless torment on the cross, but instead gave up His life. Yet if eternal burning were the punishment for sin, and Jesus paid the penalty, He would still be on the cross today suffering for us. Yet Jesus died, because that was the penalty for sin. Christ's death on Calvary is indisputable evidence against the atheistic, paganistic doctrine of eternal torment.

In Revelation 21:8, the Bible literally calls the destruction of the wicked "the second death." That is what it is. The punishment is death, not life. Over 180 texts in the scriptures declare that the time will come when the wicked will not be. They will be annihilated and cease to exist. There will be a fire, but it will be a fire of annihilation, not of endless torture.

"For yet a little while and the wicked shall be no more; indeed, you will look carefully for his place, but it shall be no more" (Psalm 37:10).

"But the wicked shall perish; and the enemies of the Lord, like the splendor of the meadows, shall vanish. Into smoke they shall vanish away" (Psalm 37:20).

Satan and his vast host of followers will be destroyed. They will cease to be. The little Bible book of Jude even likens the destruction of the wicked to God's destruction of the cities of Sodom and Gomorrah (Jude 7). The fire that destroyed those wicked cities was eternal, in the sense that no one could put it out. However, the fires are not still burning. When they had accomplished their purpose, they went out. So will the fires of hell that destroy the wicked. God does not consign the wicked to everlasting *punishing* but to everlasting *punishment*. The punishment is death that does not end after the punishing is complete.

The last chapter of the Old Testament boldly declares in unmistakable language the grand truth of the destruction of the wicked.

> "For behold, the day is coming, burning like an oven, and all the proud, yes, all who do wickedly will be stubble. And the day which is coming shall burn them up," says the Lord of hosts, "that will leave them neither root nor branch. . . . You shall trample the wicked, for they shall be ashes under the soles of your feet on the day that I do this," says the Lord of hosts. Malachi 4:1, 3.

When the fires of hell strike, nothing is left but ashes. The wicked are destroyed, root and branch. No clearer metaphors could have been used to describe the utter annihilation of the wicked than Malachi uses here—root and branch, and reduction to ashes. It is all over. Nothing is left but the ashes of the wicked. God makes an utter end to sin. Even Satan himself is totally eradicated.

> You defiled your sanctuaries by the multitude of your iniquities, by the iniquity of your trading; therefore I brought fire from your midst; it devoured you, and I turned you to ashes upon the earth in the sight of all who saw you. All who knew you among the peoples are astonished at you; you have become a horror, and shall be no more forever. Ezekiel 28:18, 19.

God brings an utter end to evil. Sin and sinners will be no more. God will totally clean up this perverted world. Some people note that they did not choose to be born. We did not choose to be born, but we can choose whether we want to spend eternity with God. If we do not choose Him, then God will do what only a just God would do—He will eliminate us from His universe. He does not want us to spend eternity with Him unless we choose to do so. That is what hell is all about.

Yet God's desire for us is not that we perish in hell but that we spend eternity with our Maker. The immortal passage of John 3:16 declares God's intentions very clearly. "For God so loved the world that He gave His only begotten Son, that whoever believes in Him should not perish but have everlasting life." Even this beloved verse clearly declares the punishment of the wicked to be perishing, not burning in hell. When one perishes, he or she ceases to exist. That is the ultimate fate of the wicked.

God can be trusted. Satan's deceptions are false. Our God is a just and loving God. He will destroy those who do not wish to spend eternity with Him, but those who choose God will enjoy His friendship throughout all eternity. Why not choose Him now?

18

Hope in the End of Sin

For 6,000 years, sin has ravaged Planet Earth. The deceitfulness and the destructiveness of sin prevail throughout the world. Are we truly sick of this sin-cursed earth? Do we truly hope that sin will soon cease to be? God longs to bring an end to sin on this planet. Yet God cannot do so until the entire universe is so fed up with sin that they will never allow it to arise the second time.

For Christians who have accepted Jesus Christ as Savior of their life, this sin-cursed earth becomes burdensome. We long for sin to be eliminated, but not as much as God desires to end the sin problem. Yet the Bible clearly indicates that the time is soon to come when sin will be no more. God will fully reclaim this world as His. Revelation 20 portrays the ultimate triumph of God over evil and the final demise of sin.

Revelation 20 also describes God's final dealing with sin in all its phases, in what is called the 1,000-year reign of Christ. At last, Satan is bound. At last, Satan is placed fully under the control of God. Notice this enticing scene described in the first few verses of Revelation 20:

> Then I saw an angel coming down from heaven, having the key to the bottomless pit and a great chain in his hand. He laid hold of the dragon, that serpent of old, who is the Devil and Satan, and bound him for a thousand years; and he cast him into the bottomless pit, and shut him up, and set a seal on him, so that he should deceive the nations no more

till the thousand years were finished. But after these things
he must be released for a little while. Verses 1-3.

An amazing conclusion to the great controversy! There
comes a time when Satan is bound. That great deceiver will
no longer be able to produce his deceptions upon the planet.
He will be fully unmasked and prevented from doing his hid-
eous deeds. For 1,000 years, the Bible proclaims, Satan is to
be bound before he has one final deception against the human race.

The Beginning of the 1,000 Years

The 1,000 years begins with the binding of Satan. Since the
devil is still alive and well on the planet, it is very obvious that
this 1,000-year period is still in the future. What else marks
its beginning? Revelation 20:6 (NASB) declares:

Blessed and holy is the one who has a part in the first
resurrection; over these the second death has no power, but
they will be priests of God and of Christ and will reign with
Him for a thousand years.

Two things happen at the beginning of the 1,000 years: the
first resurrection occurs, and the 1,000-year reign of the saints
with Jesus begins as Satan is bound. If there is a first resurrection, this implies a second resurrection. Jesus, in fact, refers to two resurrections in John 5:28, 29: a resurrection of
life, and a resurrection of damnation. Since those who rise in
the first resurrection reign with Christ, this is obviously the
resurrection of the righteous. Revelation 20:5 declares that the
rest of the dead (the wicked) rose not again till the end of the
1,000 years.

Thus, it appears that the 1,000 years divides the two resurrections: the resurrection of the righteous occurring at the
beginning of the 1,000 years, and the resurrection of the
wicked occurring at the end of the 1,000 years. During the

time between the two resurrections, Satan is bound. When do the righteous rise from their graves? As we have already studied, the resurrection of the righteous occurs at that beautiful event: the second coming of Jesus.

> For the Lord Himself will descend from heaven with a shout, with the voice of an archangel, and with the trumpet of God. And the dead in Christ will rise first. Then we who are alive and remain shall be caught up together with them in the clouds to meet the Lord in the air. And thus we shall always be with the Lord. Therefore comfort one another with these words. 1 Thess. 4:16-18.

The 1,000 years begins with the awesome event of the second coming. Jesus descends from heaven, the righteous are resurrected, the living righteous are caught up, then they meet Him in the air along with the resurrected righteous. Jesus escorts this triumphant redeemed host to the very gates of heaven itself. He then fulfills the promise He made 2,000 years ago to those early disciples:

> Let not your heart be troubled; you believe in God, believe also in Me. In My Father's house are many mansions; if it were not so, I would have told you. I go to prepare a place for you. And if I go and prepare a place for you, I will come again and receive you to Myself; that where I am, there you may be also. John 14:1-3.

At that final, climatic hour of earth's history, the Son of the Living God returns, claims His own people by resurrection and translation, and then transports them to the special place He has prepared for them in His Father's house. Imagine the excitement as that redeemed host enter through the gates of heaven itself and discover the place prepared for them by their Savior. Thus, at the beginning of the 1,000 years, the righteous are placed forever beyond the reach of Satan. In one sweeping action, Christ has bound Satan from attacking the people of

God by removing them from the planet over which Satan has such a hold.

Revelation 20:1-3 reveals that Satan is bound not just from the righteous but from all people during the 1,000 years. How is he prevented from deceiving the wicked? Revelation 20:5 declares that the rest of the dead (the wicked) don't live at all during the 1,000 years. They only rise at the end. So the wicked who are dead are unable to be deceived by the devil. The only group left are the wicked who are alive when Jesus comes. What happens to them? How are they put beyond Satan's control?

> And at that day the slain of the Lord shall be from one end of the earth even to the other end of the earth. They shall not be lamented, or gathered, or buried; they shall become refuse on the ground. Jeremiah 25:33.

Here are people who are slain by the Lord, and no one buries them. 2 Thessalonians 2:8, KJV, declares that the wicked one will be slain by the "brightness of His coming." Listen as Revelation 6:15-17 describes this awesome scene:

> And the kings of the earth, the great men, the rich men, the commanders, the mighty men, every slave and every free man, hid themselves in the caves and in the rocks of the mountains, and said to the mountains and rocks, "Fall on us and hide us from the face of Him who sits on the throne and from the wrath of the Lamb! For the great day of His wrath has come, and who is able to stand?"

Imagine the scene as Jesus descends in mighty glory. He comes in the glory of all the angels, plus His own glory, and His Father's glory (Matthew 16:27, 28). In this marvelous glory, the wicked cannot stand. They cry out to the rocks and mountains to hide them from this indescribable glory. No wonder Jeremiah declares that they are slain by the Lord.

The earth is totally void of living human beings. All the righteous have been taken to heaven for the 1,000 years, and all the wicked are now dead. No one is left alive. No wonder Satan is bound. There is no one to tempt. He has been bound by a chain of circumstances beyond his control. Satan is now given 1,000 years to think over the ruin that his way of life has caused. The evidence of earth's destruction—the natural result of Satan's rule—now stands before him on every side.

What Happens During the 1,000 Years?

At the beginning of the 1,000 years, Satan is bound, with no one to tempt. The wicked are all dead; the righteous are all in heaven. The earth is totally desolate. In fact, it seems that during the 1,000 years, the earth is reduced to the same chaotic condition that existed on the planet before God began the creative activity. As Genesis 1:2 declares: "The earth was without form, and void; and darkness was on the face of the deep." The word translated "deep" is the same basic word translated in Revelation 20 as "bottomless pit" or "abyss." This chaotic, destroyed earth, depopulated by the second coming, is now the bottomless pit (abyss) to which Satan is bound for 1,000 years.

There is no second chance for the wicked. Their probation is now completely over. Satan has won in their lives, and their bodies now lie decomposing over the surface of the globe. This picture of utter desolation on the planet is aptly described by the prophet Jeremiah:

> I beheld the earth, and indeed it was without form, and void; And the heavens, they had no light. I beheld the mountains, and indeed they trembled, and all the hills moved back and forth. I beheld, and indeed there was no man, and all the birds of the heavens had fled. I beheld, and indeed the fruitful land was a wilderness, and all its cities were broken down at the presence of the Lord, by His fierce anger. Jeremiah 4:23-26.

No one is left. Just as Revelation portrays, the earth is depopulated. Jeremiah informs us that this was caused by the coming of the Lord. He predicts that the earth is returned to the same formless and void state as described in Genesis 1. In fact, Jeremiah actually quotes Genesis 1:2 to describe this scene, linking it to the bottomless pit of Revelation 20.

As the wicked continue in unconscious sleep during the 1,000 years, the righteous are engaged in much activity. They have ascended to the throne room of the universe and are given the privilege of engaging in judgment all during these 1,000 years. But who is being judged? The righteous and wicked have already been separated. Why then this judgment?

In a previous chapter, we examined the biblical judgment, discovering its beginning in 1844. That pre-advent judgment, we learned, was a judgment of the saints for the sake of the unfallen beings of the universe. Remember, God does not need a judgment to discover who is righteous and who is wicked. He already knows that. Our loving God, however, desires all of His created beings to see that His judgments are right. So before bringing the righteous to heaven, He conducted the pre-advent judgment to satisfy the angels about the justice of God in bringing the righteous to heaven.

Now, the righteous are there, and Revelation 20:4 declares that judgment is given to them. No, they are not being judged. They are already judged in the pre-advent judgment. Now, God begins the judgment of the wicked, for the sake of the righteous. He does not want any one of His redeemed ones to question why He had to exclude some people from heaven. So He convenes part two of His final judgment—a judgment of the wicked to satisfy all doubts in the minds of the righteous. Only as everyone is fully convinced of the justice of God can sin be totally eradicated from God's great universe.

In addition to participating in the judgment of the wicked, the righteous are said to reign with Jesus for the 1,000 years (Revelation 20:6). Some have anticipated an earthly reign, but there is no one on earth to reign over. Instead, they share in the reign of Jesus over the entire universe. All that is entailed in that reign is not revealed in scripture, but it will be a wonderful adventure, we can be sure. For 1,000 years, phase two of the judgment continues. Then the 1,000 years end, and part three of the judgment occurs.

The End of the 1,000 Years

> Now when the thousand years have expired, Satan will be released from his prison and will go out to deceive the nations which are in the four corners of the earth, Gog and Magog, to gather them together to battle, whose number is as the sand of the sea. They went up on the breadth of the earth and surrounded the camp of the saints and the beloved city. And fire came down from God out of heaven and devoured them. Revelation 20:7-9.

So God describes the end of sinners. The 1,000 years are ended. The entire wicked throng has now been resurrected. The righteous have returned from heaven to Planet Earth (Revelation 21:2). Jude describes the purpose of this return:

> Now Enoch, the seventh from Adam, prophesied about these men also, saying, "Behold, the Lord comes with ten thousands of His saints, to execute judgment on all, to convict all who are ungodly among them of all their ungodly deeds which they have committed in an ungodly way, and of all the harsh things which ungodly sinners have spoken against Him." Jude 14, 15.

At the end of the 1,000 years, Jude declares, the righteous return with Jesus for the express purpose of executing judgment on the wicked. For 1,000 years they have been reviewing the judgment, until all are fully satisfied with what God is about to do. Now, they come together, and God resurrects the wicked for the final judgment. Why does God resurrect them only to destroy them again? To fully reveal the justice of God, He wants even the wicked to admit His fairness in dealing with them. This time, He conducts phase three of the judgment—a judgment of the wicked for the sake of the wicked. Revelation 20 further describes this final judgment scene:

> Then I saw a great white throne and Him who sat on it, from whose face the earth and the heaven fled away. And there was found no place for them. And I saw the dead, small and great, standing before God, and books were opened. And another book was opened, which is the Book of Life. And the dead were judged according to their works, by the things which were written in the books. The sea gave up the dead who were in it, and Death and Hades delivered up the dead who were in them. And they were judged, each one according to his works. Then Death and Hades were cast into the lake of fire. This is the second death. And anyone not found written in the Book of Life was cast into the lake of fire. Revelation 20:11-15.

Satan's heart is unchanged. As soon as the wicked are resurrected, he continues his artful work of deception. He actually leads this rebellious throng to think that they can go up and conquer God's New Jerusalem. Even if the wicked were given a second chance, this scene reveals that they would still fight against God. They are incorrigible. The only thing left is their destruction. Everyone is now fully convinced of that as they see this entire wicked family, led by Satan, surrounding their holy city. What an awesome scene—everyone who has ever lived on the planet is now alive at the same time and is in the same place: the saved inside the city, and the lost outside.

Then suddenly, Jesus appears on the great white throne at the height of the city (Revelation 20:11). The wicked are stopped in their murderous tracks. The books are opened, and God begins the final phase of the judgment. Amazingly, rather than quickly destroying the wicked, God takes the time to reveal to them all that He did to save them. The whole story of the conflict from Eden lost, to Calvary, to Eden restored is fully recounted for the wicked to behold. They must be fully satisfied that God did everything He could to save them.

At last it happens:

> That at the name of Jesus every knee should bow, of those in heaven, and of those on earth, and of those under the earth, and that every tongue should confess that Jesus Christ is Lord, to the glory of God the Father. Philippians 2:10, 11.

Everyone bows down and acknowledges the supremacy of God and His Christ. The conflict is over. All are fully satisfied. Sin will never rise again, because God has taken the pains to fully deal with the sin problem. No one will ever again distrust God. God is fully vindicated through His threefold work of judgment.

Phase one satisfied the angels concerning the righteous. Phase two satisfied the righteous concerning the wicked. And now phase three satisfies the wicked concerning their own choice to be lost. Even Satan is entranced by the scene and bows down and acknowledges the supremacy of Christ. His power is at its end. He is forever fully unmasked. The justice of God is fully vindicated. Satan becomes the object of universal abhorrence.

Yet Satan's character remains unchanged. He is still incorrigible. In one last, desperate frenzy, he rushes upon the wicked, seeking to rouse them to battle. But of the countless millions, there are none who now yield. Not one acknowledges his supremacy. His power is at an end. The wicked are filled with the same hatred of God as Satan is, but they see their case is hopeless. They cannot prevail against God, and with the fury of demons, they turn upon Satan, the deceiver. So God fulfills what He said to Ezekiel of old, under the symbolism of the king of Tyre:

> Therefore thus says the Lord God: "Because you have set your heart as the heart of a god, behold, therefore, I will bring strangers against you, the most terrible of the nations; and they shall draw their swords against the beauty of your wisdom, and defile your splendor. They shall throw

you down into the pit, and you shall die the death of the slain in the midst of the seas." Ezekiel 28:6-8.

By the abundance of your trading you became filled with violence within, and you sinned; therefore I cast you as a profane thing out of the mountain of God; and I destroyed you, O covering cherub, from the midst of the fiery stones. Your heart was lifted up because of your beauty; you corrupted your wisdom for the sake of your splendor; I cast you to the ground, I laid you before kings, that they might gaze at you. You defiled your sanctuaries by the multitude of your iniquities, by the iniquity of your trading; therefore I brought fire from your midst; it devoured you, and I turned you to ashes upon the earth in the sight of all who saw you. All who knew you among the peoples are astonished at you; you have become a horror, and shall be no more forever. Ezekiel 28:16-19.

As Satan is fully revealed, God concludes His final judgment. Now the fire can fall. Even the wicked throng turn on Satan. There is nothing left to do but forever end the sin problem. Fire descends from heaven's skies, and Satan and the wicked are eradicated from the planet.

This is hell as described in the previous chapter. God uses the fire to destroy the wicked and then to cleanse the earth of the defilement of sin. Now, the new heaven and new earth are created, forever free from the curse of sin. This recreated earth becomes the final home of the righteous of all ages. And thrill of thrills, Jesus permanently makes this earth His home. Our Redeemer will forever live among us. Glory be to God!

Dear reader, don't you want to be inside the city with Jesus? Then why don't you bow your head just now and invite Him to come in? Someday you will acknowledge the supremacy of God in your life. If you do it now, you will be inside the city. If you do it at the end of the 1,000 years, you will be outside the city. The choice is yours. Make the right choice now—make the choice to live forever with Jesus who died for you, and let Him become your dearest friend.

SECTION III

19

The Hope of Israel

I srael! These are the promised people, the inheritors of the promise, the people through whom the Messiah and most of the Bible was given. How indebted Christians are to the people God called to make His voice heard in the pre-Christian world. Many interpretations of last-day prophecy center on an understanding of the part Israel is to play in the last days; therefore, it is necessary for us to begin this exploration of last-day prophecies with a thorough understanding of who Israel is and what part they are to play in last-day events.

When the Bible predicts that earth's last conflict will center on Israel, who is this prediction referring to? Is it the nation of Israel in the Middle East? They claim to be the nation of Israel, but the nation of Israel today is really only a secular state, and most Israelites do not even believe in God. Does it refer, then, to Jews around the world, many of whom reside in the United States?

Or does it refer only to the conservative Jews who continue to maintain faith in a secular age? Perhaps it has an even wider meaning. Of course, there is only one way to discover what is meant by the prophecies referring to Israel in the last days. We must study the Bible itself for the answer. To whom does the Bible indicate these prophecies of Israel belong? Who is the true Israel at the end of time? We need to examine the nature of Israel throughout biblical history as we attempt to discover to whom the prophecies refer.

Old Testament Israel

The origin of the nation of Israel is usually traced to Abraham, who, in obedience to God, moved his tribe out of Ur and into Palestine. Upon arriving in the Promised Land, God appeared to him and entered into a covenant relationship with him. Note the terms of the covenant:

> And the Lord said to Abram, after Lot had separated from him: "Lift your eyes now and look from the place where you are—northward, southward, eastward, and westward; for all the land which you see I give to you and your descendants forever. And I will make your descendants as the dust of the earth; so that if a man could number the dust of the earth, then your descendants also could be numbered." Genesis 13:14-16

At first glance, it appears that God is offering Abraham the land of Palestine, and many descendants. However, as one studies other references to this promise, it becomes clear that more is involved than the mere possession of the war-torn Middle East and a large posterity.

The original promise given to Eve in the Garden of Eden was that the seed of the woman would bruise the serpent on the head (Genesis 3:15). This is the first intimation that the Messiah would come through the seed of the woman. Now, Abraham is promised that through his seed would come the Messiah. Genesis 13:14-16 is simply a ratification of the promise originally given to Eve. This is confirmed in the New Testament in Galatians 3:16: "Now to Abraham and his Seed were the promises made. He does not say, 'And to seeds,' as of many, but as of one, 'And to your Seed,' who is Christ."

The promise wasn't merely to assure Abraham multiple descendants but to promise that from his seed would come the ultimate Deliverer of God's people, Jesus Christ. The second promise was for land, but Hebrews 11:10-16 informs us that it was not just the land of Palestine. That land was symbolic of the ultimate inheritance that awaited Abraham's descendants—the heavenly Canaan.

Thus the promises made to Abraham, of land and seed, are not simply physical promises given to the people of God—they are spiritual promises given to a people who have entered into a covenant relationship with God. If the promises given to Abraham are referring to Christ and heaven, then ultimately all who inherit these promises will be the spiritual descendants of Abraham and therefore Israelites. So even in the Old Testament calling of Israel, we discover a spiritual calling of a spiritual people rather than a physical calling of an ethnic people.

Being spiritual promises, the fulfillment was not passed on to every child of Abraham. Abraham had two children—Isaac and Ishmael—but only Isaac, the child of promise, received the blessings and inherited the promises. Later, Isaac had two children: Esau, the firstborn, and Jacob, the one who cheated his brother out of the birthright. Even though Esau was the firstborn, he did not receive the promises, because he did not accept Isaac's God. Instead, Jacob received them, because he believed in God. This is why Jacob, as he flees from the wrath of Esau after cheating his brother out of the blessing of Isaac, is given a vision from God, who repeats the promise of Abraham to Jacob (Genesis 28:13, 14). Those promises include the land and the seed, which is Christ.

Twenty years later, Jacob returns from the land of Laban with his family. Esau comes to meet him. Jacob is concerned for the safety of his family. He spends the night praying, and the angel of God comes and wrestles with him. Jacob is unable to prevail and finally realizes that he is wrestling with a supernatural being. In his desperation, Jacob cries out to the angel:

> And He said, "Let Me go, for the day breaks." But he said, "I will not let You go unless You bless me!" So He said to him, "What is your name?" He said, "Jacob." And He said, "Your name shall no longer be called Jacob, but Israel; for you have

struggled with God and with men, and have prevailed." Genesis 32:26-28.

In his desperation, Jacob wrestles with God and prevails. It is at this time that the angel changes the name of Jacob—a name which meant "cheat"—and gives him the new covenant name "Israel," meaning "one who prevails with God." Note the spiritual nature of this calling of Jacob, which is the first use in scripture of the term *Israel*. The name is applied to Jacob only after his conversion to the true God. It is a spiritual name applied to one who has prevailed with God. The origin of the name *Israel* is spiritual in nature, rather than physical. This biblical name for a redeemed people cannot be applied to a people that are not redeemed.

Throughout Old Testament history, the term *Israel* refers primarily to the descendants of Jacob. Out of all people in the ancient world, these people were the only ones to keep alive the knowledge of the true God. The twelve tribes entered into a covenant relationship with God at Sinai. They agreed to be His people, and He agreed to be their God.

Throughout the Old Testament period, these descendants of Israel continued to be the covenant people, although non-Hebrews could become a part of the believing community. These people would not be genetically linked to Jacob, but they could still be Israelites if they possessed the faith of Israel. Individuals like Rahab, the harlot of Jericho, and Ruth, the Moabite, both became full Israelites and are even listed in the geneology of Jesus, yet they were both of pagan birth. It was possible to be born a pagan and die an Israelite. This again reveals the spiritual nature of the term *Israel*, even in the Old Testament.

After the reign of Solomon, the nation of Israel divided into two rival nations—the southern kingdom, using the name of Judah, and the northern ten tribes, taking the name of Israel. However, the ten tribes soon abandoned the Israelite faith and adopted paganistic practices. Most of the ministry of Elijah and Elisha was an attempt to bring them back to the worship of the true God. These prophets referred to the northern tribes living in apostasy as a harlot. Why? They professed to be Israel without entering into a covenant with the biblical God. You cannot claim the name and refuse to claim the God of Israel. Eventually, even Judah turns away from God, and He allows them to go into Babylonian captivity because of their failure to be true to Him.

After the Babylonian captivity, only a remnant of the Jews returned to Palestine. The rest were scattered throughout what ultimately became the Roman Empire. This remnant that returned to Palestine contained representatives of all the twelve tribes (1 Chronicles 9:3; Ezra 6:14-17; Zechariah 8:3-5). The ten tribes really were not lost—some from each tribe returned to form the new Israel that was obedient to God.

By the time of Christ, however, the term *Israel* had lost its spiritual meaning almost entirely. A Jew was one who was born of Abraham, regardless of where the person lived. Yet even in this time, it was possible to convert to Judaism and thus become an Israelite, revealing again that the term is not primarily an ethnic term, but a spiritual one.

The New Testament Israel

In the New Testament era, one quickly discovers a Judaism that was proud of its monotheism but also one that had become so exclusive that it ceased to be an effective evangelizing agency to the surrounding nations. God had brought Israel out of Egyptian captivity and placed them in Palestine, where the continents crossed, so that as people traveled between the continents, they would come in contact with Israel and learn of the true God. However, Israel failed to fulfill this mission and kept the faith almost exclusively to itself.

Now Jesus, the Jewish Messiah, appears as God's last desperate attempt to help the Jews move out of their exclusiveness and reach out to the nations around them with the good news of the true God. God expected fruit from Israel, but found none. Into this setting comes Jesus, the maker of the covenant with Israel, and announces to the startled Israelites that the time for them to be God's chosen people was about to end.

During the Babylonian captivity, God had promised His people through the prophet Daniel that they would be given another 70 weeks to get their act together. (Remember, in prophecy a day stands for a year—see page 15 of this book.) Now Jesus is appearing at the end of the 70 weeks, 483 years later, beginning His ministry during Daniel's seventieth week (see Daniel 9). His ministry is to last 3½ years, and then in the midst of that seventieth week, Jesus, the Messiah, is to die. Then for another 3½ years, the disciples are to labor for the Jews. If the Jews don't respond, they will cease to be the promised keepers of the covenant, and God will raise up a new people to reach the world for Jesus.

That is why Jesus, several times in His ministry, definitively warns the Jewish leadership that they have reached the end of their probation and that the promises were to be given to a new people who would be faithful to the covenant. Note these startling announcements:

> He also spoke this parable: "A certain man had a fig tree planted in his vineyard, and he came seeking fruit on it and found none. Then he said to the keeper of his vineyard, 'Look, for three years I have come seeking fruit on this fig tree and find none. Cut it down; why does it use up the ground?' But he answered and said to him, 'Sir, let it alone this year also, until I dig around it and fertilize it. And if it bears fruit, well. But if not, after that you can cut it down.'" Luke 13:6-9.

> O Jerusalem, Jerusalem, the one who kills the prophets and stones those who are sent to her! How often I wanted to gather your children together, as a hen gathers her brood under her wings, but you were not willing! See! Your house is left to you desolate. Luke 13:34, 35.

The fig tree was a clear symbol that all Jews understood to be a reference to their nation. They were the keepers of the vineyard that God had called to produce fruit: Gentiles, to be saved in the kingdom of God. Instead, they had become an exclusive club that reveled in their possession of the truth of God instead of sharing Him with the surrounding nations. Now Jesus announces that the fig tree that was supposed to produce fruit and did not, was going to be cut down to the ground. It would cease to be the representative of God. Yet Jesus is patient. He indicates that there is still time for them to repent. Clearly, Jesus does not want Israel to be cut off. He wants them to continue to be the people of God and to share Him with the world, yet God's passion for reaching people who do not know Him is greater than His loyalty to one people who fail to accomplish His mission. Jesus wept over Jerusalem, because He so desperately wanted to see them respond, but they would not.

Finally, Jesus delivers His most scathing rebuke to the Jewish leadership. They were following in the path of their fathers in rejecting the messages God had sent. Now they were about to reject and crucify the greatest revelation that the Father had ever sent to the world. Again, Jesus clothes His message in the language of a parable, but the Pharisees clearly see the implication of the startling words from Jesus.

> Hear another parable: There was a certain landowner who planted a vineyard and set a hedge around it, dug a winepress in it and built a tower. And he leased it to vinedressers and went into a far country. Now when vintage-time drew near, he sent his servants to the vinedressers, that they might receive its fruit. And the vinedressers took his servants, beat one, killed one, and stoned another. Again he sent other servants, more than the first, and they did likewise to them. Then last of all he sent his son to them, saying, "They will respect my son." But when the vinedressers saw the son, they said among themselves, "This is the heir. Come, let us kill him and seize his inheritance." So they took him and cast him out of the vineyard and killed him. Therefore, when the owner of the vineyard comes, what will he do to those vinedressers? Matthew 21:33-40.

In the parable, the vineyard is a clear reference to the privilege of being called by God to represent Him to the world. The term *vinedressers* is a reference to the Jewish nation, which only "rented" this privilege. Jesus then proceeds to castigate the leadership for their abuse of the privilege. They had not listened to the prophets God sent. They had done exactly as Jesus declared in the parable—they stoned and killed the prophets, and now they were ready to kill the son, Jesus. The Master now asks them a penetrating question: What should be done with these despisers of the vineyard? The leadership is quick to answer. So caught up in the injustice Jesus portrayed, they at first did not realize they were pronouncing their own demise.

"They said to Him, 'He will destroy those wicked men miserably, and lease his vineyard to other vinedressers who will render to him the fruits in their seasons'" (Matthew 21:41).

Then Jesus accurately places the responsibility squarely on the shoulders of the Jewish leadership:

"Therefore I say to you, the kingdom of God will be taken from you and given to a nation bearing the fruits of it" (Matthew 21:43).

"Now when the chief priests and Pharisees heard His parables, they perceived that He was speaking of them" (Matthew 21:45).

The events which Daniel had foretold to happen at the end of the 70 weeks are the same events which Jesus unmistakably shows are about to be fulfilled. The Jewish nation, so long God's emissary to the world, was about to be replaced by a nation that would produce fruit—a people who would share God with the world and not keep Him to themselves. Of course, the people of Israel were not rejected—only their exclusive hold on being the emissaries of God's truth.

Since the term *Israel* is a spiritual term and not an "ethnic" term in scripture, it is possible for the Jews to lose their spiritual identity as Israel, even though they maintained their cultural heritage. Jesus was not taking this heritage away—He was simply announcing what they had already done: rejected

Him as the only means to obtain spiritual vitality. For 1,500 years, God had patiently waited for this nation to accomplish the mission of God. The hope of Israel was the coming of the Messiah, but now they have rejected Him. God has no choice. He must create a new Israel—the Christian church.

The New Israel

The early Christian church did not see themselves as the inaugurators of a new religion—they were the continuation of Israel. With the Jewish leadership rejecting the Messiah, those who chose to accept Him and be gathered to Him became the new Israel. This was the self-identification of those first called to herald the risen Christ. They were now the new nation that became the continuation of Israel—the rightful inheritors of the promises of Abraham, because they had accepted the fulfillment of the promise: Jesus Christ, Himself.

Writing after the cross, the apostle Paul proclaims this new identify for Israel—the Christian church.

> For he is not a Jew who is one outwardly, nor is circumcision that which is outward in the flesh; but he is a Jew who is one inwardly; and circumcision is that of the heart, in the Spirit, not in the letter; whose praise is not from men but from God. Romans 2:28, 29.

Note Paul's clear understanding of the new Israel. It is not Israel after the flesh, but after the Spirit. In the New Testament, we discover an attempt to help the early church see clearly that God had called them to be the new Israel. Here is the restoration of the spiritual nature of Israel, just as God intended it in the Old Testament. In Romans 9, Paul continues the thought by suggesting that only those who have accepted the promise (Christ) are really the true Israel:

> But it is not that the word of God has taken no effect. For they are not all Israel who are of Israel, nor are they all chil-

dren because they are the seed of Abraham; but, "In Isaac your seed shall be called." That is, those who are the children of the flesh, these are not the children of God; but the children of the promise are counted as the seed. Romans 9:6-8.

In New Testament times, you must accept the promised one, Jesus, in order to be a true Israelite. Israel is no longer a nation of the literal descendants of Abraham, but of all those, whatever their nationality, who have accepted Jesus, the Promised One. This is the new Israel that Jesus had foretold. Paul emphatically declares that spiritual Israel has been reborn. Paul further elaborates on the stock of Israel in Romans 11. Here he references Israel as a mighty tree with many branches. The original branches, the Jews, had been cut off, and the Gentiles had now been added.

You will say then, "Branches were broken off that I might be grafted in." Well said. Because of unbelief they were broken off, and you stand by faith. Do not be haughty, but fear. For if God did not spare the natural branches, He may not spare you either… And they also, if they do not continue in unbelief, will be grafted in, for God is able to graft them in again. For if you were cut out of the olive tree which is wild by nature, and were grafted contrary to nature into a cultivated olive tree, how much more will these, who are natural branches, be grafted into their own olive tree? For I do not desire, brethren, that you should be ignorant of this mystery, lest you should be wise in your own opinion, that blindness in part has happened to Israel until the fullness of the Gentiles has come in. And so all Israel will be saved." Romans 11:19-26.

Paul's heart cry is for the native sons of Israel to return to spiritual Israel, but he is also concerned lest the newly established Christian church, the new Israel, composed of Jews and Gentiles, follow a path similar to that of the original Israel. He did not want to see the church repeat the error of neglecting to share the message with others and failing to reach out to lost people. The new Israel has no better election than the first. They must produce fruit—souls for the kingdom of God. If they fail, God will raise up someone else to do it and will elect a new Israel. God never promises unconditional election.

This new Israel that Jesus has called out is composed of people of all nationalities. Its uniqueness is not built on ethnicity, but on acceptance of the Promised One and sharing Him with the world. Christ has forever broken down the wall that divides people by race and brought them together into one new body—the church built on the foundation of Jesus Christ, Himself (Ephesians 2:14-16; 19-22).

"There is neither Jew nor Greek, there is neither slave nor free, there is neither male nor female; for you are all one in Christ Jesus" (Galatians 3:28).

This is the radical new body that Jesus has created. It is not built on ethnicity, but on faith in Jesus Christ. There are no racial dividers with God. There are no status dividers with Jesus. And there are no gender dividers with Him. All are one in Christ at the cross. Jesus has forever removed all differences between people in the church. Everyone is now on equal footing. Not only is equality theirs, but Paul now emphatically claims this new body to be the new Israel and the inheritors of all the promises made to Abraham.

"And if you are Christ's, then you are Abraham's seed, and heirs according to the promise" (Galatians 3:29).

The promise of the Seed in Genesis has found fulfillment in Jesus, and those who believe in Jesus are the children of the promise. Paul calls them the seed of Abraham: Israelites. Thus, in unmistakable language, Paul has redefined Israel for the church. Once we are past the 70-week probationary period, a new Israel emerges, composed of Jews and Gentiles. It is the Christian church. They are the new Israel.

However, as Paul warned, the church could also turn away from Jesus, just as the ancient Jews did. If they turned away, Paul warned, they would cease to be Israel. During the Dark

Ages, for example, the church left the truth about Jesus and incorporated paganistic beliefs into the church. According to Paul's definition, the church then ceased to be Israel, even though it still claimed to be the church. One must be faithful to Jesus, or one cannot claim to be the nation of God.

As a result of the Reformation, churches came into being as part of another new Israel destined to bring the traditional Christian church back to the truth about Jesus and salvation through grace alone in Him. Yet even for the Reformation churches, there is no guarantee of unconditional election. If they turn from the truth about Jesus, they too cease to be God's "Israel," and God raises up another, new "Israel" to complete His work. God's work is bigger than any one organization. God demands faithfulness, not merely a name, national label, or traceable apostolic heritage.

Finally, at the end of time, God's final remnant appears and finishes the work of God by carrying the gospel to all the world as Jesus commanded. John the Revelator describes them:

> And the dragon was enraged with the woman, and he went to make war with the rest of her offspring, who keep the commandments of God and have the testimony of Jesus Christ. Revelation 12:17.

Amazingly, at the end of time, God still has His faithful Israel—a people who hold high the truth about Jesus in the most degenerate age in this planet's history. God describes them as the "rest of God's people" or the "remnant." They maintain loyalty to Jesus by keeping the commandments of God through their living faith in Jesus, the Christ. They are the final, faithful people of God—the last Israel.

20

The Prophecies of the Hope of Israel

In view of the various entities that have possessed the term *Israel* down through the ages, one must be careful when interpreting the prophecies of scripture referring to Israel. Any prophecy finding fulfillment after A.D. 34, when the 70-week prophecy ended, must find fulfillment, not in literal Israel of the Middle East, but in the new Israel—those who are loyal to Christ. As a consequence, all the prophecies of Israel in the last days would apply to the people of Revelation 12:17—the final loyal Israel belonging to God.

To be faithful to scripture, we cannot apply the last-day prophecies of Israel to the people of the Middle East. These prophecies find fulfillment instead in the loyal Christians of the last days. Let us examine some of these prophecies in light of the emergence of the new Israel.

The Old Testament contains many prophecies concerning Israel. Some of them foretell a glorious future, while others indicate that they will be dispersed among the nations. Obviously, both of them cannot be fulfilled. As one studies these prophecies, it becomes clear that God held out two futures for Israel—one if they were faithful; the other if they were not. Since they were not faithful, the prophecies of their glorious future will never be fulfilled. Biblical scholars refer to this as conditional prophecy. Scripture itself, through the prophet Jeremiah, details this very kind of prophecy.

> The instant I speak concerning a nation and concerning a kingdom, to pluck up, to pull down, and to destroy it, if

that nation against whom I have spoken turns from its evil, I will relent of the disaster that I thought to bring upon it. And the instant I speak concerning a nation and concerning a kingdom, to build and to plant it, if it does evil in My sight so that it does not obey My voice, then I will relent concerning the good with which I said I would benefit it. Jeremiah 18:7-10.

God here declares that all prophecy involving people and nations is always conditional. God does not have to mention conditionality in each prophecy. This one statement clearly indicates that all prophecy is conditional, based upon human obedience.

For example, when God asked Jonah to preach to the Ninevites "forty days and Ninevah shall be overthrown" (Jonah 3:4), no condition was stated. Yet the Ninevites repented, and God did not destroy the city. Did that make Jonah a false prophet? Absolutely not! The conditions changed, and God did not destroy the city. Likewise, God predicted a glorious future for Israel, but they did not repent, so God could never bring the glorious future to fruition.

The Return of Israel to Palestine

Today Israel has returned as a nation to the Middle East and the land of Palestine. Is this a fulfillment of prophecy? No. The present-day return of Israel is not predicted, even though some have attempted to apply certain prophecies to the present situation by removing them from their historical context. This misuse of prophecy will only and ultimately bring reproach upon the Bible. Notice one of the prophecies often quoted in support of the present-day return to Palestine:

"For behold, the days are coming," says the Lord, "that I will bring back from captivity My people Israel and Judah," says the Lord. "And I will cause them to return to the land that I gave to their fathers, and they shall possess it." Jeremiah 30:3.

Behold, I will bring them from the north country, and gather them from the ends of the earth, among them the blind and the lame, the woman with child and the one who labors with child, together; a great throng shall return there. Jeremiah 31:8.

At first glance, these prophecies do appear to indicate that the time will come when God will restore the Israelites to the land of Palestine. Yet one who is honest with scripture must examine the context. The book of Jeremiah was written in the days just prior to and during the Babylonian captivity of the Jews. Jeremiah even predicted that the captivity would last seventy years. Although Jeremiah predicted doom for Israel because of their sins, he held out hope that they would someday return to Palestine following the Babylonian captivity. Just as predicted, seventy years later, they were released and returned to Palestine in total fulfillment of these tremendous prophecies of Jeremiah.

All prophecies concerning the return of Israel to Palestine are given in the context of the Babylonian captivity. To apply already-fulfilled prophecies to a modern-day return to Palestine is not only avoiding the biblical context but is actually a perverted use of scripture. There is nothing in the biblical text to indicate that there will be a latter-day, dual fulfillment of these prophecies. Without biblical authorization, no person has the right to apply these texts to the modern-day return of the Jews. There is no doubt that the nation of Israel is in Palestine today, but that return is not a fulfillment of prophecy.

The New Israel and the Prophecies

Several Old Testament prophecies of Israel are reinterpreted in the New Testament in light of the emergence of the new Israel. Yet one cannot necessarily reinterpret all prophecies of Israel. The New Testament itself must provide the reinterpretation. The glorious future promised to Israel is now to be fulfilled through the church rather than literal Israel, because the New Testament has clearly affirmed the church as the new spiritual Israel.

For example, in Joel 2:32, the prophet declares that in the last days, salvation will be found on Mt. Zion and in Jerusalem. Some have taken that text literally to mean that one must be on the holy Mt. Zion in Jerusalem at the second coming in order to be saved. Yet in the New Testament, Mt. Zion and Jerusalem no longer carry geographic significance. As these terms were symbolic of God's Old Testament people, they have now become symbolic of the Christian church, through which the salvation is being proclaimed. Thus the text, applied to our day, simply declares the church, the new Israel, to be the evangelizing agency with the message of God's salvation.

Likewise, in Luke 21:24, Jerusalem is predicted by Jesus to be trodden under the feet of Gentiles until the time of the Gentiles is fulfilled. Since Jerusalem in the New Testament era refers to the church, the text is telling us that the church will be dominated by a Gentile (apostate) power for a certain period of time. Revelation 11:2 gives further amplification to this prophecy: "But leave out the court which is outside the temple, and do not measure it, for it has been given to the Gentiles. And they will tread the holy city underfoot for forty-two months."

This passage repeats Jesus' prophecy, but adds that the time of the Gentiles is 42 months. One quickly recognizes that this is the same time period predicted by Daniel for the little horn or the beast of Revelation 13 to dominate the church. Thus, the prediction of Jesus is a warning to the church that for 1,260 years, this false power will dominate the church of Jesus, treading under its feet the truth of God.

These prophecies have been given a new understanding by the New Testament. Actually, all prophecy pertaining to Israel after A.D. 34 (the end of the 70-week prophecy) refers not to the literal descendants of Abraham, but to the spiritual descendents—those who have accepted Jesus, whether they be Jew or Gentile. There is no special significance to literal Israel today.

Armageddon

One of the most fascinating prophecies of Revelation is the prophecy of the battle of Armageddon in Revelation 16.

> Then the sixth angel poured out his bowl on the great river Euphrates, and its water was dried up, so that the way of the kings from the east might be prepared. And I saw three unclean spirits like frogs coming out of the mouth of the dragon, out of the mouth of the beast, and out of the mouth of the false prophet. For they are spirits of demons, performing signs, which go out to the kings of the earth and of the whole world, to gather them to the battle of that great day of God Almighty. "Behold, I am coming as a thief. Blessed is he who watches, and keeps his garments, lest he walk naked and they see his shame." And they gathered them together to the place called in Hebrew, Armageddon. Revelation 16:12-16.

The battle of Armageddon occurs during the sixth plague of the seven final plagues to be poured out upon Planet Earth. It is the final battle of the planet. Since the seven last plagues have not yet begun to fall, it is obvious that the battle of Armageddon is still future. Early in our study, we referred to the battle of Armageddon briefly as we noted the fall of ancient Babylon. The connection between the two was obvious.

Involved in the battle of Armageddon is the final spiritual Babylon, which we have seen to be a worldwide apostasy from God. Just as spiritual Israel refers to the worldwide church, so Babylon, the enemy of God, is worldwide at the end. The sixth plague records the drying up of the Euphrates in preparation for the final fall of spiritual Babylon. As in ancient Babylon, the river Euphrates was the life-giving support of Babylon, even so, the spiritual Euphrates refers to those powers supporting the final great Babylon. The river being dried up refers to the support of Babylon being withdrawn—the powers that have sustained her suddenly withdraw that sustenance.

All of this happens, according to verse 12, to prepare the way for the kings of the east. In ancient Babylon, the king of the East referred to Cyrus, who came and destroyed ancient Babylon and then released God's people. The ancient king of the East was symbolic of the deliverer of God's people. Of course, the ultimate Deliverer of God's people is Jesus, who will come to deliver His people from the East.

The sixth plague opens with the startling prediction that mighty spiritual Babylon loses her support and is thrown into confusion. All this is in preparation for the mighty Deliverer, Jesus Christ, to come and deliver His people, held captive by modern spiritual Babylon.

In the confusion, mighty spiritual Babylon, composed of three parts—the dragon, the false prophet, and the beast—loses its unity, and the three parts move out with great fury to regain the support of the powers that have just abandoned them. Thus, verses 13 and 14 portray these three parts of Babylon frantically seeking the support of the kings of the earth. To convince them of their power, the three parts perform all kinds of miracles. Finally, they actually convince them that if they could wipe out the true followers of Jesus from the face of the earth, their power would then be absolute. The Bible calls this earth's final battle—the battle of the great day of God Almighty (verse 14).

In the midst of all this turmoil, God gives His people the assurance that He is with them and that soon He will return to deliver them from the power of Babylon. This assurance does not stop Babylon the great from unleashing its fury upon the people of God. Instead, all the powers of Babylon gather themselves to destroy God's people at a place called Armageddon (verse 16). It is the place where the final annihilation of the people of God will be attempted.

Some have interpreted Armageddon as a plain in the Middle East, particularly in Palestine, declaring this to be the place of the final battle. However, in the last days, Israel is the church, and it is everywhere. The final battle must be everywhere that God's people are. So what does Armageddon mean?

Only once does the Bible use this word. There has never been, nor is there now, anyplace in Palestine called Armageddon, which clearly indicates that the very word is a symbol, especially since it only appears in the highly symbolic book of Revelation. The word is derived from two Hebrew words. The first word is *har,* meaning "mountain" or "hill." No scholar has any doubt regarding this meaning.

The second part of the word has two possibilities, and scholars are divided over the actual word from which it is derived. Some suggest that the word is from *Meggidon,* meaning "Megiddo." Since Megiddo is mentioned as a literal place in the Old Testament, it is assumed that this is the meaning of the word—the mount of Megiddo. Most who interpret the battle of Armageddon as a literal battle in Palestine have accepted this possibility.

However, there is no "hill of Megiddo" in Palestine. There is a plain of Megiddo and a valley of Megiddo and even a town of Megiddo—but no mount of Megiddo. Interpreters of this position assume they are all one and the same. Yet the scriptures are never that imprecise. If town, plain, or valley had been meant, Bible writers would not have used the term *mount.* Therefore, a literal interpretation pointing to a location in the Middle East rests on very inexact information.

The second possibility is that it is derived from the Hebrew word *mo'ed,* which means "assembly." Thus the meaning would be the "mount of the assembly." Interestingly, this phrase does appear one time in the Old Testament. Remember that Revelation 16:16 indicated it was an Old Testament term. Isaiah 14:13 contains this phrase:

How you are fallen from heaven, O Lucifer, son of the morning! How you are cut down to the ground, You who weakened the nations! For you have said in your heart: "I will ascend into heaven, I will exalt my throne above the stars of God; I will also sit on the mount of the congregation On the farthest sides of the north; I will ascend above the heights of the clouds, I will be like the Most High." Isaiah 14:12-14.

Here is the only place in the Old Testament where the word translated "Armageddon" appears. It is in the setting of Lucifer's attempt to conquer God and sit where God sits, ruling the nations. Lucifer desires to sit in the "mount of the congregation" (Isaiah 14:13)—the place from which God rules. Revelation 16:16 is simply telling us that in the final battle of the great controversy, the same issues raised by Satan in the beginning are still being waged. Satan has not changed—he still desires to conquer God's people. The final battle by Babylon is simply her last attempt to destroy the people of God and conquer the mount of the congregation.

The mount of the congregation in ancient Israel was Mt. Zion—the symbol of God's people. The New Testament Mt. Zion is God's church, and the battle of Armageddon is simply Satan's final attempt to destroy the church of God in the end of time. All the powers of earth are thus lined up to bring destruction to God's final, faithful remnant. All appears hopeless until God intervenes and wins the battle of Armageddon.

As the powers of Babylon arrive at the mount of the congregation (wherever God's people have assembled), they are intent on their annihilation. But at that moment, God raises His mighty hand, signaling the end of the great controversy.

"Then the seventh angel poured out his bowl into the air, and a loud voice came out of the temple of heaven, from the throne, saying, 'It is done!'" (Revelation 16:17).

In the hour of extremity, when all appears lost for God's people, He intervenes. Instead of becoming a time of destruction for the people of God, the battle of Armageddon ends up in the destruction of Babylon and the mighty deliverance of God's people. There is therefore no need to fear the battle of Armageddon. It is not a day of defeat but of tremendous victory for the people of God. With His mighty hand, God intercedes and delivers His faithful, final Israel—the loyal ones who, at the end of time, keep the commandments of God and have the testimony of Jesus (Revelation 12:17). This is the final great day of victory. The end has come. God has delivered His people. Praise His mighty name!

21

The Culmination of Our Hope

What a glorious day is coming! The day in which all those powers that have oppressed and opposed God's people throughout the ages will come to their utter end. Only Jesus will reign supreme in that awesome hour.

The Bible calls this hope in the personal second coming of Jesus, the blessed hope (Titus 2:13). What a blessed hope it is, indeed! The one who died for us will return in majestic splendor to redeem those who are faithful to Him. Every emotion in our body cries out to behold the day of our Redeemer.

What will this day be like? It is a day that marks the demise of the Antichrist—that power that dominated the people of God in the end time. It is also the hour in which all the wicked are slain by the brightness of Christ's coming (Revelation 6:14-16). Even nature itself unleashes its fury in the day of God. Revelation 6:14 mentions that every mountain and island are moved out of their places. It is the day of God's judgment, and the entire world collapses under the power of the visitation of God Almighty.

Yet to the Christian, it is a day of glorious hope. The dead in Christ are resurrected (1 Thessalonians 4:16-18), the wicked enemies of God's people are destroyed (Revelation 16:14-17), and Jesus comes again to take His people home (John 14:1-3). Listen to these marvelous descriptions of the event from the pages of scripture:

> Behold, He is coming with clouds, and every eye will see Him, even they who pierced Him. And all the tribes of the

earth will mourn because of Him. Even so, Amen. Revelation 1:7.

For the Lord Himself will descend from heaven with a shout, with the voice of an archangel, and with the trumpet of God. And the dead in Christ will rise first. Then we who are alive and remain shall be caught up together with them in the clouds to meet the Lord in the air. And thus we shall always be with the Lord. 1 Thess. 4:16, 17.

Our God shall come, and shall not keep silent; a fire shall devour before Him, and it shall be very tempestuous all around Him. Psalm 50:3.

Therefore if they say to you, "Look, He is in the desert!" do not go out; or "Look, He is in the inner rooms!" do not believe it. For as the lightning comes from the east and flashes to the west, so also will the coming of the Son of Man be. Matthew 24:26, 27.

And while they looked steadfastly toward heaven as He went up, behold, two men stood by them in white apparel, who also said, "Men of Galilee, why do you stand gazing up into heaven? This same Jesus, who was taken up from you into heaven, will so come in like manner as you saw Him go into heaven." Acts 1:10, 11.

What marvelous descriptions of the coming of the Lord. Notice the details of His coming revealed in these passages.

1. He comes visibly in the clouds.

2. Every eye, including the wicked, sees His return.

3. There is a lot of noise associated with His coming to awaken the dead—the voice of the archangel and the trump of God.

4. He does not keep silence, and a fire goes before Him, destroying the wicked.

5. It is not a secret return. It is open and visible. Jesus warns against anyone teaching that He has come secretly.

6. His coming is as visible as lightning.

7. He will return the same way He left—visibly and personally.

Just a quick examination of these few texts describes for us the absolute certainty and visibility of this climactic event. When He comes, the whole world will know it instantaneously. Every text of scripture that talks about the return of Jesus clearly indicates that this is an event unparalleled in the history of the world. Remember, when it is all over, the wicked are all dead, and the righteous have all gone to heaven. So this is the event that depopulates the earth.

A Secret Return

Amazingly, a popular view of the second coming of Jesus suggests that it will be a secret event. The righteous will just suddenly disappear from the planet, while life continues. As we have seen, such a notion is contrary to all the evidence of scripture.

What has led people to create a false understanding of the return of Jesus—one that Jesus Himself warned us about? Jesus declared it would be one of the last-day deceptions (Matthew 24:26, 27).

This view of the end times is often referred to as the "secret rapture." The word *rapture* does not even appear in the Bible. It means a "snatching away." And of course, it is true that the church of Jesus is snatched away when Jesus comes and destroys the wicked. The question is not whether there is a rapture or not, but whether it is secret. All of the texts examined above indicate that it is the opposite of secret.

According to the secret rapture model, Jesus unexpectedly comes and snatches away His church, while everyone else who is left wonders what happened to the ones taken away. The world is then plunged into a seven-year tribulation period, during which Antichrist rules the world. The Jews are converted, rebuild the ancient temple, and once again become God's evangelizing agency. After 3 ½ years, the Antichrist stops the animal sacrifices that have been reinstated in the Jewish temple. The world is then plunged into another 3 ½ years of trouble, at the end of which Christ visibly comes for those who respond to Him in the second-chance offer.

As wild as these ideas seem, they have gained wide acceptance today. They are not supported by any scripture and are actually totally contrary to the biblical description of the second coming that we have seen. This theory makes some claims that seem preposterous, such as the idea that the Jewish temple sacrifices of animals will be reintroduced. When Jesus died, He forever ended such sacrifices. The use of sacrifices today would be an attempt to absolutely nullify the sacrifice of Jesus.

This theory divides the second coming into two parts—a secret and a visible return, separated by seven years. However, there is not a line anywhere in the Bible separating the second coming into two parts. As we have seen, the Bible always reveals one coming—visible and personal. If there was even one text suggesting this order of events, we might look at it to study the context, but there is none. It is a purely nonbiblical fiction, totally unsupported by even one verse of scripture.

This theory also suggests that after the secret coming, the Antichrist will be revealed. In other words, you don't have to worry about the Antichrist because, if you are a Christian, you will be raptured before the Antichrist even appears. Yet time and time again, as we have studied throughout this book, we have seen that God's people are here to the very end of earth's history. The last days may be troublesome for the people of

God, but God will go through the fire with them, just as He did with the three Hebrews in the fiery furnace. God did not deliver them out of trouble, but in the midst of trouble. In fact, Daniel 12:1 specifically states that God will deliver His last-day people in the midst of the great time of trouble:

> At that time Michael shall stand up, the great prince who stands watch over the sons of your people; and there shall be a time of trouble, such as never was since there was a nation, even to that time. And at that time your people shall be delivered, every one who is found written in the book. Daniel 12:1.

This text is emphatic. God's people are still here during the final time of trouble. God delivers them in the midst of this great tribulation. Just as the ancient Hebrews were in Egypt during the ten Egyptian plagues, yet God preserved His people during that tribulation, so shall it be at the end of the world.

Furthermore, the Bible teaches that the Antichrist is not one individual at the end of the world, but a religious system that stands in opposition to the truth of God. We have studied the Antichrist elsewhere in this book and have discovered it to be the religious system of the Dark Ages that will be reinvented in the end time. It is a system that spans the ages. So the righteous cannot escape it. They have to deal with the deceptions of the Antichrist. How happy Satan would be if Christians pretended the Antichrist did not exist. How easy it would be to ensnare them. The Antichrist will be fully unmasked and exposed before the time Jesus comes to gather His people home. Note how the apostle Paul warns us against deception on this very point:

> Now, brethren, concerning the coming of our Lord Jesus Christ and our gathering together to Him, we ask you, not to be soon shaken in mind or troubled, either by spirit or by word or by letter, as if from us, as though the day of Christ had come. Let no one deceive you by any means; for that

Day will not come unless the falling away comes first, and the man of sin is revealed, the son of perdition. 2 Thess. 2:1-3.

Paul's emphatic point is that God's people should not be deceived into thinking that the Antichrist will be revealed after the return of Christ to gather His people to Him. The Antichrist will be exposed before God's people are gathered home. With such an emphatic warning that we should not be deceived on this point, we must not be misled by the rapture theory, promising us that the Antichrist comes after the rapture. Such a clear distortion of scripture is exactly what Paul warned about.

Why has this entire structure called the rapture been invented without any scriptural basis? The root of the problem lies in an understanding of Israel. These theorists refuse to accept the clear New Testament teaching that a new spiritual Israel has replaced the ethnic Israel of the Old Testament. Therefore, they believe that all the promises made to the literal Jews must still be literally fulfilled, in spite of the clear, ringing language of the New Testament to the contrary. It is almost as if they have never read the New Testament with its clear statements such as: "And if you are Christ's, then you are Abraham's seed, and heirs according to the promise" (Galatians 3:29).

According to this distorted view, God is going to use ethnic Israel as His evangelizing agency in the last days. What is the church to do when God uses Israel? Are Christians to just be silent? Impossible! Therefore, God has to get His church out of the world so He can use Israel. As wild as it may seem, this is the foundation of the theory. The whole rapture concept is based on this one point. If the church is God's evangelizing agency until the very end, as the Bible teaches, then there is absolutely no justification for this far-fetched, unbiblical teaching of the secret rapture. It is merely an attempt to justify the belief that God uses literal Israel instead of the church in the last days.

There is one text that theologians who support the rapture misuse to try to prove their point. Look at it in context:

> But as the days of Noah were, so also will the coming of the Son of Man be. For as in the days before the flood, they were eating and drinking, marrying and giving in marriage, until the day that Noah entered the ark, and did not know until the flood came and took them all away, so also will thecoming of the Son of Man be. Then two men will be in the field: one will be taken and theother left. Two women will be grinding at the mill: one will be taken and the other left Matthew 24:37-41.

> I tell you, on that night there will be two men in one bed; one will be taken, and the other will be left. There will be two women grinding at the same place; one will be taken, and the other will be left. Two men will be in the field; one will be taken and the other will be left. And answering they said to Him, "Where Lord?" And He said to them, "Where the body is, there also will the vultures be gathered" Luke 17:34-37, NASB.

Both passages are recording the same words from Jesus. Matthew and Luke both record the event and the message. A few words are different, but the message is the same. In Matthew's account, the context centers on Noah and the flood, during which Noah was kept safe in the ark while the flood came and took away all the wicked. Then Jesus draws the parallel with the last days, suggesting that, as in Noah's day, two people can be together—one will be taken, the other left. As in Noah's time, they were taken by the flood and destroyed, so shall they be taken and destroyed at the second coming, while the righteous will be left for the coming of the Lord. The parallel with the flood makes it very clear that the ones taken are the wicked, not the righteous, as the rapturists claim.

The passage in Luke conveys a similar thought; however, the context in this case is not the flood of Noah. Again, Jesus repeats the thought that one shall be taken and the other left. The disciples in wonder ask the question: "Where?" Where will they be taken? Jesus immediately returns the answer: "Where the body is, there also will the vultures be gathered" (Luke 17:37, NASB).

The ones taken in this passage obviously are the wicked, for they become dead bodies that the vultures destroy. No matter which passage one looks at, it is very clear that the ones taken are the wicked, not the righteous. And just as in the case of the flood, and also during the last days, the wicked are destroyed and not left for seven additional years to receive another chance.

The Hope of the Church

Instead of the wild, fanciful teaching of the secret rapture, the Bible offers the believer a glorious hope. That hope is in a personal, visible, real return of Jesus. One day, the sky will break wide open. In the distance, Jesus will be seen coming in the clouds of heaven with power and great glory. The dead in Christ rise, and the living are caught up and meet Him in the air. The wicked are slain.

This is the real hope of scripture. It is the same hope that filled the hearts of the first believers in the risen Christ. This advent hope still fills the hearts of God's last-day people, who will see the ultimate fulfillment of their dreams in the soon return of Jesus.

All heaven explodes in one rapturous shout of victory when Jesus returns. Revelation 19 boldly proclaims this ultimate victory of the risen Lord. Note just a few of the shouts of praise recorded here at the return of Jesus:

> After these things I heard a loud voice of a great multitude in heaven, saying, "Alleluia! Salvation and glory and honor and power belong to the Lord our God! For true and righteous are His judgments, because He has judged the great harlot who corrupted the earth with her fornication;

and He has avenged on her the blood of His servants shed by her." Again they said, "Alleluia!" . . . And the twenty-four elders and the four living creatures fell down and worshiped God who sat on the throne, saying, "Amen! Alleluia!" Then a voice came from the throne, saying, "Praise our God, all you His servants and those who fear Him, both small and great!" And I heard, as it were, the voice of a great multitude, as the sound of many waters and as the sound of mighty thunderings, saying, "Alleluia! For the Lord God Omnipotent reigns! Let us be glad and rejoice and give Him glory, for the marriage of the Lamb has come, and His wife has made herself ready." Revelation 19:1-7.

What marvelous praise! God has brought an end to the great controversy. Revelation 19 is one of the greatest praise chapters in scripture. Why do they praise Him? God is lauded because He has dealt fully with the Antichrist and now comes to deliver His people. Read the whole chapter, and it is clear that when Jesus returns, He claims His people by bringing them to the marriage supper of the Lamb, while at the same time, He destroys the wicked, taking them to the feast of vultures.

Yes, Jesus is coming—and coming soon. The most important thing for us today is to be prepared for this momentous event. How can you be ready? By inviting Jesus into your heart right now, accepting Him as your Savior, and letting Him save you—not because of anything you have done, but because of what He has done. Will you invite Him in right now?

22

Hope When the King of the North Reigns

One of the most intriguing prophecies of the book of Daniel is the prophecy of the eleventh chapter. It appears as the fourth in a series of grand outline prophecies. The second chapter of Daniel portrayed world history through the great image of gold, brass, silver, iron, and a mix of iron and clay, culminating in the stone that strikes the image. We discovered that these represented the empires of Babylon, Media-Persia, Greece, Rome, and divided Europe, respectively—and finally, the second coming of Christ.

The second great prophecy in Daniel 7 unveiled four ferocious beasts: lion, bear, leopard, and the dragon with ten horns, representing Babylon, Media-Persia, Greece and Rome, with the ten horns representing the ten divisions of Rome into Europe. Then came the little horn, representing the church of the Dark Ages, followed by the judgment scene, which represents God's final pre-advent judgment. Daniel 8 and 9 portrayed the same sequence a third time through the ram, he-goat, and little horn, culminating in the cleansing of the sanctuary. These we discovered represented Media-Persia, Greece, Rome in its two phases—pagan and Christian, and then the beginning of the pre-advent judgment in 1844.

All the prophecies of Daniel go through the same sequence of empires, leading up to the judgment and the second coming of Christ. Likewise, in Daniel 11, the sequence is repeated again. This time, however, two basic symbols are used—the king of the North and the king of the South. Yet the power represented by each keeps changing through history. Thus the king of the north begins in Daniel 11:2 with Persia and ends up in verses 31-39 being the church of the Dark Ages. The king of the south, on the other hand, begins with Egypt and maintains Egypt as the power until verse 31, when the church of the Dark Ages begins. Then the king of the south disappears, only to reappear in verse 40.

This poses some interesting questions. Why does the power change, but the symbol remain unchanged? Why does Egypt disappear in verse 31? We will look at Egypt's disappearance and reemergence later in this chapter. This strange use of one symbol to represent different powers is not new in Daniel. We found it in Daniel 8, when the little horn represented Rome in its two phases: Christian and pagan. The same symbol was used to show their connection with each other.

Likewise, different symbols were employed in the other chapters of Daniel to help us understand that they are separate powers. But in Daniel 11, the prophet is revealing to us that behind all the powers seeking to oppress the people of God is the same primary power—the devil. So while the other chapters indicate outwardly separate powers, Daniel 11 presents to us a unified system—the unifying factor being Satan himself.

There is no need to repeat the historical background of Daniel 11:1-39. One can examine any commentary on Daniel, and the sequence is clear. We have already carefully examined this sequence of the empires in the beginning chapters of this book. At present, we wish to focus on the new revelation given in the eleventh chapter of Daniel.

At the time of the end the king of the South shall attack him; and the king of the North shall come against him like a whirlwind, with chariots, horsemen, and with many ships; and he shall enter the countries, overwhelm them, and pass through. He shall also enter the Glorious Land, and many countries shall be overthrown; but these shall escape from his hand: Edom, Moab, and the prominent people of Ammon. He shall stretch out his hand against the countries, and the land of Egypt shall not escape. He shall have power over the treasures of gold and silver, and over all the precious things of Egypt; also the Libyans and Ethiopians shall follow at his heels. But news from the east and the north shall trouble him; therefore he shall go out with great fury to destroy and annihilate many. And he shall plant the tents of his palace between the seas and the glorious holy mountain; yet he shall come to his end, and no one will help him. Daniel 11:40-45.

This is the climax of the message of the book of Daniel. The power referred to in this passage is the final power to oppress the people of God. It is the power that God destroys at the second coming of Christ. He will come to his end. This is the good news of the final chapter of the book of Daniel. In order to fully understand these final scenes, we will need first of all to make three clear identifications of the symbols used in this chapter:

1. What is the "glorious holy mountain?" It is the object of the attack of this final king of the north.

2. Who is this final king of the north that eliminates the king of the south and then attacks the glorious holy mountain?

3. Who is the revived king of the south who is only briefly mentioned and then destroyed by the king of the north?

The "Glorious Holy Mountain"

This symbol is very easy to identify, because we have already studied Israel. The term *glorious holy mountain* is described clearly in Psalm 48:1, 2 as a reference to Mt. Zion:

Great is the Lord, and greatly to be praised In the city of

our God, In His holy mountain. Beautiful in elevation, the joy of the whole earth, is Mount Zion on the sides of the north, the city of the great King.

Every Israelite reading Daniel's words would know immediately that he was referring to Mt. Zion—the symbol of the people of God, Israel. Originally, Mt. Zion was the place where the temple was built, but by Daniel's time it was the symbol for all of God's people, wherever they were.

In our study of Israel, we discovered that the term *Israel* is a spiritual term referencing the people of God who are loyal and faithful to God. Since Daniel 11:40-45 is portraying God's people at the time of the end, the glorious holy mountain would be a reference to the people of God in the last days—the final spiritual Israel who are loyal and faithful to Jesus by keeping His commandments and having the testimony of Jesus (Revelation 12:17). They are not literal Jews but Christians (Jew and Gentile) who have accepted the promise of Abraham—the Christ.

Note in Daniel 11 that the final attack of the king of the north is against the glorious holy mountain. Thus, Daniel 11 is describing earth's final battle. We have in this passage the Old Testament version of the battle of Armageddon. In fact, in the next few chapters, we will be looking at the battle of Armageddon from several different perspectives, yet all contain the same message. Daniel 11:40-45, Revelation 12:17, Revelation 13:11-18, and Revelation 16:12-16 are all depicting the same scene—earth's final battle. The participants are identical in each passage. We will gain further insights into each participant as we study these great chapters.

The focus of Daniel 11 is the loyal, faithful, remnant people of God—the glorious holy mountain of the last days. The good news revealed in each passage is that God wins this battle and the king of the North will be unsuccessful in his attempt to place his tabernacle in the glorious holy mountain. God's people will not be defeated. The king of the North will be overcome.

The King of the North

The king of the North is a symbolism unique in Daniel 11. The same symbol is used to represent all the powers of history that have been arrayed against God's people. What lies behind the use of this symbol that indicates the unity of the powers arrayed against God and His people down through the ages?

In the Old Testament, the north is referred to as the point of the compass from which God ruled. The ancient Israelites looked to the north as the seat of the divine government. In Leviticus 1:11, for example, it was commanded that the sacrifice be slain on the north side of the altar, which was declared to be before God. In Psalm 48:1, 2, Zion, city of the great King, is declared to be located in the far north. In Ezekiel 8:3, 4, the glory of God was declared to be in the north. Thus, the north became the point of the compass that the Israelite looked to for the presence of God. This would make God the one and only true King of the North. Any others claiming to be the king of the North would be usurpers.

Daniel 11 is not presenting God as the king of the North but is detailing for us the history of those powers that have attempted to usurp God's throne and rule in the place of God. Thus, Daniel 11 would be the history of the false kings of the north. That is the reason for the use of one symbol: Each individual representation of the king of the north is a different face of the ultimate counterfeit king of the North—Satan.

The scriptures present Satan's original attempt to rule above God as claiming that Satan alone was to rule from the north:

> How you are fallen from heaven, O Lucifer, son of the morning! How you are cut down to the ground, you who weakened the nations! For you have said in your heart: "I will ascend into heaven, I will exalt my throne above the stars of God; I will also sit on the mount of the congregation on the farthest sides of the north; I will ascend above the heights

of the clouds, I will be like the Most High." Isaiah 14:12-14

Here is a reference to Satan's original attempt to take over the government of heaven. What did Satan wish to do? He wanted to sit on the mount of the assembly in the recesses of the north. He wanted to plant his tabernacle on the mount of the assembly. At the end of the world, Satan will make one final attempt to control God and His people. Daniel 11 is describing this final assault of Satan against God, as Satan renews his claim to be the king of the North. The final battle of the king of the North in Daniel 11 is the continuation of the battle of the great controversy, begun in heaven when Satan rebelled, and continued on earth. Daniel 11:40-45 describes the end of the controversy. The issue at stake in the great controversy is who is the rightful ruler, the true king of the North—Christ or Satan?

Daniel 11 rehearses Satan's usurped role as the king of the North, as Satan worked through ancient Babylon, Persia, Greece, Rome, and the fallen church of the Dark Ages. In each case, Satan has worked through these powers to harass and destroy the covenant people. Finally, in verses 40-45, Daniel portrays Satan's final assault against God's people of the last days, who keep the commandments of God and have the testimony of Jesus (Revelation 12:17).

Who then is the final king of the North through whom Satan works in the last days? It is the same power described in Revelation 13:11-18 as the land-roaming beast and in Revelation 16 as final, spiritual Babylon. This final Babylon is portrayed as consisting of three parts: the beast, the false prophet, and the dragon.

This final threefold union is therefore the final king of the North described in Daniel 11:40-45. The first part we have already identified: the beast. Revelation 13:1-10 refers to the beast as the church of the Dark Ages with its political power. Now at the time of the end, this Roman beast reappears, not as a single beast, but in coalition with two other powers, which will be identified in an upcoming chapter.

The King of the South

It is clear from the first few verses of Daniel 11 that the original king of the South is a reference to Egypt. However, in verse 31, when the church of the Dark Ages is introduced, the king of the South disappears, only to reappear in verse 40 as a major power attacking the king of the North at the end of the Dark Ages, around 1798.

Ancient Egypt, however, basically ended as a major power after the battle of Accius in 31 B.C., when Octavius defeated the forces of Marcus Antonius and Cleopatra. Egypt was transformed into a Roman province. Today it is just one of the countries of the Arab world, and it was certainly not a major player in the world at the end of the Dark Ages when it was to attack the church of the Middle Ages. Who then is the king of the South that would attack the king of the North (political papacy) around 1798 and inflict the deadly wound from which the political arm of the church would eventually recover?

Instead of looking for a rebirth of Egypt, we must examine what kind of power Egypt was when it first came in contact with God's people. The Egypt (king of the South) of Daniel 11:40 would therefore be a power akin to ancient Egypt when it assailed God's ancient people. The most vicious attack against God's people by ancient Egypt was clearly during the time of the Egyptian bondage. The defiance of Egypt to the biblical God is seen clearly in Exodus.

> Afterward Moses and Aaron went in and told Pharaoh, "Thus says the Lord God of Israel: 'Let My people go, that they may hold a feast to Me in the wilderness.'" And Pharaoh said, "Who is the Lord, that I should obey His voice to let Israel go? I do not know the Lord, nor will I let Israel go." Exodus 5:1, 2.

This is the most direct confrontation that the ancient king of the South had with the biblical God. It was a denial of the existence of the biblical God and a defiance of His claims. It is an exaltation of paganism above the biblical God and total denial of His supremacy. Throughout the Old Testament, Egypt, then, becomes a symbol of those who deny the existence of the biblical God and claim to have made the world apart from God. Daniel 11 is predicting that around 1798, an atheistic power similar to Egypt and symbolized by Egypt, would arise and attack the political arm of the medieval church.

Revelation 11 helps us better understand Daniel 11, for Revelation 11 predicts in greater detail the modern rise of the king of the South. In Revelation 11:3, God's two witnesses are said to prophesy for 1,260 years, clothed in sackcloth. The fact that they prophesy for 1,260 years clearly indicates that they are symbols, rather than a specific person. What are God's two witnesses? Revelation 11:4 declares them to be the two olive trees and two lampstands that stand before the Lord. The olive tree is a symbol of the Holy Spirit in scripture, and the lampstands are symbols of the Word of God (Psalm 119:105). Since the Holy Spirit is the source of the Word of God, the two symbols are both referring to the same thing—the Word of God found in two testaments. An attack against the two witnesses is thus an attack against the Bible. All during the 1,260 years, the Bible was kept from the people, hidden in obscurity, clothed indeed in sackcloth.

At the end of the 1,260 years, the Bible is attacked by the beast that comes up out of the abyss, and this beast kills it (Revelation 11:7-9). This beast that ascends out of the abyss is none other than the modern rise of the king of the South. The nation here represented is France, which greatly attacked the Bible during the French Revolution in the 1790s—the very time the modern king of the South is to reappear.

At the height of the French Revolution, the Bible was banned. In its stead, the goddess of reason—a naked woman—was enthroned, and a ten-day week was initiated. All this was in defiance of the biblical God. Revelation 11:9 predicted that this attack would continue for 3 ½ days, or years. Interestingly, France's abolishment of religion lasted exactly

3 ½ years. The decree abolishing religion was enacted on November 26, 1793 and was repealed on June 17, 1797—exactly 3 ½ years later. The linkage to the king of the South, and Egypt specifically, is clearly stated in verse 8:

"And their dead bodies will lie in the street of the great city which spiritually is called Sodom and Egypt, where also our Lord was crucified" (Revelation 11:8).

Here is a power arising at the time of the end (1798—the end of the Dark Ages) with an atheistic emphasis and an attack on religion. This power then attacks the political papacy and inflicts the deadly would. It was Berthier, the French general under Napoleon, who, in the aftermath of the French Revolution, invaded the Vatican, took the pope prisoner, and ended the political power of the church in 1798. That was an exact fulfillment of Daniel 11:40.

Today, the French Revolution is recognized as the beginning of the modern atheistic and secular revolution. The modern attack against the Bible can be traced to the French Revolution. Since 1798, there has been a worldwide dissemination of the ideas of the French Revolution. Georg Hegel, coming out of the French Revolution, became the father of modern atheism in philosophy and theology, openly questioning the validity of the Bible. Charles Darwin, influenced likewise by the French Revolution, proposed evolution as an alternative to biblical creationism, questioning the very uniqueness of God as Creator. Then there was Karl Marx, who read Darwin and united it with his philosophy to create communism—the school of thought that dominated a good share of the world during the twentieth century.

Thus since 1798, the king of the South has reappeared. We have seen the worldwide penetration of the ideas of the French Revolution. As a result, atheism and secularism have become the major worldview, replacing a biblical worldview that had always dominated the earth prior to 1798. This secular worldview took over primarily western society and the communist bloc. How long will it continue before the world returns to a religious worldview?

From the Bible, we have learned the meaning of the symbols of Daniel 11:40-45. The glorious holy mountain is a symbol of God's loyal people of the last days. The king of the North, while originally referring to God, is used in Daniel 11 to describe Lucifer and the powers through which he has worked as the usurped king of the North. The final power that he works through is the final threefold union united against God's people. The king of the South refers to the atheistic, secularist state that dominated a good share of the world during the twentieth century. Let's now examine the prophecy with these identifications in mind.

The Prophecy of Daniel 11:40-45

At the time of the end the king of the South shall attack him; and the king of the North shall come against him like a whirlwind, with chariots, horsemen, and with many ships; and he shall enter the countries, overwhelm them, and pass through. He shall also enter the Glorious Land, and many countries shall be overthrown; but these shall escape from his hand: Edom, Moab, and the prominent people of Ammon. Daniel 11:40, 41.

Verse 40 opens with the king of the South attacking the king of the North (him)—a reference to the king of the North in the previous verse, which was the political power of the Dark Ages church. This is a clear prediction of the French attacking the papacy and destroying its political power in 1798. The Bible calls this the time of the end. All time after the Dark Ages is referred to in scripture as the time of the end. The papacy is given a deadly wound. During this time of a weakened papacy, atheistic and secularistic philosophy penetrates the world. However, the dormant papacy is revived and launches a vicious counterattack against the king of the South, totally annihilating him, according to verse 40. The revived political power of the church then proceeds to conquer and dominate a good share of the world. This is the prediction of

Daniel 11:40, 41. Amazingly, in the latter part of the twentieth century, the world witnessed the beginning of the counterattack as the revived political church began to destroy the atheistic/secularistic philosophy that ruled the world during that time. This revived political power of the church is part one of the final threefold union.

The 1990s witnessed the downfall of almost the entire communist empire—and it happened overnight. Who caused it? According to Daniel 11, it would be this revived political power of the church that would soon develop into the threefold union.

But the election of John Paul II, a Polish Pope, in 1978 was the signal event. When he visited Poland in 1979, six million of his countrymen, a sixth of the population, turned out to see him. He proclaimed Christianity and communism incompatible. The church became the center of political protest in Poland.

> With the Pope's support, Solidarity was formed, and John Paul II sent word to Moscow that if Soviet forces crushed Solidarity, he would go to Poland and stand with his people. The Soviets were so alarmed they hatched a plot to kill him. In 1982 the Pope was shot by a professional killer in St. Peter's Square, miraculously he survived.—"Communism's Incredible Collapse: How It Happened" by Fred Barnes, *Reader's Digest*, March 1990.

According to Daniel 11, the king of the South is to be eliminated. There is to be no atheism, at least outwardly, in the final conflict. In the next chapter, we will examine the mark of the beast—a religious mark that all will receive in the last days. Such a scenario would mean that a religious worldview would once again dominate the earth at the end time.

The part that the pope played in the defeat of communism was one of the amazing stories to emerge in the aftermath of the defeat of communism in the early 1990s. In fact, in 1992,

Time magazine produced a cover story detailing the union of the pope and President Reagan to defeat communism. The article was entitled: "The Holy Alliance: How Reagan and the Pope conspired to assist Poland's Solidarity movement and hasten the demise of Communism."

> In that meeting, Reagan and the Pope agreed to undertake a clandestine campaign to hasten the dissolution of the communist empire. Declares Richard Allen, Reagan's first National Security Adviser: "This was one of the great secret alliances of all time."—*Time*, February 24, 1992, p. 28.

> The key administration players were all devout Roman Catholics—CIA chief William Casey, Allen, Clark, Haig, Walters, and William Wilson, Reagan's first ambassador to the Vatican. They regarded the US-Vatican relationship as a holy alliance: the moral force of the Pope and the teachings of their church combined with their fierce anticommunism and their notion of American democracy. Yet the mission would have been impossible without the full support of Reagan, who believed fervently in both the benefits and the practical application of Washington's relationship with the Vatican. One of his earliest goals as President, Reagan says, was to recognize the Vatican as a state "and make them an ally."—*Time*, February 24, 1992, p. 31.

> "Nobody believed the collapse of communism would happen this fast or on this timetable," says a cardinal who is one of the Pope's closest aides. "But in their first meeting, the Holy Father and the President committed themselves and the institutions of the church and America to such a goal. And from that day, the focus was to bring it about in Poland."—*Time*, February 24, 1992, p. 35.

> In response to concerns of the Vatican, the Reagan Administration agreed to alter its foreign-aid program to com-

ply with the church's teachings on birth control.—*Time*, February 24, 1992, p. 35.

What an amazing union! A Roman pope and an American president, united together to defeat communism. Since the time of Reagan, every U.S. president has continued this special relationship with Rome, and each appointed a full ambassador to the Vatican. No other denomination is given such status in the United States. Only the Vatican is accorded such high diplomatic status, where the United States recognizes its political power with ambassador status.

In a fascinating book, *Keys of This Blood*, published before the collapse of communism, Malachi Martin describes the political aims of Pope John Paul II. The book cover states: "Pope John Paul II Versus Russia and The West for Control of the New World Order," and the subtitle reads: *The Struggle for World Dominion Between Pope John Paul II, Mikhail Gorbachev, and the Capitalist West.*

This book states that the objective of Pope John Paul II was first to conquer communism and then to conquer the west. What gives the book tremendous credence is the fact that the pope was able to accomplish the first part by eliminating communism, just as Daniel 11 predicted. He hasn't been able to conquer the west, but he has created a partnership with America, which is an interesting arrangement for a country founded on the separation of church and state. Yet in America today, we have a "holy alliance" between the pope and America. Note the conclusion Martin draws:

> This is why John Paul is waiting. God must first intervene, before John Paul's major ministry to all men can start. …It will be the death and entombment of Leninist Marxism and the effective liquidation of the long—centuries-long—war that the forces of this civilized world have waged against the Church Christ founded and the religious belief of that Church. The battle between the Gospel and the anti-Gospel will be over. The other two major contenders in the millen-

nium endgame will be eliminated.—*Keys of This Blood*, p. 657.

Of course, the Bible does not predict, as we shall soon see, that America will be eliminated. Instead, we will discover that the Bible predicts America will join hands with Rome in this final, threefold union. The first inklings of this have been demonstrated by the "holy alliance" created to eliminate communism. The king of the North and this final threefold union may well be beginning in our day.

Daniel 11 predicted that around 1798, the king of the South would strike a deadly blow against the then-reigning king of the North (papacy). This was fulfilled when the political power of the papacy ended. Daniel 11 further predicts that the king of the North will regroup and counterattack the king of the South and wipe him out. We have seen that striking fulfillment of prophecy in the early 1990s. Not only does the Bible predict that the king of the North will conquer communism, it also says he will do it with great rapidity. Anyone familiar with the demise of communism recognized that it indeed happened in a very short period of time, just as Daniel 11 predicted.

As this final king of the North (the final threefold union) goes forth making great headway among the nations (verses 41-43), something happens that quickly turns the tide against this final king of the North:

> But news from the east and the north shall trouble him; therefore he shall go out with great fury to destroy and annihilate many. And he shall plant the tents of his palace between the seas and the glorious holy mountain; yet he shall come to his end, and no one will help him. Daniel 11:44, 45.

Interesting words predicted here. Tidings out of the north and east disturb the king of the North. Why? This false king of the North feels that he is in control of the world—that it all belongs to him—yet tidings out of the north and east trouble him. The north is the point of the compass from which God rules, and the east is the point of the compass from which Christ comes. Just as the false king of the North feels that all is in his hands, the true king of the North is about to speak, and Christ is about to come out of the east, as the king of the East (Revelation 16:12). Just when the false king of the North appears to be in full control of the world, the sign of the approaching Christ is seen. Knowing the prophecies, the devil is alarmed, because his end is now near.

Realizing that the intervention of God is about to happen, Satan provokes the final king of the North to go forth with great rapidity and place his seat in Mt. Zion by conquering the final faithful people of God who keep his commandments and have the testimony of Jesus at the end of time. This is Satan's final attempt to place his seat in the glorious holy mountain. If he could wipe out the saints, his triumph would be complete. This plunges the world into the final battle of Armageddon that was described in the previous chapter.

As in Revelation 16, the Bible pictures God intervening as the king of the North plays his last card and attempts to annihilate God's saints. God brings down the curtain by interrupting the battle of Armageddon with the second coming of Christ. Daniel 12:1, 2 concludes this divine intervention described in the prophecy of Daniel 11.

> At that time Michael shall stand up, the great prince who stands watch over the sons of your people; and there shall be a time of trouble, such as never was since there was a nation, even to that time. And at that time your people shall be delivered, every one who is found written in the book. And many of those who sleep in the dust of the earth shall awake, some to everlasting life, some to shame and everlasting contempt. Daniel 12:1, 2.

Note again that it is in the midst of this final attempt to destroy God's people (the glorious holy mountain) that God intervenes and delivers His people. They are not delivered *from* trouble and distress. But *in the midst* of this awesome time of distress—the worst in the history of the world—God mightily delivers His people. When it seems impossible, God intervenes and provides a marvelous deliverance.

Therefore, we do not need to fear this final threefold king of the North. He will come to his end, and none shall help him. But God's faithful people will be delivered. The important thing for me to remember is that I have given my life to Jesus, and all the powers of hell arrayed against me cannot be victorious, because Jesus is greater than any other power. The overwhelming testimony of scripture is that God wins. Praise God! We know the outcome of earth's final battle. Why not decide to join Jesus and be on the winning side?

23

Hope in the Time of the Mark of the Beast

Then a third angel followed them, saying with a loud voice, "If anyone worships the beast and his image, and receives his mark on his forehead or on his hand, he himself shall also drink of the wine of the wrath of God, which is poured out full strength into the cup of His indignation. He shall be tormented with fire and brimstone in the presence of the holy angels and in the presence of the Lamb. And the smoke of their torment ascends forever and ever; and they have no rest day or night, who worship the beast and his image, and whoever receives the mark of his name." Here is the patience of the saints; here are those who keep the commandments of God and the faith of Jesus. Revelation 14:9-12.

This is the most solemn warning in all of scripture. God provides fearful consequences for those who receive the mark of the beast. Obviously, it is not God's intention that any of His creatures receive this awful mark. In the book of Revelation, the mark of the beast and the seal of God stand as opposites. The faithful, loyal people of God receive the seal of God, while the unfaithful people end up receiving the mark of the beast. Note in verse 12 that those who receive the mark of the beast stand in sharp contrast to those who keep the commandments of God and have the faith of Jesus. Possessing these two latter characteristics is the opposite of worshiping the beast and receiving his mark.

The seal of God and the mark of the beast are issues during the last generation of time. No one today has the mark of the beast. Only in the final conflict is it imposed by civil legislation. However, what we do today is preparing us for which sign we will receive in the last days—the mark of the beast, or the seal of God. Certainly, all of us desire to be a part of those that keep the commandments of God and have the faith of Jesus.

Identity of the Beast

In order to discover what the mark of the beast is, one must first of all note who the beast is, for the mark of the beast is simply the sign of loyalty to the beast power. The beast has already been clearly identified as the church of the Dark Ages, when it united the church and the state and persecuted dissenters. There were several identifying marks of this false religious system that we noted earlier. Let us quickly review them:

1. It is a religious power that receives worship (Revelation 13:4). The church in its apostasy during the Dark Ages indeed was a religious power that received the worship of the people.

2. It is a blasphemous power (Revelation 13:1, 5, 6). Blasphemy was for a man to claim the power to forgive sins. (Mark 2:7). The church made the claim that even God had to abide by its judgment in the forgiveness of sins. Blasphemy was for a man to claim equality with God. So blasphemous did the church become that it actually claimed to be the creator of God. Furthermore, blasphemy was to mix paganism with Christianity, which the church did throughout the Dark Ages.

3. It is a persecuting power (Revelation 13:7). The Dark Ages Church shed more innocent blood than any other institution that has ever existed among humankind.

4. The number of its name adds up to 666 (Revelation 13:18). The official title of the head of the church in Latin was *Vicarius Filii Dei*. Taking the Roman numerals of the name, it adds up to the biblical 666.

5. Daniel indicated that the beast power would attempt to change times and laws (Daniel 7:25). It not only did this but also proudly boasted that it had done so. The church eliminated the second commandment forbidding the worship of images and divided the tenth into two parts, in order to retain ten commandments. It also changed the seventh-day Sabbath contained in the fourth commandment to Sunday, the first day of the week.

Probably the boldest thing that the church of the Dark Ages did was to change God's seventh-day Sabbath—the sign of the time of our relationship with God—into a human-made institution. It took the church, as studied earlier, over six hundred years to complete, but then, looking back over those years, the church today proudly proclaims that it changed the day.

Q: What is the Third Commandment?

A: The Third Commandment is: Remember that thou keep holy the Sabbath day.

Q: Which is the Sabbath day?

A: Saturday is the Sabbath day.

Q: Why do we observe Sunday instead of Saturday?

A: We observe Sunday instead of Saturday because the Catholic Church transferred the solemnity from Saturday to Sunday.

—Peter Guierman. *The Convert's Catechism of Catholic Doctrine*, 1951, p. 50.

There is no question in Rome's mind but that it changed

the Sabbath to Sunday. History confirms that Rome accomplished what it claimed. However, this issue for Rome is the proof of its authority and power. Note the bold claims of authority based on its supposed change of the Sabbath:

Q: How prove you that the Church hath power to command feasts and holy days?

A: By the very act of changing the Sabbath into Sunday, which Protestants allow of and therefore they fondly contradict themselves, by keeping Sunday strictly, and breaking most other feasts commanded by the same church.

—Henry Tuberville, *An Abridgment of the Christian Doctrine,* 1833, p. 58.

You will tell me that Saturday was the Jewish Sabbath, but that the Christian Sabbath has been changed to Sunday. Changed! But by whom? Who has authority to change an express commandment of Almighty God? When God has spoken and said, Thou shalt keep holy the seventh day, who shall dare to say, Nay, thou mayest work and do all manner of worldly business on the seventh day, but thou shalt keep holy the first day in its stead. This is a most important question which I know not how you can answer.

You are a Protestant, and you profess to go by the Bible and the Bible only; and yet in so important a matter as the observance of one day in seven as a holy day, you go against the plain letter of the Bible, and put another day in the place of that day which the Bible has commanded. The command to keep holy the seventh day is one of the ten commandments; you believe that the other nine are still binding; who gave you authority to tamper with the fourth? If you are consistent with your own principles, if you really follow the Bible and the Bible only, you ought to be able to produce some portion of the New Testament in which this fourth commandment is expressly altered.

—*Library of Christian Doctrine: Why Don't You Keep Holy the Sabbath Day?* p. 3.

There is no question that the issue of the change in the Sabbath is not a minor topic with Rome. It is the defining issue that gives the church the authority to be above scripture. If it can change the Sabbath by its authority, then the church would be supreme over scripture rather than the church having to answer to scripture. Several years ago, someone sent a letter to Pope Pius XI questioning if it were true that the church had changed the Sabbath to Sunday. The following reply was reported in *The Catholic Extension Magazine* by Peter R. Tramer, editor:

Dear Sir,

Regarding the change from the observance of the Jewish Sabbath to the Christian Sunday, I wish to draw your attention to the facts:

A. That Protestants who accept the Bible as the only rule of faith and religion, should by all means go back to the observance of the Sabbath. The fact that they do not, but on the contrary observe Sunday, stultifies them in the eyes of every thinking man.

B. We Catholics do not accept the Bible as the only rule of faith. Besides the Bible we have the living Church, the authority of the Church, as a rule to guide us. We say, this Church, instituted by Christ, to teach and guide men through life, has the right to change the ceremonial laws of the Old Testament and hence, we accept her change of the Sabbath to Sunday. We frankly say "yes," the Church made this change, made this law, as she made many other laws, for instance, the Friday Abstinence, the unmarried priesthood, the laws concerning mixed marriages, the regulations of Catholic marriages, and a thousand other laws.

C. We also say that of all Protestants, the Seventh-day Adventists are the only group that reason correctly and are consistent with their teachings. It is always somewhat laughable to see the Protestant Churches, in pulpit and legislature, demand the observance of Sundays of which there is nothing in the Bible.

> With best wishes,
> (Signed) Peter R. Tramer, editor

Rome's challenge is significant. If one goes by the Bible and the Bible only, one must observe the seventh-day Sabbath. During the sixteenth-century Protestant Reformation, the reformed faith was making significant headway against Rome. The Roman church convened the Council of Trent to attempt to find an answer to the Protestant menace of the Bible and the Bible only. Somehow, they had to prove that even the Protestants obeyed the authority of the Roman church.

> Finally at the last opening on the eighteenth of January, 1562, all hesitation was set aside: the archbishop of Reggio made a speech in which he openly declared that tradition stood above Scripture. The authority of the church could therefore not be bound to the authority of the Scriptures, because the church had changed Sabbath into Sunday, not by the command of Christ, but by its own authority.
> —Heinrich Julius Holtzmann, *Kanon and Tradition*, 1859, p. 263 in German.

That settled it. The church left the council with that argument and stopped the Protestant reformation in its tracks, for the Protestants had no answer. It was true. There was no biblical authority for Sunday—only the tradition of the Roman church. It is Rome's contention that tradition is on equal footing with scripture. The fact that the church changed the Sabbath into Sunday, she declares, proves that point. Today, Rome still proudly announces its change of the Sabbath as proof of its power and authority.

It is often claimed on the radio nowadays that Christianity should not be a matter of tradition, as the Catholics perversely make it, but be based rather solely on the Bible. And yet it is quite obvious that Christianity always was a matter of tradition.

One in every thousand Christians perhaps keeps the day the Bible says. The other 999 keep the day tradition says. And how significant it is that no one ever questioned the switch. We read of no violent controversies or schism over it. Each generation simply followed the previous generation…

Huge sums have been offered for a Scripture text for Sunday worship. None have been won. None will be. The Bible has been combed from Genesis to Revelation. It offers numerous texts commanding us to worship on the seventh day, but not a single one for the first day. It tells us how God commanded the seventh day to be kept as a memorial of Creation. It tells how the command was repeated on Sinai. It tells how the Son of God Himself kept the seventh day. It says nowhere that Christians should keep a different day from the Jews, His chosen people.

Some people have been misled by the term "Lord's Day." This they take in the Christian sense, and, in the light of tradition, assume to be Sunday. They forget that, minus tradition, the Lord's Day means only what it meant to Adam and Eve – the seventh day. In the very act of interpreting "Lord's Day," not in the Biblical sense but as Sunday, they are traditionalists.

Then there are those who say—"Well, what does it matter? Saturday, Sunday, any day will do. If Sunday was good enough for the early Christians, it is good enough for us." They forget that it is not the early Christians who will judge us but God and it was God who laid on mankind the strict obligation of keeping the seventh day, which His chosen people will keep. Who could change that command? Obviously only God Himself. How? He has not done it in the Bible, but there is also the church, which He made just as surely as He made the Bible. To suggest that men could change it is absurd. To argue that there are good reasons for it is nonsense, for what are man's puny reasons beside God's commands. If it has been done it has been done in virtue of the power he entrusted to the Apostles, and especially to St. Peter…Why do some modern Christians doubt it?

—Prefectuire Apostolic, Very Reverend R. S. Dehler, C. R., published in the *Catholic Bulletin of Bermuda*, February 7, 1954.

The Mark of the Beast

An examination of the identification marks leaves no doubt that the beast described in Revelation 13 and Daniel 7 is none other than the great Roman apostasy of the Dark Ages. The mark of the beast would then be the mark or sign of the authority of this power. As we have just seen, Rome claims that the mark or sign of its authority is its change of the Sabbath from Saturday to Sunday, not by the authority of the Bible or Christ, but simply by the authority of the church. Thus, the mark of the authority of this power is its change of the Sabbath from Saturday to Sunday. Rome proudly proclaims this to be the ultimate sign of its authority.

Of course the Catholic Church claims that the change (from Sabbath to Sunday) was her act. . . . And the act is a mark of her ecclesiastical power and authority in religious matters.

—Reply to a letter dated October 28, 1895 and addressed from Cardinal Gibbons, by Chancellor C. F. Thomas.

It was the Catholic Church which . . . transferred this rest to the Sunday . . . thus the observance of Sunday by the Protestants is an homage they pay, in spite of themselves, to the authority of the [Catholic] Church.

—*Plain Talk About Protestantism of Today*, p. 213. Monsignor Louis Segur.

What bold claims Rome makes! The change of the Sabbath, it declares to be a mark of its authority and power, and states that Protestants who keep Sunday are bowing in homage to the authority of the Catholic Church. Remember that no one has the mark of the beast yet. It only applies when it is enforced by civil legislation in the last days. But make no mistake about this issue—it is not a minor one. The clear issue is, who is the rightful authority in the life of Christians: a rebellious church, haughtily claiming an authority above God—or is our authority truly Jesus Christ and His word?

The Seal of God

Directly opposite to the mark of the beast is the seal of God in the book of Revelation. Revelation 7:2, 3 describes an angel coming down from heaven with the seal of the living God to place upon the foreheads of those who are ready to meet Jesus in the last days. A seal is a sign of authority. Just as the mark of the beast is the sign of the beast's authority, so the seal of God is the sign of God's authority.

A seal on a document indicates it to be authentic. The seal of the president of the United States, for example, will have the president's name, his title, and the territory over which he rules. So must the seal of God. Where can we find God's seal? Revelation 7:3 indicates that God's people are sealed in their forehead. The mind is located within the forehead, and Hebrews 8:10 indicates that God writes His law in our minds. Thus the logical place to discover the seal of God would be in the law of God, the Ten Commandments.

In one of those commandments, the fourth, God has placed His seal:

> Remember the Sabbath day, to keep it holy. Six days you shall labor and do all your work, but the seventh day is the Sabbath of the Lord your God. In it you shall do no work: you, nor your son, nor your daughter, nor your male ser-

vant, nor your female servant, nor your cattle, nor your stranger who is within your gates. For in six days the Lord made the heavens and the earth, the sea, and all that is in them, and rested the seventh day. Therefore the Lord blessed the Sabbath day and hallowed it. Exodus 20:8-11.

In verse 11, we find all three elements of the seal: God's name, title, and dominion—Lord God, Maker of heaven and earth.

Interestingly, God has placed His seal in the Sabbath commandment, while the beast has placed his mark in the Sunday commandment. The issue could not be drawn more clearly. The issue in the Sabbath/Sunday controversy is the issue of the authority of the beast versus the authority of Christ.

But who is the seal of God? Who is Lord God, Maker of heaven and earth? It is Jesus. John 1:1-3 and 14 declares unequivocally that Jesus is the Creator. Thus, Jesus is the Seal of the Living God.

When we accept Jesus on a personal level, He enters our life and, like a seal, when His character is impressed onto us, we bear His likeness. To have the seal is to have the character of Jesus in our life. And, interestingly, He places the seal in the Sabbath command.

The Sabbath is the one commandment that addresses our relationship with Jesus. The reason the seal is in the Sabbath is because we need to take this weekly, twenty-four-hour period and spend it with Jesus if we are to have His character reflected in our lives. That is why the Sabbath is such a significant issue in the last days. God's last-day people must have this deep, abiding relationship with Jesus, and it can only be obtained through spending significant time with Jesus.

"Moreover I also gave them My Sabbaths, to be a sign between them and Me, that they might know that I am the Lord who sanctifies them" (Ezekiel 20:12).

"Hallow My Sabbaths, and they will be a sign between Me

and you, that you may know that I am the Lord your God" (Ezekiel 20:20).

The Sabbath is the sign of sanctification—the sign that we know the Lord. Note again—the Sabbath is all about our relationship with Jesus. The devil wishes to destroy this relationship with Jesus, which is why the Sabbath is the object of his special attack in the last days.

The Issue of the Last Days

The issue of the last days is between the mark of the beast and the seal of God. It is not about the observance of days, but about loyalty. The observance of days is merely the outward manifestation.

The real issue is determining the ultimate authority in the life of the Christian: Christ, or Rome. Thus, in the last days, God asks us to choose between the seal of God and His Sabbath, and the mark of the beast and its Sabbath.

Why is this issue so important? It is because the issue involves the authority of God and a relationship with Jesus. There is no such thing as an insignificant issue when our relationship with God is at stake. That is why God attaches such a fearful warning to the issue of the mark of the beast. To accept the mark of the beast when one knows the difference between the seal of God and the mark of the beast is to denigrate the relationship with Jesus and declare that it is not important whether this relationship exists or not. Those who make that choice in the final hour receive the mark of the beast and suffer the wrath of God.

When Rome and Protestantism quote the Sabbath commandment, they usually quote only the first part: "Remember the Sabbath day to keep it holy." They leave out the rest of the commandment that tells which day is the Sabbath. Yet, in leaving out the part that tells which day it is, they end up leaving out the seal of God.

This is the great crime: They have left Jesus out of the Sabbath. Emphasizing the seal of God and God's Sabbath is merely trying to place Jesus back in the heart and center of the Sabbath where He belongs, for He declares that He is Lord of the Sabbath.

God invites us today to make a choice between the seal of God and the mark of the beast. It is not just a question of days, but of who is the object of our allegiance. Who is the ultimate authority in your life—Christ, or Antichrist? As for me and my house, we will serve the Lord. How about you? Will you now declare that you will honor God's Sabbath and develop that deep relationship with Him? Will you be a part of His last-day people that keep the commandments of God and have the faith of Jesus?

24

Hope When the Mark of the Beast Is Enforced

I magine a time when no one can buy or sell products without a special mark. The Bible declares that such a time is coming. This is why it is so important to develop a relationship with Jesus now through daily time with Him and a weekly Sabbath experience. It is the only way to remain strong in the trying times soon to break upon Planet Earth.

Revelation 13 pictures two different beasts: one comes up out of the sea, while the other rises from the earth. The first beast has been clearly identified as the church of the Dark Ages with its union of church and state. John describes the rise of the second beast in graphic terms:

> He who leads into captivity shall go into captivity; he who kills with the sword must be killed with the sword. Here is the patience and the faith of the saints. Then I saw another beast coming up out of the earth, and he had two horns like a lamb and spoke like a dragon. And he exercises all the authority of the first beast in his presence, and causes the earth and those who dwell in it to worship the first beast, whose deadly wound was healed. Revelation 13:10-12.

There are several identifying marks of this second beast. He arises as the first beast is being taken captive. He rises out of the earth instead of the sea. This beast is lamblike, not ferocious like the other beasts, yet ultimately, this beast speaks like the dragon and forces people to worship the first beast. He does it after the healing of the deadly wound.

The second beast is as easy to identify as the first was. Only one power meets all the marks of identification that we find in these few verses. First of all, this beast arises as the first beast goes into captivity. That happened in 1798. Therefore, the second beast must arise around 1798.

The first beast rose out of the sea—a representation of populated Europe (Revelation 17:15). The earth being the opposite of the sea would represent a land not as populated as Europe. In addition, this power was to be lamblike—innocent and freedom-loving rather than a kingly power. Sometime in the future, the deadly wound of the first beast would be healed, and this beast would become its partner to enforce the worship of the first beast. Thus, this second beast represents the second power of the unholy trinity that forms the final threefold union.

There is only one power that arose around 1798 in a new land, characterized as lamblike in its beginnings. That power can only be the United States of America. As strange as it may seem, the Bible clearly identifies America as this second beast. Of course, America has not yet fulfilled all the details of this prophecy; however, it did arise as a lamblike power, with its strong emphasis on freedom and liberty.

The tragedy is that someday in the future, all this will vanish, as the United States ultimately repudiates every principle of its constitution and forces its population to worship the first beast that had the deadly wound healed. The healing of the wound is the restoration of political power to the church. Evidently, the United States is to play a major role in the healing of that wound. We have already seen how America sends an ambassador to the Vatican, recognizing its political power. In addition, we noted that America also formed a "holy alliance" with Rome to defeat communism. So it should not surprise us if in the future, this relationship deepens, and America becomes a pawn in the hands of the political power of the church to force people to worship Rome's way.

Revelation 13:12 indicates that the second beast causes the people to worship the first beast. That does not mean that all are forced to become members of the Roman Church. In order to worship the beast, all one has to do is to honor an institution that has the church as its only authority, and one is thereby worshiping the beast. In the last chapter, we noticed that the Roman Church claimed that when Protestants keep Sunday, they pay homage (worship) to the authority of the church. Ultimately, Revelation 13 declares that America will be foremost in enforcing the mark of the beast—Sunday worship by legislation—which would be worshiping the beast.

One wonders how this is possible in freedom-loving America. The constitution guarantees Americans freedom of religion and the separation of church and state. Yet that same constitution did not prevent America from recognizing the Roman church above all other churches by sending an ambassador to sit in the Vatican. That very act established a tie with Rome that no other denomination enjoys. Amazingly, in the aftermath of the tragedy of September 11, 2001, Americans seem willing to give up some of their freedoms for the sake of safety from terrorism. Where this will lead, no one knows, but it may be one more step down the road to the ultimate loss of our freedoms.

If the Bible says this will happen, it will happen. However, the scripture actually continues by detailing exactly how America will agree to even greater recognition of the authority of Rome.

> He performs great signs, so that he even makes fire come down from heaven on the earth in the sight of men. And he deceives those who dwell on the earth by those signs which he was granted to do in the sight of the beast, telling those who dwell on the earth to make an image to the beast who was wounded by the sword and lived. Revelation 13:13, 14.

In order to convince Americans to follow the second beast as he leads people to worship Rome, the first beast, the Bible declares, performs signs and wonders—miracles—even bringing fire down from heaven. All this is done to convince people that God is leading in this new direction. Then people willingly concede their freedoms to follow this new god, who performs mighty acts.

The last time fire fell from heaven was on Mt. Carmel in the Old Testament, when Elijah brought fire down to prove that God was with him. Now, the beast brings this fire down to prove that God is with him, but this is not genuine fire—it is false fire. Some have suggested that this fire is a nuclear bomb; however, a bomb would obliterate people, but this fire deceives people. Perhaps we should not look for physical fire, but a symbolic fire that deceives.

Fire is a symbol used in the book of Revelation. In Revelation 4:5, the perfect Holy Spirit in heaven is symbolized by seven lamps of fire burning. In Matthew 3:11, John the Baptist foretold that when Messiah came, He would baptize people with the Holy Spirit and fire. All of these texts indicate that there seems to be a scriptural connection between fire and the Holy Spirit. Throughout the New Testament, fire seems to be used symbolically to represent the outpouring of the Holy Spirit. Even at Pentecost, in Acts 2:1-4, the Holy Spirit is poured out on the early disciples as tongues of fire. This was the initial "speaking in tongues" in the early church.

Revelation 13:12-14 indicates that at the time of the end, false fire (false tongues), miracles, signs, and lying wonders will be poured out in an attempt to deceive people into worshiping the first beast. Here is the third party of the unholy trinity—the power of the dragon to deceive people through miracles, signs, and wonders. The dragon will not only use counterfeit miracles and tongues but will also make use of the occult in an all-out assault upon America and the world. It is this miracle-working power of the dragon that convinces people that God is bringing a new revival of spirit power. Thus they willingly give up their freedoms to make certain all in America receive the blessings of this false revival with all its false miracles.

Here then is the unholy trinity that makes up the final threefold union that becomes the power that inflicts the mark of the beast. This is the power that will meet its end in the battle of Armageddon. What are the three parts to this power? The beast (a revived political Romanism); second, the false prophet (the second beast, representing America); and third, the dragon, representing the spiritualistic phenomena associated with false signs, wonders, miracles, and tongues—as well as occult manifestations. It is the power of the dragon that pulls the other two together, according to Revelation 13:12-14.

Genuine Versus Counterfeit Miracles

One of the major characteristics of this unholy trinity is the performance of miracles and wonders, as well as tongues speaking, as they seek to attract the world's attention. One must always remember that biblically, these are gifts that God at times gives to His church. At the end, the unholy trinity counterfeits these signs, wonders, and miracles. At the same time, signs and wonders will also become the order of the day among God's people.

This creates confusion, which is Satan's aim. Genuine tongues and miracles will be performed alongside the counterfeit tongues and miracles. That is why one cannot make a decision for truth based on the miraculous. The devil will attempt to duplicate every genuine miracle or tongue God supplies. The Christian in the last days must test everything by the Word of God. Miracles, signs, wonders, and tongues can never determine truth.

The gift of tongues was prominent in the early church, along with all the other spiritual gifts, because the church was empowered by the Holy Spirit. The Holy Spirit manifests Himself with the outpouring of spiritual gifts, one of which is the gift of tongues. However, the gift of tongues in the early church was the very least of the gifts that were given, and never was regarded as an absolute necessity for every believer (1 Corinthians 12:28-31). Yet in the modern usage of this gift, some make it the defining gift of the Spirit and the authenticator of the baptism of the Spirit. This belief is totally contrary to scripture, and when employed, should signal the presence of the counterfeit gift of tongues.

In fact, Paul argues in 1 Corinthians 14:22, 23 against undue use of the gift of tongues. Paul claims that the gift of tongues is not to be used in the church but in the world. As believers would come in contact with individuals in the world who did not speak their language, God would miraculously give them the gift of tongues in order to communicate the gospel to them. Since that was the biblical function of the gift, Paul declares that when believers who all spoke the same language came together, there was no need of utilizing the gift of tongues.

How can one tell the genuine from the counterfeit? It is not always easy. However, if someone uses miracles and tongues to supersede the plainly revealed truth of God, we can be certain that the manifestations are not genuine. In John 16:13, Jesus declares that the genuine Holy Spirit will not speak about Himself and will lead believers into all truth. One should be cautious of those who speak in tongues and only talk about the Spirit. The Holy Spirit doesn't push Himself into the spotlight—He exalts Jesus. The only spirit that is always uplifting himself is Lucifer (Isaiah 14:13). The Holy Spirit leads people into truth. God's truth is contained in His Word—the Bible. Anyone who uses a manifestation of the Spirit, such as speaking in tongues, to avoid keeping and following the Bible, has a false gift. That is certain. The genuine Holy Spirit will lead us into the truth of the Word, never away from it.

The true evidence of Spirit possession is not the physical phenomena of shouting, dancing, falling prostrate, speaking in tongues, or even miracles. The true evidence of the indwelling of the Holy Spirit is seen in the fruit of the Spirit in the lives of transformed individuals who implicitly follow the Word of God (Galatians 5:22, 23).

In the last days when the unholy trinity exerts its power, it will use miracles, signs, wonders, and tongues to deceive people into worshiping the Roman beast. The ultimate end of all these counterfeit miracles is the attempt to enforce by legislation the mark of the beast. Immediately after describing all the miraculous things the unholy trinity does, John declares what happens as a result of all these miracles:

> And he deceives those who dwell on the earth by those signs which he was granted to do in the sight of the beast, telling those who dwell on the earth to make an image to the beast who was wounded by the sword and lived. Revelation 13:14.

Note that it is the purpose of the miracles to enable the unholy trinity to gain credence among the people and persuade them to make an image to the beast. The beast power, as described in Revelation 13:1-10, was a union of church and state. Therefore, an image to the beast would be an American likeness to the first beast—an American union of church and state. How does this happen? It occurs because the performance of false miracles and tongues influences people to believe that God is leading in this movement.

Today, the vast majority of church-going people are biblically illiterate. Most cannot name even half of the Ten Commandments. George Barna, respected researcher, has discovered that as many as three out of four regular attenders in the churches are not biblical Christians—they are simply attending the most visible of Christian events: the weekly service (*Ministry Currents,* George Barna, Oct.-Dec. 1992, p. 3). These people are ignorant of the very faith they profess to embrace. No wonder people today are wide open for deception.

Many are caught up in the emotion of a worship service rather than enjoying the Bible study aspect. They take pleasure in all the miracles, signs, and tongues being manifested in many services, but lack a genuine Christian experience based on the Word of God.

On the other hand, many unchurched people today are dabbling in the occult and New Age philosophy. In reality, there may be little difference between the religion of the New Age and much of what is being presented as Christianity in today's churches. We are witnessing a mixture of Christianity with pagan practices that is unprecedented in Christian history.

> Such new spiritual capacities intrigue old-style social-gospel liberals from mainline denominations. White House spokesman Neil Lattimore denied that there were séances; but official sources have acknowledged that Jean Houston led Mrs. Clinton, a United Methodist, in "imaginary conversations" with figures of the past, such as Eleanor Roosevelt and Hindu peace activist Mahatma Gandhi. "We have to draw strength from wherever we can, to make it from day to day," said the White House chief of staff, underplaying the enormity of these revelations. Nancy Reagan's dalliance with astrology pales to insignificance compared with Hillary Clinton's "reaching out and searching hard" away from her Christian roots into the pagan core of the new Religious Left's occult spirituality.
> —Peter Jones. *Pagans in the Pews*. Regal: Ventura, California. 2001.

What is happening in modern American Christianity appears to be two separate movements. Among the liberal branch of Christianity in America, there is this movement to raw paganism and occult behavior as testified to above. On the other hand, the tongues, miracles, and wonders of the religious right also appear to be a form of spiritualism. Note how a person speaking in tongues and a spiritualistic medium describe identical experiences:

> As my friends began to pray over me, I felt a strange physical sensation start in my hands and feet and gradually spread over my whole body. It was like an electrical current or as though the inside of my body were shaking against my skin.
> —Roger Alexander, describing his experience in speaking in tongues. Roger Alexander, "The Holy Spirit at Michigan State," *Act: Today's News of the Holy Spirit's Renewal*, Sept.-Oct. 1967, p.23.

In entering the trance condition, your hands and body may twist and jerk, as if you were being treated to a series of galvanic shocks. When the spirit enters, in the arms are felt peculiar, tingling sensations, like needles and pins, something akin to a current of electricity passing through from head to foot."

—Vishita, Bhakta Swami, *Genuine Mediumship*. Chas. T. Powner, Publisher, Chicago 1941, p. 37.

It is fascinating to see the similarities between these two experiences. Could it be the same spirit in both? Amazingly, the two extreme wings of Christianity—the radical right and the liberal left—are both dabbling in the spirit world. Revelation 13 predicted that the power of the dragon in spiritualistic phenomena would bring together the two powers that will unite for the final enforcing of the mark of the beast. Perhaps it is starting to happen.

A person who formerly spoke in tongues describes what happened in a couple of meetings where people were speaking in tongues. What happened here caused him to leave. You can understand why.

"But," someone might ask, "didn't the interpretation of the tongues benefit the church?" To answer that let me tell a couple of incidents with which I am personally familiar. In one meeting I was in, a certain person spoke in a tongue and another gave the interpretation. Then a third person stood up, a visitor. He said, "I am a Jew. I have heard of this gift of tongues and I came to see what it was all about. That was Hebrew that that person was speaking, but he was not praising God as the so-called interpreter said he was doing. Instead he was cursing God!"

—*Praise the Lord*, pp. 108, 109.

On another occasion when I was present, a local member gave an utterance, and he was interpreted as saying, "I am God, give me your worship and praise." But there was a couple visiting that night from New York. The man stood and introduced himself. He said, "I have visited Pentecostal meetings several times, but I have never before heard anyone speaking in tongues. I came tonight because I wanted to hear what it was like. I am Italian, and that message was in Italian. But instead of "I am God," as the interpreter said, the message actually was, "I am Satan—I am your lord and master."

—James Beshires Jr., *Praise the Lord*, p. 109.

Note the clear connection between this false speaking in tongues and the power of Satan. The religious right has been caught up in spirit manifestations that are consistent with its view of Christianity. Yet the source of the manifestations in many cases appears to be the devil himself. On the other hand, the liberal left, without a biblical anchor, has substituted paganism for the Bible and intertwined their religion with occult spiritualism. But the two are not as far apart as they appear outwardly—both groups are being controlled by demonic spirits.

The 60s movement did not rebel against religion. It rebelled against the *Christian* religion. The dust of history has settled enough to see that the counterculture movement of the '60s did not seek secularization but a radically different spirituality.

Baby Boomers were "a generation of seekers." Only 4 percent of them are atheists or agnostics. The rest follow some religion. Our declining moral standards are not because we are no longer religious but because we have changed religions. The noble search for expanded consciousness and alternate spiritualities in the '60s led East, where seekers discovered mysticism and returned to spawn a relativistic religious hybrid: Western spiritual monism.

This new pagan monism joins the Eastern religious idea that "all is one and one is all" to Western technology, democratic self-determination and the ideal of autonomous egalitarianism. The whole is clothed in "Christian" dress for general Western consumption. The mix has created a potent elixir that fires the minds and hearts of social transformers in this new millennium.

—Peter Jones, *Pagans in the Pews*, p. 30.

Thus a new paganism, laced with spiritualistic phenomena, has taken control of much of the liberal wing of Christianity. Without the sure anchor of God's Word, these people have left their Christian moorings and returned to medieval paganism.

At the same time, much of the religious right has moved into a dependence upon spiritualistic phenomena in the shape of tongues and miracles instead of the Bible. What these two opposite groups have failed to realize is that they have both ended up in the same place: controlled by the power of demons instead of the Word of God. Could it be that soon these two extremes will discover their common roots and then unite to bring about the establishment of the image of the beast?

The Fulfillment

The liberal wing of Christianity has always been politically active, whereas the more conservative wing has stood firm on the principle of the separation of church and state. It would not be difficult for the liberal wing to maintain a political agenda, since they are already involved; however, what is fascinating today is to observe the religious right also seeking a political agenda. When the religious right inaugurated the Moral Majority in the early 1980s, an editorial appeared in the Washington state chapter of the Moral Majority. It made this startling statement:

Separation of church and state is a dangerous concept
. . . . Our constitution prohibits the establishment of religion and guarantees the free exercise thereof. The "establishment

clause" means that the Baptists, Assemblies of God, Catholics, Lutherans, or Mormon church can never become the "official church" in America. The free exercise clause means that the government is powerless to be involved in the regulation of belief or church activities. It does not mean that our beliefs cannot be legislated or church attending people elected to office. A thorough understanding of our constitution is vital to our survival. Let's talk more like the constitution and less like a bumper sticker. Wipe the phrase separation of church and state out of your vocabulary.

—*Editorial for Moral Majority*, Washington State, August 1980.

It is clear that at the heart of what the religious right has been unsuccessful thus far in attempting is to enforce their version of Christianity upon America. Their ideal is to return America to the days before the constitution was enacted, when religion was enforced upon the citizenry. Listen to Pat Robertson describe this goal:

The founders of America—at Plymouth Rock and in the Massachusetts Colony—felt that they were organizing a society based on the Ten Commandments and the Sermon on the Mount. They perceived this new land as a successor to the nation of Israel, and they tried their best to model their institutions of governmental order after the Bible. In fact the man who interpreted the meaning of Scripture to them, the pastor, was given a higher place than the governor of the colony. These people built an incredible society because they exalted "the mountain of the Lord's house" above the other mountains.

There is no other way to explain the success of this experiment in liberty other than to realize that for almost two hundred years prior to our Constitution, all of the leadership of this nation had been steeped in the biblical principles of the Old and New Testaments. Their new order was a nation founded squarely on concepts of the nature of God, the

nature of man, the role of the family, and the moral order as
established by the God of Jacob.
—Pat Robertson, *The New World Order*, 1991, p. 246.

Make no mistake about the aims of the religious right. Pat
Robertson has left us in little doubt. He feels that the best days
of America were when religion was enforced by the state. According to him, America lost it when she inaugurated the Constitution providing for the separation of church and state. To
save America, we must recreate the religious state of early
America. That was when people were placed in the stocks for
Sabbath-breaking. Why does Pat Robertson desire to move
America back there? His answer is unnerving:

The next obligation that a citizen of God's world order
owes is to himself. "Remember the Sabbath day, to keep it
holy," is a command for the personal benefit of each citizen.
… Only when people are permitted to rest from their labors,
to meditate on God, to consider His way, to dream of a better world can there be progress and genuine human better-
ment.… Laws in America that mandated a day of rest from
incessant commerce have been nullified as a violation of the
separation of church and state.
—Pat Robertson, *The New World Order*, 1991, p. 236.

This issue that is driving the religious right is made clear
by Pat Robertson. They cannot enforce Sunday worship as long
as we have the protection of the separation of church and state.
No wonder they want to eliminate this separation. In light of
the prediction of Revelation 13 that this second beast would
someday enforce the worship of the first beast (Sunday worship), this statement by Pat Robertson is chillingly clear.

Have we reached the fulfillment of Revelation 13 yet? No,
but there are movements occurring that certainly are leading
in that direction. The Roman church and the religious right
have become more closely associated in recent years than in
the entire history of the Reformation.

A group of 40 prominent evangelical and Catholic scholars and leaders has agreed that Christians must stop aggressive proselytizing of one another's flocks and work together more closely to "contend against all that opposes Christ and His cause...."

Not since the 16th century have Protestants and Catholics "joined in a declaration so clear in respect to their common faith and common responsibility." Said Richard John Neuhaus, a Catholic priest and head of the Institute on Religion and Public Life...

What brought the two communities together to this point, some signers said, are the experiences of worshiping together in the charismatic movement and working together for political causes, such as the pro-life movement. Evangelical Protestants have much more in common with Bible-believing Catholics than with liberal Protestants."

—*National & International Religion Report*, April 4, 1994, p. 1.

With the religious right joining hands with Romanists, it would take no stretch of the imagination to see how the new paganism of the religious left could easily join the coalition, ultimately creating the unholy trinity. How soon this will happen, no one knows, but certainly Bible-believing Christians ought to watch these developments very carefully.

Having joined together in common cause, they will then attempt to enforce their religion on everyone else, with dire consequences for non-compliance. Notice how Revelation 13 concludes with the enforcement of the mark of the beast:

He was granted power to give breath to the image of the beast, that the image of the beast should both speak and cause as many as would not worship the image of the beast to be killed. He causes all, both small and great, rich and poor, free and slave, to receive a mark on their right hand or on their foreheads, and that no one may buy or sell except one who has the mark or the name of the beast, or the number of his name. Revelation 13:15-17.

The ultimate end of all these miraculous, occult, spiritualistic phenomena is the enforcement of the mark of the beast. The ultimate penalty will be death to those who fail to follow, but first there will be severe economic restrictions so that no one can buy or sell unless they have the mark of the beast. The attempt to inflict these penalties is what is described in Revelation 16 and Daniel 11 that we have already studied. Revelation 13 is simply providing greater details of the issues involved in the final conflict that results in the battle of Armageddon.

The New Testament always correlates doctrine and experience. When I have God's truth, it leads to an experience with this God. It never moves from experience to truth. That can only lead to the acceptance of a counterfeit. But people will argue that because it is supernatural, it must be from God. Once we admit the presence of the counterfeit, the argument from experience to truth fails. It must always be the truth of God's Word first that leads me to an experience with the living God. The Bible must always be first. That is how we judge what is truth and what is error.

People may say that God is with them when they keep man's Sunday because of the gift of tongues, miracles, or spiritualistic séances among them. Thus, all who accept physical manifestations above the plainly revealed will of God in scripture will be deceived. Matthew 24:24 indicates that if it were possible, these false signs and miracles would deceive even the very elect.

God's people, the saints of Revelation 14:12 who keep the commandments, can maintain the position "It is written," in spite of the miracles and the tongues. Their defense is biblical revelation, not supernatural physical manifestations. And God honors them. Revelation 14:18-20 reveals one final angel coming down, who has power over this fire, and when earth's harvest is reaped, those who have accepted the spurious revival of tongues and miracles instead of biblical revival will be cast into the winepress of God's wrath. And the outward issue dividing the two camps will be the Sabbath of the fourth commandment. Those who have kept the Sabbath commandment have naturally developed a deep experience with God through obedience to His Word. Why not choose right now to prepare for this final hour by finding the intense relationship with Jesus inherent in biblical Sabbath keeping?

Hope for God's Remnant People

Hardship, persecution, and even death have confronted the followers of Jesus throughout the 2,000-year journey of the Christian church. Yet amid the storms that have buffeted God's church, hope always springs to life amid the most discouraging of situations. That hope is an unshakable faith in the return of Jesus. No matter how difficult the situation, the hope of seeing Jesus the second time has encouraged God's faithful ones to present a consistent witness throughout the ages. Even while being burned at the stake, that hope caused them to sing forth with joyous praise.

In all of the uncertain times of history, God has always had a faithful people who have remained loyal and true to Jesus no matter how difficult the situation. Even in the darkest hours of persecution when it appeared that Satan's counterfeit would surely dominate the church, God had His faithful witnesses who held true to the gospel.

Revelation 12 traces the history of God's faithful people down through the Christian age. It depicts the struggles, conflicts, and victories of the loyal followers of Jesus in every age.

The story of God's church revealed here provides courage and hope to the people of God as they face the final conflict of the ages. Just as God has been with His servants in times past, God's last-day people can know that He will be with them in the last crisis.

Now a great sign appeared in heaven: a woman clothed

with the sun, with the moon under her feet, and on her head a garland of twelve stars. Then being with child, she cried out in labor and in pain to give birth. Revelation 12:1, 2.

In prophecy, a woman is symbolic of the church (Jeremiah 6:2). Revelation 12 depicts the church at the time of the birth of Christ. The Old Testament church is here depicted as giving birth to the Messiah, the Christ. The woman is revealed as standing on the moon and clothed with the sun. The moon is a reflected light, while the sun would denote full reality.

Since the moon reflects the light of the sun, the woman standing on the moon would indicate that the New Testament church does not abolish the Old Testament, with its reflected light of sacrifices and ordinances. Instead, the New Testament church builds on the foundation laid in the Old Testament. The system of animal sacrifices dimly reflects, like the moon, the reality of the gospel of Christ. That is why Revelation 12 pictures the church standing on the moon. It is built upon the foundation of the Old Testament, yet it clothes that foundation with the glory and reality of the gospel of Christ, the Sun of Righteousness (Malachi 4:2). The church in both testaments is one. The church of God in the Old Testament continues in the New Testament but now is clothed in the bright beams of the light of Calvary.

Revelation 12 is depicting the church at the time of the birth of Christ. The woman is with child, and that child is clearly Jesus (Revelation 12:5). The enemy, Satan, is quickly introduced in verses 3 and 4 as he attempts to attack the church and destroy the child that the woman produces. Here is the theme of this great chapter. There is a mighty controversy between Christ and Satan. This chapter depicts that conflict from the birth of Christ and continuing throughout the Christian era. The dragon is used to symbolize Satan, the archenemy of God and His people.

The introductory verses give us the historical setting for the conflict that will be portrayed in this chapter. Satan attempts to destroy the man-child (Christ). Yet he is unsuccessful, for the man-child is victorious and escapes the dragon by ascending into heaven as Victor over death and the grave. The passage very quickly passes over the history of the life of Christ, for its purpose is to reveal this great controversy that continues behind the scenes in every era.

With the ascension of Jesus, Satan turns his vicious attacks on the church that Jesus leaves behind. Revelation 12:6 describes the church fleeing into the wilderness to escape the fierce assaults of its adversary. Even though Jesus won the battle at Calvary, Satan still continues the war as a defeated foe.

The Great Controversy

The first six verses of Revelation 12 have revealed a powerful conflict going on between Jesus and Satan. The church gives birth to the Christ-child, but Satan attacks him. The child wins the battle and escapes to heaven, but Satan continues the aggression against the church left behind. The church flees to the wilderness, but Satan follows. All this is the setting for the main theme of the chapter and of the entire book of Revelation. It is depicted clearly in the verses 7-12, which is the very apex of the message of the book of Revelation.

> And war broke out in heaven: Michael and his angels fought with the dragon; and the dragon and his angels fought, but they did not prevail, nor was a place found for them in heaven any longer. So the great dragon was cast out, that serpent of old, called the Devil and Satan, who deceives the whole world; he was cast to the earth, and his angels were cast out with him. Then I heard a loud voice saying in heaven, "Now salvation, and strength, and the kingdom of our God, and the power of His Christ have come, for the accuser of our brethren, who accused them before our God day and night, has been cast down. And they overcame him by the blood of the Lamb and by the word of their testimony, and they did not

love their lives to the death. Therefore rejoice, O heavens, and you who dwell in them! Woe to the inhabitants of the earth and the sea! For the devil has come down to you, having great wrath, because he knows that he has a short time." Revelation 12:7-12.

Imagine that scene—war in heaven. Satan, originally named Lucifer, was the highest of created beings, but he rebelled, and war ensued in heaven. Satan was cast down to this earth, successfully tempted Adam and Eve to sin, and thereby regained entrance into heaven to represent this world, claiming that this world belonged to him. Yet God did not give up on Planet Earth. He sent His Son, Jesus, who died and gained the victory on every point that caused Adam to fall. The second Adam successfully won the battle over Satan and then died as humankind's Redeemer. Revelation 12 depicts the final victory of Calvary, gained by Jesus on the cross. As a result, the accuser of the brethren is cast down.

Jesus is victorious over Satan. The battle has been won. Satan is defeated. That is the resounding message of Revelation 12. It is the heart and center of this passage, but it also encapsulates the entire book of Revelation. In some respects, verses 7-12 summarize the entire Bible story. The ones who follow Jesus claim His victory. They overcome the devil through the blood of the Lamb and the word of their testimony.

There may be a great controversy going on between Christ and Satan, and the human race may be caught in the middle, but the message of this chapter rings out loud and clear: Jesus and His people will win the great controversy. The battle was won on Calvary. God's people need only to claim that tremendous victory of Jesus. Just because Jesus won at Calvary does not mean the end of Satan. That victory of Calvary must also be demonstrated by the loyalty of the followers of Jesus throughout history. The rest of Revelation 12 depicts the awesome story of God's church down through the ages, revealing that in spite of all the persecution thrown at the church by the adversary, God has always had victorious, faithful people on His side.

The Story of the Faithful

Now when the dragon saw that he had been cast to the earth, he persecuted the woman who gave birth to the male Child. But the woman was given two wings of a great eagle, that she might fly into the wilderness to her place, where she is nourished for a time and times and half a time, from the presence of the serpent. Revelation 12:13, 14.

Notice that in Revelation 12, verses 13 and 14 repeat verse 6. Verses 7-12 are parenthetical to the story but have actually given us the background to understand what is occurring in the relentless conflict of the church. Now the Revelator returns to the story of the church under the attack of Satan. The devil persecutes, but the faithful are nourished in the wilderness for the 1,260 years of the church's apostasy.

Persecution for the church of Jesus began very early. In A.D. 34, Stephen became the first of the Christian martyrs, but persecution was to continue for nearly three hundred years under the relentless rule of Rome. Christianity became an outlawed sect. Those who remained loyal to Jesus had property confiscated, and many were tortured and killed for their faith. In Rome, Christians were burned at the stake in the arena as living torches to illuminate the scene below, as other Christians were torn apart by wild animals. To be a Christian in such a time required a steadfast faith in the One who is the ultimate Deliverer.

Yet these Christians died with such tremendous victory that many pagans took their places, inspired by a faith that persecution could not kill. The blood of the martyrs indeed became the seed of the church. In A.D. 313, when the persecution ended under the Edict of Milan, a council of the church was held. Many leaders attended. What a sight they were! Some had limbs torn from their bodies; others suffered from eyes that had been gouged out during the persecution, but all were happy in the service of the Lord Jesus. How precious they were in the sight of God!

Satan was not happy with the advance of Christianity. In spite of the persecution, the church was growing everywhere. The enemy of the church realized that the persecution of believers was not eradicating the church but increasing it. So the devil decided to change tactics. Instead of overtly persecuting the church, the devil decided to enter the church and corrupt it from within. The church may have more to fear from compromise within than all the overt persecution that confronts it.

Over the course of the next hundred years, great changes entered the church. With the conversion of Constantine, the Roman emperor, to Christianity, the persecuted religion soon became the legislated religion of the Roman Empire. With pagans flooding into the church, many changes were made to the Christian faith to make it easier for the pagans to adjust.

Pagans had been used to multiple gods and goddesses, whereas Christians worshiped only one God. To make it easier for the pagans, the martyrs of the church were elevated, and people were told that they could pray to the martyrs, who were made saints. This quickly replaced the household gods of ancient paganism. In place of a female deity, Mary, the mother of Jesus, was elevated, and Christians were told to pray to her. The veneration of relics of early Christianity provided something tangible for Christians to worship—such as a splinter of wood that was said to come from the cross, or a morsel of bread that was declared to be used at the Last Supper.

Further compromises followed quickly. Pagans were accustomed to sacrificing to their gods, but Christianity worshiped a God who Himself became the Sacrifice, once and for all. Therefore, there was no need of a continual office of sacrifice. To appease the pagans, the beautiful symbolism of the Lord's Supper was changed by declaring that the bread, instead of being a symbol of the body of Jesus, was instead His actual body. And the wine, likewise, was transformed into the actual blood of Jesus. Thus, when the priest consecrated the emblems, they became the actual body and blood of Jesus, which was then uplifted in a form of sacrifice. So instead of the once-for-all sacrifice of Jesus, Christians now had the daily sacrifice of the mass.

Other doctrines soon were introduced or expanded that conflicted with early Christianity. The counterfeit Sabbath on Sunday that was already being practiced at Rome was now expanded and forced upon all Christians. Likewise, the pagan doctrine of natural immortality and eternal torment were popularized and made a part of the Christian faith.

The result was that by the end of the fourth century, Christianity no longer resembled the faith that was persecuted in the third century. Dark Ages Christianity had become the accepted norm. What were the true followers of Jesus to do in the midst of all this apostasy? Flee to the wilderness. Revelation 12:6,13, 14 declared that the true church indeed would have to flee to obscurity during the reign of the Dark Ages Church. Therefore, we find Christ's followers worshiping in mountain strongholds and caves for the next 1,260 years, while apostate Christianity dominated the church.

The Church in the Wilderness

The true church of Jesus dwindled during the reign of apostate Rome. Faithful servants of God continued to worship Him according to scripture, but they were few. It was indeed a period of hiding for the church. Copies of scripture were rare, and if one had even a small portion, it was well hidden. If the authorities discovered anyone with scripture, they could be killed. The Bible was only in the hands of the apostate church. When one possessed even the smallest part of scripture, it was always concealed and only pulled out and read when it was safe. How precious was the Bible in those days.

The devil was not happy. Even though he had conquered most of the church, there still remained those who held high the truth of God. Thus Satan must do all he could to eliminate these believers so his control would be complete.

"So the serpent spewed water out of his mouth like a flood after the woman, that he might cause her to be carried away by the flood" (Revelation 12:15).

Soon, Satan unleashed a flood of persecution in an attempt to drown the church of the wilderness. Families worshiping God in secret caves were flushed out and killed, and the relentless persecution of dissenters began, which continued for over one thousand years. Once again, to be a Christian was punishable by death. The irony of this persecution was that it was accomplished by those who claimed to be followers of the meek and mild Jesus.

Yet in spite of all the persecution, God's true church of the wilderness prevailed. It appeared as if it would be snuffed out, but it remained true. After nearly one thousand years of persecution, truth again began to illuminate the darkness of the Middle Ages. Martin Luther, the great Reformer, discovered the grand truth that one is saved not by works performed but solely by the grace of Christ. This light hit the established church like a lightning strike. Attempts were made to silence his voice, but this truth was unstoppable. As Luther declared:

> Unless I am convinced by Scripture and plain reason—I do not accept the authority of the popes and councils, for they have contradicted each other—my conscience is captive to the Word of God. I cannot and I will not recant anything for to go against conscience is neither right nor safe. God help me. Amen.
>
> —Martin Luther at the Imperial Diet of Worms, 1521.

His moving stand aroused the princes of Germany to come to his defense against Rome, and the Protestant Reformation was born. Light once again began to emerge from the darkness of the hour.

Yet even Luther's strong stand did not stop the relentless persecution. For another two hundred years it continued throughout Europe. Even the young Protestant churches followed the example of Mother Rome in persecuting those who disagreed with her. It appeared as if the true faith would never be allowed to emerge from the darkness of persecution. Yet God had promised in Revelation 12:16 that the earth (symbol of the United States) would open her doors and swallow up the flood of persecution. Thus at the end of the 1,260-year period of the church in the wilderness, the Constitution of the United States was voted, with its Bill of Rights, separating state from church and providing a place of freedom for the persecuted church of Jesus. At last, the time was ripe for the church to reemerge out of the wilderness. Here at the end of time, God would still have a faithful remnant who would remain loyal and true to Jesus amid the final onslaught of the enemy.

The Emergence of the Remnant

> And the dragon was enraged with the woman, and he went to make war with the rest of her offspring, who keep the commandments of God and have the testimony of Jesus Christ. Revelation 12:17.

At the end of the 1,260 years, the church is to emerge out of the wilderness. God had miraculously preserved His church during this time of deep apostasy. All the threats against the church, both internal and external, could not destroy the church that Christ had established. Yet even this long wilderness pilgrimage, in which Satan seemed to be in control and the church was in hiding, did not destroy Satan's desire to eliminate the church.

The final days arrive, and Satan unleashes his last great fury against the church Christ established. This time, Revelation 12:17 declares Satan is enraged and engages the church in one final onslaught of war. This war is waged against the "rest" of the woman's offspring—the remnant, as other translations render it. The remnant is the last end of the church—

the church of the last days. Against this final true church of Jesus, all the fiery darts of the wicked one will be hurled, but God's faithful people will still prevail. The resounding message of this chapter is that God's church and God's truth will prevail against whatever Satan throws against the church.

The battle of Revelation 12:17 is the same one described in Daniel 11:40-45, Revelation 13:11-17, and Revelation 16:16. Each of these passages describes earth's final battle in different ways, but each one contains the same ultimate truth: God's church will triumph. The question is: will we triumph with it?

God will have a people who will be loyal to Him in earth's last hour. They are identified here as the remnant who keep the commandments of God and have the testimony of Jesus. Evidently, commandment keeping is to be the telltale sign of God's church in the end time. One must always remember that God has honest people in all churches who are serving Christ to the best of their knowledge. However, in the end time, God will ultimately call all of His people into full obedience to all the commandments of God.

To be a commandment-keeping church, the church must obviously keep all the commandments of God, including the fourth commandment that requires the observance of the seventh-day Sabbath. Revelation 12:17 indicates that this will be the telltale evidence that the church is loyal to Jesus. Despite the fact that not all Christians are obeying all of God's Ten Commandments, they still remain God's people. That's why God wants us to proclaim this message, so that all God's children can enjoy this deep personal relationship with Jesus that Sabbath keeping brings. Ultimately, all the faithful will see this great Sabbath blessing and become a part of what will be the final remnant that keep the commandments of God.

As we have mentioned, God's people are in all churches of all denominations. Interestingly, even though many churches are not living in full harmony with scripture, God continues to use them where they are to bring people to some knowledge of Himself. However, God has called into being a special people in the last days who preach a full message of Bible truth, including the keeping of all the commandments of God. They are not better than any other church, but God has called them into existence to proclaim this special message at the end time. That church is the Seventh-day Adventist church.

The Seventh-day Adventist church is one of the few churches calling people to keep the seventh-day Sabbath of scripture. It is not the individuals who have been called, it is the message they proclaim, that makes them special. The people are just like anyone else, but they proclaim a distinct end-time message to share with the world. In addition to keeping the commandments of God, the church that proclaims the last message will also have these characteristics:

1. They will hold to the testimony of Jesus (Revelation 12:17). The testimony of Jesus is the spirit of prophecy. Revelation 19:10. We will examine this characteristic in the next chapter.

2. They preach the special message of the three angels (Revelation 14:6-12). These three messages center on the everlasting gospel. So the remnant message is a gospel-centered message revealing the awesome truth of the pre-advent judgment, the fall of Babylon, and the warning against the mark of the beast.

3. This unique message is proclaimed worldwide (Revelation 14:6).

As one examines these characteristics, it is clear that only the Seventh-day Adventist church is in harmony with these characteristics. While God continues to use all churches to advance His cause, He has called the Seventh-day Adventist church into existence in these final days to proclaim this unique message and call God's people to full obedience to all the commandments of God.

As you come to know Jesus better and understand His

message for the end time through the pages of this book, it will become clear to you that the unique message of the Seventh-day Adventist Church is true and biblical. Knowing this, we invite you to join us as we proclaim this special message. To become a part of this final movement is not to renounce your past Christian experience but to build on it. God has led you in the past. Now He continues to lead you into the future. Remember that God always leads you in harmony with His Word. Now He calls you to a deeper walk with Him through full obedience to all His commandments and sharing the message of the three angels with others.

As you prepare for the final days of earth's history, God invites you to be a part of a movement that today encircles the earth, with a message being proclaimed in nearly every country on the planet. Will you respond to God's call to you to follow this message of truth by contacting your local Seventh-day Adventist Church and inquiring how you can have a part in sharing this last message to the world?

26

The Prophetic Word Brings Hope

The last days of Planet Earth are filled with calamity and trouble on every side. Yet in the midst of these troublous times, the people of God find hope and peace. The assurance of Revelation 12 that God is with His people throughout their persecuted history provides hope for Christ's followers who keep the commandments of God in the last days. They are no different than Christ's followers in every age. The only difference is that they will witness the visible return of Jesus to this earth.

Revelation 12:17 identifies these people as the ones who keep the commandments of God and have the testimony of Jesus. Keeping all the commandments, including the seventh-day Sabbath, has helped them develop such a relationship with Jesus that they trust Him implicitly in this final journey of faith. In addition, God has given them the testimony of Jesus to strengthen and encourage them in the last days. What is the testimony of Jesus? Revelation 19:10 declares it to be the spirit of prophecy.

God has always encouraged His people through the gift of prophecy. In every age of the church, throughout both testaments, the gift of prophecy was given to the faithful people of God to bring encouragement and strength to them. It would not therefore be unusual for God once again to comfort His last-day people with the prophetic gift. Revelation 12:17 indicates that He will do this and that the presence of this precious gift of prophecy will be another sign that God is with them.

How God Communicates

Since the prophetic gift is to be given in the last days, let us briefly examine how God communicates with His people in any age. God declares that He will do nothing in the earth without first revealing what He will do through His servants, the prophets (Amos 3:7). The prophets were to be spokespeople for God. God communicated with the prophets through the Holy Spirit (2 Peter 1:21). The messages of the biblical prophets did not come from human origins, but were the result of the impression of the Holy Spirit on the minds of the prophets.

This Holy Spirit impressed the minds of the prophets through visions and dreams (Numbers 12:6). A dream or vision is an impression made on the mind of a prophet, in which God reveals things to this person. The prophet may then write out what has been shown. God inspires the thoughts of each prophet, but the messages are written in their own words. This is why two prophets seeing the same vision would each use different words to express it, much as two people observing the same accident would report it differently. Yet each recounting would be an inspired description of the vision. In the life of Christ, four gospel writers tell the gospel story, each in their own words, but all are inspired of God.

God uses different people as prophets. Sometimes God utilizes educated people like Moses and Paul. Other times, He uses humble shepherds like Amos. Sometimes God uses men; other times women, as His spokespersons. The Bible records that Miriam, Deborah, Huldah, Anna, and Philip's daughters were given the gift of prophecy.

There also appear to be two groups of prophets in the Bible: those whose writings are preserved in the canon of scripture—and those who were equally inspired, but whose writings have not been preserved. For example, Elijah was a mighty prophet, but there is no book of Elijah in scripture. This would indicate that one could be an inspired prophet without adding to the unique collection of the Bible.

The gift of prophecy is one of the spiritual gifts God has given to guide the church to the very end of time:

> And He Himself gave some to be apostles, some prophets, some evangelists, and some pastors and teachers, for the equipping of the saints for the work of ministry, for the edifying of the body of Christ, till we all come to the unity of the faith and of the knowledge of the Son of God, to a perfect man, to the measure of the stature of the fullness of Christ. Ephesians 4:11-13.

Note that all these gifts, including the gift of prophecy, are to remain in the church until it reaches the full unity of its faith, which will not happen until the second coming of Jesus. This is why the gift of prophecy remains in the church until the very end of human history. The gift is needed to help the church develop into maturity.

Today, many have misunderstood the gift of prophecy, feeling that it refers to one who predicts the future. That is a possible meaning of the word, and some Bible prophets did predict the future. However, that was never the main work of the prophets. The New Testament declares that the main work of the prophetic gift is edification, exhortation, and comfort (1 Corinthians 14:3).

Prophets After Bible Times

Was the prophetic gift to continue in the church after the New Testament was written? There are several indications in the scripture that this gift will continue to the very end. Ephesians 4:11-13 clearly indicates this to be the case. However, other passages also declare this to be true. First Thessalonians 5:19-21 tells us not to despise prophesyings. Obviously, if the gift was to be eliminated from the church after Bible times, Paul would have warned us to avoid all prophets. But instead, he tells us not to despise them, but to test them to see if they are from God. The fact that they must be tested indicates the presence of both genuine and counterfeit. Thus arises the need to verify the claim by the previous revelations of God's Word, the Bible. Jesus gives a similar indication in Matthew 7:15, where He provides a warning, not against all prophets, but against false prophets.

Malachi 4:5, 6 predicts that before the great and dreadful day of the Lord, God would send Elijah, the prophet. Note it is not just Elijah, but Elijah the prophet. This prediction is not of the reincarnation of Elijah, but of one who comes as Elijah came. The first fulfillment occurred before the first coming of Jesus. God sent the second Elijah, John the Baptist, whom Jesus declared was the Elijah (Matthew 17:11-13). Accompanying John the Baptist was the gift of prophecy. Likewise, Malachi indicates that before the dreadful day of the Lord's second coming, God will again send the Elijah. Therefore we can expect that at the end of time, God will again send the prophetic gift to His people.

Joel 2:28-32 predicts a time when there will be a renewal of spiritual gifts—especially the gift of prophecy. This is to happen near the end when the sun is darkened and the moon turned to blood. At that time, Joel declares that God will call forth a remnant, and in this remnant there will be the prophetic gift. The final remnant was identified in the last chapter as those who keep the commandments of God and have the testimony of Jesus (Revelation 12:17). Revelation 19:10 indicates that the testimony of Jesus is the spirit of prophecy, and Revelation 22:9 utilizes the same words as Revelation 19:10, but instead of spirit of prophecy, uses the word *prophet*. Thus, God's last-day people are identified by the fact that they keep all of God's commandments and have the gift of a prophet in their midst. Has the gift of a prophet been given to God's last-day church, as He promised?

The Prophetic Gift Regiven

Throughout the Middle Ages, the prophetic gift appears to have disappeared from the church. Throughout the period of great apostasy, this spiritual gift seems to have been in obscurity. However, once the church emerges from the darkness of that era, the prophetic gift is to reappear.

In 1842, an African-American pastor, William Foy, was given several visions that he claimed to be from the Lord. He was then given a third vision, which he did not understand and did not relate. That ended his visions. Later, in 1844, Hazen Foss was also given this third vision, which later was discovered to be the same that William Foy had received. He too could not understand it and refused to relate it. Ultimately, his refusal caused the Holy Spirit to tell him that he had grieved the Spirit and that the visions would be taken from him and given to the weakest of the weak.

A few months later, in December 1844, as a group of young Methodist ladies were kneeling in prayer in Portland, Maine, one of their number—a seventeen-year-old girl in poor health—was taken off in vision. Her name was Ellen Harmon, later to be known as Ellen White. She was one who, at the time, could be described as the weakest of the weak.

Like those before her, she shrank back from the prophetic office, but being a sincere Christian, she dared not be disobedient to the heavenly vision. As she related the vision she had received, she continued to receive others, until her death in 1915.

For 69 years, she continued in the prophetic office, writing out what she declared to be visions from the Lord. As a result, she produced more literature than any other woman in American history. Was this a genuine manifestation of the gift of prophecy—or a counterfeit? Only as we test the claim can we verify its authenticity.

The first authentication needs to be in the supernaturalness of the gift. Can it be accounted for by natural means, or is there the evidence of the supernatural? Ellen White had certain physical phenomena that accompanied her in vision. For example, during a vision, she did not breathe. Some of her visions lasted for as long as four hours. Obviously, going without breathing for four hours, yet remaining alive, is evidence of a supernatural occurrence. On other occasions, Ellen White was given supernatural strength. While in vision once, she held a large family Bible weighing 17 pounds, extended on her arms for thirty minutes, and she was only a 97-pound weakling at the time—evidence again of the presence of supernatural power. The physical phenomena, however, do not indicate whether the prophet is genuine or counterfeit. They only reveal that we are dealing with a supernatural occurrence. Since there are two supernatural powers, one must apply the biblical tests of a prophet to discover which supernatural power is at work.

Tests of the Prophet

There are four biblical tests of a prophet. The first is Isaiah 8:20: "To the law and to the testimony! If they do not speak according to this word, it is because there is no light in them." The "law and the testimony" is an expression the Bible writers use for scripture. Therefore, this test indicates that a prophet must agree with scripture. The Bible must be first. If God speaks to a prophet today, that revelation must be in agreement with all previous revelations. You don't test the Bible by the modern-day prophet, but you do test the prophet by the Bible. In this case, Ellen White is consistent with scripture. All of her writings are in complete harmony with the Bible.

The second test of the prophet appears in 1 John 4:2: "By this you know the Spirit of God: Every spirit that confesses that Jesus Christ has come in the flesh is of God." The second tests call for the prophet to ring true on the full humanity and divinity of Christ. The prophet must uplift Jesus as the center of the Christian faith.

Here again, Ellen White shines. Everything she has written expresses a continual uplifting of Christ in all areas. Some of her books that especially illustrate this point are: *The Desire of Ages, Steps to Christ, Thoughts From the Mount of Blessing*, and *Christ's Object Lessons*. All of these books deal with the life of Jesus. In counseling pastors how they should preach, Ellen White wrote:

> Lift up Jesus, you that teach the people, lift Him up in sermon, in song, in prayer. Let all your powers be directed to pointing souls, confused, bewildered, lost, to the Lamb of God. Lift Him up, the risen Saviour, and say to all who hear, come to Him who "hath loved us, and hath given Himself for us." Let the science of salvation be the burden of every sermon, the theme of every song. Let it be poured forth in every supplication. Bring nothing into your preaching to supplement Christ, the wisdom and power of God. Hold forth the word of life, presenting Jesus as the hope of the penitent and the stronghold of every believer. Reveal the way of peace to the troubled and the despondent, and show forth the grace and completeness of the Saviour.—*Gospel Workers,* p. 160.

Obviously, Ellen White uplifts Jesus in all His fullness.

Jesus, in Matthew 7:16, gives the third test of a prophet: "You will know them by their fruits." Prophets were not perfect, but there would be consistency in their lives. Here is what the press said about Ellen White at her death:

> The life of Mrs. White is an example worthy of emulation by all. . . . She was a humble, devout disciple of Christ, and ever went about doing good . . . honored and respected by all who appreciate noble womanhood consecrated to unselfish labor for the uplifting and betterment of mankind. —*St. Helena Star,* St. Helena, California, July 23, 1915.

The fourth biblical test is found in Jeremiah 28:9: "When the word of the prophet comes to pass, the prophet will be known as one whom the Lord has truly sent." As noted earlier, biblical prophets did not always give predictions, but when they did, they can be tested by their fulfillment. Like most biblical prophets, Ellen White did not major in predictions, but she gave some, and here she can be tested. In 1890, long before the advent of modern transportation, Ellen White wrote:

> Disasters by rail will become more and more frequent; confusion, collision, and death without a moment's warning will occur on the great lines of travel.—*Messages to Young People*, p. 89. April 21, 1890.

Nearly one hundred years before September 11, 2001, Ellen White described the following scene in vision:

> In the night I was, I thought, in a room but not in my own house. I was in a city, where I knew not, and I heard expression after expression. I rose up quickly in bed, and saw from my window large balls of fire. Jetting out were sparks, in the form of arrows, and buildings were being consumed, and in a very few minutes the entire block of buildings was falling and the screeching and mournful groans came distinctly to my ears. I cried out, in my raised position, to learn what was happening: Where am I? And where are our family circle? Then I awoke. But I could not tell where I was for I was in another place than home.—*Manuscript Releases*, vol. 11, page 361. 1906.

Ellen White warned extensively about the rise of spiritualism as a major perversion of God's truth in the last days. When modern spiritualism began with the mysterious knockings in New York by the Fox sisters, Ellen White wrote:

> I saw that the mysterious knocking in New York . . . was the power of Satan, and that such things would be more and more common, clothed in a religious garb so as to lull the deceived to greater security.—*Early Writings*, p. 43.

Ellen White predicted that spiritualism, which had no religious overtones in its early days, would become more and more religious. A hundred years later, in 1948, when the centennial book of modern spiritualism was published, it made this astonishing claim:

> Spiritualism, with its signs, wonders, visions, and healing gifts was the religion of the apostles, of the post apostolic fathers, and the primitive Christians.—*Centennial Book of Modern Spiritualism in America* (1948), p. 115

Ellen White wrote volumes in the field of health and nutrition. Every one of her claims has proven true. In 1905 she wrote: "Tobacco is a slow, insidious, but most malignant poison"—*The Ministry of Healing*, p. 327. It still would be fifty years before science would catch up with Ellen White and know that tobacco caused cancer.

A very quick examination of these four tests indicates that Ellen White indeed meets every one of the biblical tests of a prophet. The only conclusion one can reach is that Ellen White's prophetic ministry is genuine and in harmony with scripture. However, her writings are not an addition to scripture. The Bible is a unique collection and cannot be added to. As noted earlier, one can be a truly inspired prophet and not add to the sacred canon. Ellen White fits that category.

Relationship to the Bible

Ellen White, herself, was very careful about how people viewed her relationship to the Bible and refused to allow her writings to be used in place of the Bible. All Bible truth must be discovered from the scripture alone. She described her work as being that of a lesser light to lead people to the greater light. Her last publicly recorded words were these:

> Thus closed the last sermon Ellen White was to make at a General Conference session. She moved away from the desk and started to her seat, then turned and came back, picked

up the Bible from which she had read, opened it, and held it out on extended hands that trembled with age. She admonished, "Brethren and Sisters, I commend unto you this Book."
—Reported by W. A. Spicer, then secretary of the General Conference, in *The Spirit of Prophecy in the Advent Movement*, p. 30.

At times during her life, people attempted to use Ellen White's writings in place of the Bible. She always condemned such approaches. The Bible was always to be first. She was not an inspired commentary on the Bible. The Bible stood firm by itself. Her job was to lead people back to the Bible as the only source of truth.

> The written testimonies are not to give new light, but to impress vividly upon the heart the truths of inspiration already revealed. Man's duty to God and to his fellow man has been distinctly specified in God's word; yet but few of you are obedient to the light given. Additional truth is not brought out; but God has through the Testimonies simplified the great truths already given and in His own chosen way brought them before the people to awaken and impress the mind with them, that all may be left without excuse.—*Testimonies for the Church*, vol. 2, p. 605.

Bible truth is not discovered through the writings of Ellen White. Truths are discovered by Bible study alone. What then is the purpose of her writings? Listen to her:

> In our time there is a wide departure from their doctrines and precepts, and there is need of a return to the great Protestant principle,—the Bible, and the Bible only, as the rule of faith and duty.—*The Great Controversy*, pp. 204, 205.

> I took the precious Bible, and surrounded it with the several "Testimonies for the Church," given for the people of God. "Here," said I, "the cases of nearly all are met. The sins

they are to shun are pointed out. The counsel that they desire can be found here, given for other cases situated similarly to themselves. God has been pleased to give you line upon line and precept upon precept. But there are not many of you that really know what is contained in the Testimonies. You are not familiar with the Scriptures. If you had made God's word your study, with a desire to reach the Bible standard and attain to Christian perfection, you would not have needed the Testimonies. It is because you have neglected to acquaint yourselves with God's inspired book that He has sought to reach you by simple, direct testimonies, calling your attention to the words of inspiration which you had neglected to obey, and urging you to fashion your lives in accordance with its pure and elevated teachings."—*Life Sketches,* p. 198.

Since the work of Ellen White was not to give new light but simply to bring out the great truths in the Bible, Ellen White can never be used to decide Bible truth. The Bible must be the only standard. Ellen White, however, does provide many wonderful insights into the scriptures that help God's people on their spiritual journey.

In addition, Ellen White was a great influence on the developing Seventh-day Adventist Church, helping it remain a Bible movement. She pressed the church to develop a Christian educational system, a medical work, a welfare work, and a publishing work that belts the earth today. Her guidance today continues to help the church maintain itself as a biblical movement.

The blessings of the gift of prophecy in the Adventist church have been abundant. It indeed has provided hope and comfort to people who are attempting to keep the commandments of God through their faith in Jesus. The Seventh-day Adventist Church relies on scripture alone for its doctrines, not on the writings of Ellen White.

Yet these writings have helped the church to keep loyal to scripture. They are as fully inspired as scripture, but the Bible always has the greater authority. You too will find these counsels to be of help to you in your spiritual journey. Why not pick up one of Ellen White's beautiful volumes and discover an even deeper relationship with Jesus? We can thank God that He has fulfilled His Word and provided the gift of prophecy to His last-day church, just as He promised in Revelation 12:17.

27

Hope in the Midst of Disappointment

Hope runs high. Expectations send a surge of electricity throughout our being as we contemplate the ultimate fulfillment of our hopes and dreams. It is the consummation of such hope that keeps the human spirit alive during periods of greatest discouragement. The ultimate hope for the Christian is the second coming of Jesus. The Bible calls it the "blessed hope," but it is a hope that has kept faith alive in the hearts of millions of Christians during discouraging times.

God never promised His church a bed of roses, but He did promise them that the ultimate hope of seeing Jesus again will become a reality. The study of prophecy brings a special hope and joy to the hearts of God's people as we contemplate the final consummation of our hope—the second coming of Jesus.

Revelation 10 pictures the beginnings of God's last-day movement—one that is fraught with hope and disappointment. Revelation 10 appears as one of two chapters describing two movements that are to play a major role in last-day events.

Revelation 11 describes the rise of the modern king of the south, with its secularistic philosophy, that we have already examined. At the same time, however, another movement begins that is to prepare a people for the coming of the Lord. That movement is described in Revelation 10:

> I saw still another mighty angel coming down from heaven, clothed with a cloud. And a rainbow was on his head,

his face was like the sun, and his feet like pillars of fire. He had a little book open in his hand. And he set his right foot on the sea and his left foot on the land. Revelation 10:1, 2.

The message of Revelation 10 is not revealed by an ordinary angel but by a "mighty" angel. The word *angel* means "messenger" and does not necessarily imply one of the created beings we normally refer to as angels. Several clues in the description of this strong angel indicate that this reference is possibly to Jesus Himself, who appears to John as the mighty angel. In the description John gives, this mighty angel is described as clothed with a cloud, a rainbow above his head, face shining like the sun, and feet like pillars of fire.

Revelation 1 describes Jesus, the Son of God, utilizing almost the same description as found in Revelation 10, but in this case there is no doubt whatever about it being a reference to Jesus:

His head and hair were white like wool, as white as snow, and His eyes like a flame of fire; His feet were like fine brass, as if refined in a furnace, and His voice as the sound of many waters. Revelation 1:14, 15.

Of the four elements in the Revelation 10 description, three of them are coming directly from the description of Jesus in Revelation 1. In other places in Revelation, particularly in Revelation 2 and 3, John has drawn from this description repeatedly in describing the one giving the message of Revelation.

Through repeated usage of the Revelation 1 description, John is reassuring his readers that the same One who began the message of Revelation is still giving it. Thus the message of Revelation 10 has not been entrusted to any ordinary angel, but Jesus Himself comes with this message.

The Movement of Revelation 10 Described

I saw still another mighty angel coming down from

heaven, clothed with a cloud. And a rainbow was on his head, his face was like the sun, and his feet like pillars of fire. He had a little book open in his hand. And he set his right foot on the sea and his left foot on the land, and cried with a loud voice, as when a lion roars. When he cried out, seven thunders uttered their voices. Now when the seven thunders uttered their voices, I was about to write; but I heard a voice from heaven saying to me, "Seal up the things which the seven thunders uttered, and do not write them." The angel whom I saw standing on the sea and on the land raised up his hand to heaven and swore by Him who lives forever and ever, who created heaven and the things that are in it, the earth and the things that are in it, and the sea and the things that are in it, that there should be delay no longer, but in the days of the sounding of the seventh angel, when he is about to sound, the mystery of God would be finished, as He declared to His servants the prophets. Then the voice which I heard from heaven spoke to me again and said, "Go, take the little book which is open in the hand of the angel who stands on the sea and on the earth." So I went to the angel and said to him, "Give me the little book." And he said to me, "Take and eat it; and it will make your stomach bitter, but it will be as sweet as honey in your mouth." Then I took the little book out of the angel's hand and ate it, and it was as sweet as honey in my mouth. But when I had eaten it, my stomach became bitter. And he said to me, "You must prophesy again about many peoples, nations, tongues, and kings." Revelation 10:1-11.

The following points should be noted in this passage:

1. There is an open book in the angel's hand.

2. The angel stands on land and sea.

3. Seven thunders speak.

4. John is told to cover up what the thunders revealed.

5. At this time, there will be no more delay or time.

6. The message comes from the Creator-God.

7. John is told to eat the book.

8. It is sweet as honey to the mouth.

9. It turns bitter in the stomach.

10. They must once again preach the message.

These are indeed strange descriptions, but let us decipher them one by one.

1. There is an open book in the angel's hand. The fact that the book is opened indicates that at one time, it was closed. The only Bible book ever sealed up was the book of Daniel (Daniel 12:4). Yet even the whole book of Daniel was not sealed. A closer examination reveals that the main portion sealed was that dealing with the time prophecies. The open book indicates the opening of the time prophecies of the book of Daniel. Since Daniel 12:4 indicates that they will be opened in the time of the end, it would indicate that the movement described in Revelation 10 must arise at the biblical time of the end (after 1798) and deal with the unsealing of the time prophecies of the book of Daniel.

2. The angel standing on the land and sea would indicate the worldwide extent of the proclamation of the unsealing of the book of Daniel.

3. Seven thunders roar. A message is given to John—he hears it and is about to write it down.

4. God instructs John not to write out what he saw. Something is hidden from view regarding the time prophecies. John saw it but never wrote it down.

5. The mighty angel then proclaims that there shall be no more delay, or, as some translations read, "there shall be time no longer." This is obviously not announcing the end of the world, because the world continues after this utterance. In the context of Revelation 10, it is describing the time prophecies and then announces the end of those prophetic time periods. The longest of Daniel's time prophecies is the 2,300-year prophecy ending in 1844. Thus the movement here described must arise around 1844 and deal with the unsealing of the time prophecies.

6. The message is certain, because it comes from the Creator-God. However, the words used in Revelation 10 to describe the Creator-God are a direct quotation from the fourth commandment (Exodus 20:11). The usage of the Sabbath commandment to describe God in this passage is another indication that the movement of Revelation 10 would ultimately restore the Sabbath truth.

7. John is told to eat the book in the angel's hand. Eating the book is not literal, obviously, but is an indication of the joy and enthusiasm the people discovered as they devoured the time prophecies of the book of Daniel.

8. It was a sweet and blessed experience to finally understand all these great time prophecies of Daniel.

9. However, they were to go through a bitter disappointment over these time prophecies of Daniel.

10. After the disappointment, they would arise again

and go into the entire world with the message of the book of Daniel.

Thus there was to arise a movement in the early nineteenth century that would decipher the time prophecies of Daniel, restore the Sabbath truth, go through a bitter disappointment over the time prophecies, and then arise again with the message of the book of Daniel and carry it to the entire world. Did such a movement arise?

The Fulfillment of Revelation 10

At the dawn of the nineteenth century, the religious world held primarily to post-millennialism—a view that expected the second coming to occur after a 1,000-year period of peace and prosperity. Premillennialism—a view held by the majority of Christians today—was held by only a few people at the beginning of the nineteenth century. However, things changed rapidly as the movement of Revelation 10 emerged and forever shattered post-millennialism.

At the sunset of the eighteenth century in Europe, scholars began researching the time prophecies of Daniel, reaching the conclusion that a day in prophecy equaled one literal year. Thus the 1,260-days prophecy they concluded would end in 1798. When the pope was taken prisoner in 1798, it ratified their method of interpretation. They then began to focus on the other great time prophecy of Daniel—the 2,300 years— reaching the conclusion that it would end around the mid-nineteenth century. There was a general feeling that the second coming of Christ would take place around that time. This view was espoused by some of the great preachers of the era in England: Edward Irving, Joseph Wolf, and Henry Drummond.

By 1820, three hundred of the Church of England clergy and six hundred of the nonconformist clergy were preaching the near return of Jesus based on the fulfillment of the time prophecies of Daniel. However, the movement in Europe was primarily among the scholars and never took a popular course.

However, in America it was different. Rather than a scholarly movement, it was a popular movement. It was not led by clergy, but by a devoted farmer, William Miller. Miller was a Baptist from upstate New York. He was not educated in the schools of his day but self-educated, through reading library books. The result was that Miller became a Deist (a group that felt God created the world, but then left it to care for itself). Witnessing the carnage of the war of 1812, Miller returned to his farm in Low Hampton, New York, and began attending the local Baptist church, where he ultimately was converted to the Savior.

His old deist friends chided him on his new beliefs. In an effort to answer their questions, Miller began an intensive investigation of scripture that was to last for fifteen years. He dispensed with all commentaries and used only *Cruden's Concordance* and his Bible, but it was the books of Daniel and Revelation that particularly interested him. Prophecy was one area that would help him prove the Bible true to his deist friends. In his study, he discovered Daniel 8:14—the 2,300-year prophecy. As he figured it out, he reached the conclusion that the 2,300 days would end around 1843 to 1844. Accepting the popular notion of the era that the sanctuary referred to the earth, he reached the conclusion that Christ would come around 1844.

Amazingly, independent of Miller, others were arriving at the same conclusion at the same time. We have already mentioned the European scholars, but American preachers were coming to that conclusion as well. William Davis in South Carolina and Alexander Campbell, the founder of the Disciples of Christ movement, both were teaching the end of the 2,300 days. Seemingly, this was a message ripe for proclamation, as a multitude of individuals arrived at the same conclusion about the same time.

In 1831, the conviction pressed on Miller to begin to share with the world what he had learned. Not being a trained preacher, he passed off the impression and continued his study. Yet he could not shake the conviction and finally knelt in prayer to tell the Lord that he would go if someone invited him. Immediately, a knock came at his door. Answering the knock, he was met by his nephew, Irving Guilford, inviting him to preach in a nearby church. Dumbfounded by the quick answer, Miller escaped to the grove behind his house and agonized again with the Lord. Overwhelmed by the call of God, he accepted the invitation and began his ministry.

The Dresden Baptist church, hearing the message on the conclusion of the 2,300 days in the mid-nineteenth century, and the possible coming of Christ at the time, was electrified. People were converted to Jesus, and invitations began to pour in requesting that Miller come and share his message. Miller only went where he was invited, mostly in upstate New York and New England. In 1833, he met a preacher, Joshua V. Himes, who invited Miller to preach in his church in Boston, thus beginning Miller's ministry to the large cities. Himes also became the first of nearly two thousand clergy who were ultimately to join Miller in the proclamation of the soon coming advent of Jesus Christ.

Many who joined Miller did not necessarily subscribe to his date setting but joined in his proclamation because of the truth of the premillennial return of Christ. The rediscovery of the truth of premillennialism was a major breakthrough in the nineteenth century. In fact, most conservative Christians today who believe in the near return of Jesus before the millennium are indebted to William Miller for the rediscovery of this truth.

Quickly, the Millerite movement spread throughout America and around the world. The news of the soon coming of Jesus thrilled people's hearts with joy and anticipation. One historian has said:

> As early as 1842, second advent publications had been sent to every missionary station in Europe, Asia, Africa, and America both sides of the Rocky Mountains…The com-

manders of our vessels and the sailors tell us that they touch at no port where they find this proclamation has not preceded them, and frequent inquires respecting it are made of them. —J. N. Loughborough. *The Great Second Advent Movement.* p. 105.

The movement was inter-denominational. People of all faiths and no faith embraced the sweet message—Jesus is coming soon. Thousands of conversions quickly followed as people came to faith in Jesus. However, by the early 1840s, a change occurred in the popular denominational churches. At first open to the Millerites, they now were closed, and people who believed in the premillennial return of Jesus were disfellowshipped from their churches. This setback did not delay the advent proclamation. Instead of churches, the Millerites hired halls and erected tents to proclaim the certainty of the soon return of Jesus.

Being an inter-denominational movement, they saw no need of a separate organization, but when the churches turned away from their message, they organized themselves as the "Second Advent Association." They settled on no specific date for the coming of Jesus, feeling only that He would return during the Jewish year 1844—from March 21, 1843 to March 21, 1844. When Jesus did not return by March 21, 1844, the Millerites experienced their first disappointment. However, their faith was founded on Bible study, so they simply went back and studied their Bibles to find the answer to their disappointment.

At a Millerite camp meeting on August 12, 1844, as they were restudying the prophecies, one of the attendees shared a possible connection between the ancient Jewish sanctuary and the cleansing of the sanctuary in Daniel 8:14. Brother S.N. Snow then suggested that since in the Levitical sanctuary, it was cleansed on the tenth day of the seventh month, then would it not be logical for the sanctuary of Daniel 8:14 to be cleansed on the tenth day of the seventh Jewish month, which would be October 22, 1844. The truth of this suggestion hit the

Millerites like a bolt of lightning. They left the Exeter, New Hampshire, camp meeting with the startling news that Jesus was coming on October 22, 1844.

It is amazing to note the vast numbers of people who were awaiting the advent of Christ on October 22. Some historians suggest that nearly one million people somehow expected Christ to return on that date, and around 200,000 were ardent followers of William Miller. Considering that the United States population at the time was only around seventeen million, it is apparent that the Millerite movement had shaken America to its core.

On October 22, 1844, the Millerites gathered in homes, churches, or in the outdoors to await the Advent. All day they waited in vain. By midnight, they realized that Christ was not coming that day, and they experienced their second disappointment. The hope of the advent had been a sweet and blessed experience, indeed, as honey to the mouth, but how bitter the disappointment when it reached their bellies—just as Revelation 10 had predicted.

The Results of the Disappointment

As a result of the disappointment, the Millerites divided into various factions. Many renounced their faith in the advent and left the movement. There were two major, lasting results of the Millerite movement. First, most Christians became believers in premillennialism, and postmillennialism was relegated to the rubbish heap of history. Second, the movement resulted in the rise of the Seventh-day Adventist Church.

In the aftermath of the disappointment, the majority of the followers of Miller organized themselves into what became the Advent Christian denomination. At their organization in 1848, there were 50,000 Millerites who joined that denomination. At the same time, the smallest of the Millerite factions, numbering only three hundred in 1848, was beginning to develop into what would become the Seventh-day Adventist

Church.

The great disappointment wounded but did not destroy the second-advent movement. The date was right, but the event was wrong. Miller himself never saw the truth of the judgment, but he did keep his faith in the advent until his death in 1849. Soon after the disappointment, the great truths of scripture came to light.

In Port Gibson, New York, there was a group of Millerites who awaited the advent on October 22 at Hiram Edson's home. After midnight, when it became obvious that Christ was not coming that day, several of them went out to the barn behind Edson's home and prayed the rest of the night, asking for wisdom. The next morning, they crossed the cornfield to another Millerite home to encourage them, as they felt encouraged from their time in prayer. As they crossed the cornfield, the thought began to dawn on them that the sanctuary was not the earth but that the sanctuary was in heaven, and that Christ had a work to do there before coming to earth. They went home and spent much time studying the Bible on the sanctuary question. As they continued to study, the ministry of Christ in heaven began to open to their understanding, and they saw that 1844 marked not the end of the world, but the beginning of Christ's final phase of ministry in the heavenly sanctuary— His work of judgment. As their view became crystallized, they wrote it out in a little paper called the *Day Dawn* and mailed it to many Millerites. Among those who received it were Joseph Bates and James White, who accepted their explanation of the disappointment and the truth of the pre-advent judgment.

In Washington, New Hampshire, another group of Millerites were confronted with the truth of the seventh-day Sabbath by a Seventh-Day Baptist, Rachel Oakes Preston. After diligent Bible study, the little group in New Hampshire began keeping the seventh-day Sabbath. After the disappointment, one of their number, T. M. Prebble, wrote a little tract on the seventh-day Sabbath and mailed it to several Millerites. Among those receiving the Sabbath tract was Joseph Bates, who immediately made a trip to Washington, New Hampshire, studied with the believers there, and made his decision to begin keeping God's Sabbath. Later, James and Ellen White visited Bates and heard him speak on the Sabbath. At first they thought he erred by emphasizing the Sabbath more than the other commandments, but after Bible study, they too declared their acceptance of the seventh-day Sabbath.

Joseph Bates and James and Ellen White ultimately became the three founders of what was to be the Seventh-day Adventist Church. All the Millerites were totally united on the fundamentals of Christianity: the deity of Christ, the sinlessness of Jesus, salvation by grace alone, etc. These three now became united on the truth of the pre-advent judgment and the seventh-day Sabbath. Soon others joined with them in these great truths. Various Bible conferences were held, where more of the great truths of the scriptures were rediscovered.

In 1860, this small group had grown to three thousand members. At Battle Creek, Michigan, in 1860, they chose the name Seventh-day Adventists to indicate the two great truths that were to distinguish this movement: the soon return of Jesus and the seventh-day Sabbath. Over the next couple of years, they organized themselves into a denomination. With their resources united, they now went forth to proclaim their message. Today, the members of this denomination belt the earth, numbering in the millions and growing by over one million per year. The Seventh-day Adventist Church is today one of the fastest-growing Christian denominations in the world.

As these early Adventists studied, they came across Revelation 10. There they saw the Millerite movement foretold in graphic detail. Then they read verse 11, and they saw their marching orders: they must again preach this message to the entire earth. As a result, Adventists today exist in just about every country on the globe, a truly international religious movement—the tenth-largest Christian denomination in the world (*www.adherents.com* website, 2002). Yet it remains a movement, recognizing that it is not just another religious denomination but a mighty movement, foretold by God Himself to give this special message to the earth at the end of time.

One may feel that this is a strange way to start a church—through a disappointment—yet it appears that God has always begun His movements this way. When Israel was about to leave Egypt, God allowed them to go through a disappointment when Moses asked Pharaoh to let Israel go. Instead, he said make bricks without straw. But out of that disappointment, Moses and the people learned to trust God.

When it was time for Jesus to establish His church, He allowed the people to assume a false expectation—that the Messiah was going to deliver people from the bondage of Rome. Of course, they were bitterly disappointed when Jesus died on the cross. Yet from this disappointment, they were humbled enough for God to use them, and the result was the mighty Christian church of the first century.

When it came time for God to call forth His final movement, He was true to the way He had led in the past. He allowed His people to experience a great disappointment over the time of Christ's coming, but from the ashes of that disappointment, He led forth His church into all the world. The ways of God are not the ways of humans, yet God's hand is in it all. Revelation 10 predicted the whole disappointment, but they did not see it until after the frustration of October 22.

Clearly, God led in the establishment of His last-day church. He has led you, dear reader, through these pages. You too have discovered this marvelous truth of the three angels' messages. Why not decide right now to join this movement in proclaiming the final message to earth's billions?

Hope in a Look to Calvary

There is life in a look at the cross. There is hope when we focus our attention upon Calvary's tree. In the course of these pages, we have traversed the books of Daniel and Revelation and have understood the closing scenes of Planet Earth. Mighty biblical truths have been rediscovered, yet truth is only meaningful as it refocuses our attention on the mighty act of Jesus on Golgotha's hill. In this final chapter, we wish again to look at the great truths we have discovered in these pages and discover anew how they focus our attention on the cross.

Satan is alive and well in the twenty-first century. He is still enticing people into yet more sophisticated deceptions. However, all of Satan's amalgamations are ultimately designed to make the cross of Jesus irrelevant. Today, Satan has developed a clever counterfeit system of truth that completely nullifies the cross of Christ.

Satan's Counterfeit System

The first teaching that forms a part of Satan's counterfeit system is the teaching of evolution. Evolution's basic premise is that humanity began as a very simple life form and then over millions of years gradually emerged into human beings. Its basic teaching is that humanity can save itself. People can improve all by themselves, provided they are given enough time. Thus, humanity is getting better and better all by itself. In contrast, the Bible teaches that humanity began as perfect beings, but fell from that high estate.

If evolution were true, there would be no need of the cross, for humanity would ultimately save itself. But if creation and the fall are true, then humanity desperately needs the cross to lift us up from the pit of sin. One is the insidious doctrine of salvation by works—the other is the redemptive truth of salvation by grace alone.

The second teaching in Satan's counterfeit system is the doctrine of the natural immortality of the soul. It declares that every human being is born with an immortal soul (eternal life). If we are born with eternal life, then we do not need the cross to receive eternal life. If natural immortality is true, then there is no need of the cross, and once again, humanity can save themselves by something inherent in them—an immortal soul. The doctrine of natural immortality is thus the opposite of the biblical teaching of immortality bestowed only at the second coming of Christ. It is simply another insidious variation of the doctrine of salvation by works. There is something within the human being that grants him eternal life. Instead, the Bible teaches life is available only in Jesus and acceptance of Calvary's cross. The doctrine of natural immortality denies both Christ and the cross.

The third teaching that forms a part of Satan's clever counterfeit is closely related to the doctrine of natural immortality. It proclaims that the wicked burn in hell throughout all eternity because they possess an immortal soul that God cannot destroy. Ultimately, this falsehood proclaims that everyone receives eternal life, whether they are righteous or wicked. In other words, you can have eternal life without the cross. Yet the Bible is clear that only those who accept Jesus have life (1 John 5:11, 12). Thus the doctrine of eternal torment refutes the doctrine of the cross. The cross proclaims that the only way to have eternal life in any form is by acceptance of the cross. Of course, this doctrine also is linked to salvation by works, for it implies that the reason all receive eternal life is that there is something within the human being (an immortal soul) that gives the person eternal life even if they do not accept Jesus and the cross. This paganistic doctrine is totally opposed to the biblical truth of Calvary.

The fourth teaching Satan has laid hold of in these last days to invalidate the doctrine of Calvary is the teaching that the Ten Commandments—the law of God—has been abolished or changed. The Bible, however, defines sin as the transgression of the law (1 John 3:4). If there is no law, then there is no sin, and if there is no sin, there is no need of a Savior from sin. The attempt to abolish the law of God is a direct attack on the cross itself. The fact that Jesus died revealed that sin (transgression of the law) could only be atoned for by the infinite sacrifice of Jesus Himself. To abolish the law or to change the law would be to change the character of God, for the law is the transcript of the divine character. If there is no law, then there is no sin and no Calvary, and the death of Jesus on the cross is a farce. If the law is abolished, humanity becomes a law unto itself, another insidious form of salvation by works.

The fifth and final teaching that forms a part of Satan's counterfeit system is the false Sabbath kept on Sunday, the first day of the week, taking the place of God's seventh-day Sabbath. To keep Sunday declares that human beings have the power to change a command of God. It declares that humans do not need to spend a 24-hour period building a relationship with God. Finally, this false Sabbath is the basis for the deception that a relationship with Jesus is not that critical. Yet the scripture is plain: A relationship with Jesus is the foundation of all that God wishes to do with humanity. Sunday keeping is ultimately about salvation by works, while Sabbath keeping is ultimately about salvation by grace alone.

How does a false Sabbath mitigate against the cross? In six days, God created the heavens and the earth and then rested on the seventh day—a sign of His finished work of creation. Yet this created race turned from God and sinned. Jesus came to this earth to redeem those that were lost. On the sixth day, Friday, He went to the cross and cried out "It is finished!" (John 19:30) just as He did on the sixth day of creation. Then Jesus went into the tomb and rested on the seventh day, a sign now of His finished work of creation and redemption.

Satan does not want us to discover the link between the Creator and the Redeemer. Yet the One who created us is the same One who redeemed us on Calvary's tree. Keeping the seventh-day Sabbath is a recognition of the Creator-Redeemer link; whereas the keeping of Sunday has no linkage to Calvary and the great work accomplished for us there. The restoration of the Sabbath truth is one of the ways God uses to keep us focused on Calvary, the only source of our redemption.

The Message of the Cross

The message you have been reading in this book centers totally on the cross of Jesus. Every truth we have examined is somehow linked to Calvary. Satan knows this well, and he will do everything in his power to prevent us from accepting this great message centered on the cross of Christ.

If there ever was a time when the world needed the message of the cross, that time is now. God hears the cries from the desperate hearts of the human race, and He responds with His final message of love to the world—a message of the everlasting gospel. It is time for this message to be heard with a loud cry throughout the nations of the earth. It is our ultimate need at this point in earth's history. It is time to wave its banner high.

This message that centers in the cross also focuses on salvation by grace alone. Every truth we have discovered here drives home the certainty that humankind cannot save itself. Every truth we have studied is rooted and grounded in the foundation of the cross and reveals that humanity is saved by grace alone.

It is time for Christians to proclaim this message of the cross in all its glory. Will you pick up the cross and follow Jesus in full obedience to the message of salvation by grace alone through faith in Jesus Christ?

The Road to Calvary

The cross was the only way to redeem humanity. Nothing can diminish the importance of the decision Jesus made to go through with this sacrifice and provide a way by which humanity might be redeemed. Yet in Gethsemane, He came face to face with the decision to leave humanity in sin, or to die and provide a way of release. He chose the road to Calvary.

Jesus had arrived with His disciples outside the walls of Jerusalem in the garden of Gethsemane. Olive trees witnessed the scene as Jesus requested His disciples to wait outside the garden area while He went in to pray. For untold minutes, Jesus was entirely alone with His Father, agonizing over the struggle that was just before Him. I can imagine that Satan was there also, tempting the Son of God to leave humanity on this earth and call for a legion of angels to escort Him back to heaven. How Satan wished that Jesus would not go through with the ransom! Yet Jesus prayed: "Not my will, but thine" (Luke 22:42, KJV). Still, the devil tempted Him: "Do you think you are the only one who is right? Could all the religious leaders be wrong? All the important people and all the great men are against you. How could you be the only one who is right and all the others wrong? No one is ever going to believe in you. Even your own disciples are asleep outside the garden, and they all will soon forsake you. Give it up, Jesus—go back to heaven where you belong, and leave this world to me."

Can you imagine the strength of this temptation? Everything Satan said was true, yet Jesus decided to go through with Calvary. So He prayed: "Not my will, but thine be done." As Jesus made this decision, the Father began to separate Himself from His Son. As Jesus became sin for our race, He had to bear the curse of God on sin. He must tread this winepress alone without the assurance of His Father's love. He must die the death of sinners—a death of eternal separation from God. To Him who was one with God, separation from God and bearing the curse of God on sin caused unimaginable pain. So great was this load of sin being placed on Jesus—the sins of the entire world—that Jesus fell fainting to the ground, sweating great drops of blood.

Having made the decision, Jesus staggered out of the garden, finding His disciples sound asleep. He awakened them and urged them to pray, but it was too late. Already, the crowd approached to arrest Jesus. Led by Judas, the crowd drew near as Judas betrayed the Son of God with a kiss. Jesus was seized, and those hands so often outstretched on errands of mercy were tied behind His back as He was led off to the house of Annas and Caiphas, the two highest religious leaders in the nation.

Sometimes people trust their religious leaders for their salvation, but we can trust only Jesus. The religious leaders in the time of Christ crucified the Son of God. That night, Jesus underwent the mockery of a trial. Witnesses were hired to testify falsely against Him. Ultimately, He was convicted on His own testimony that He was the Son of God. Imagine the scene as paltry, sinful humanity stands in judgment against the infinite Creator-God of the universe. How far Satan went in his attempt to destroy Jesus.

Yet the Jewish leaders were unable to secure the death penalty. Early the next morning, they stood in Pilate's court asking for a judgment of death against the Creator-God. Pilate sensed the false accusations being made against Jesus and tried to avoid pronouncing judgment. He learned that Christ was from Galilee, so he sent Him over to Herod. Herod also wanted nothing to do with Jesus, so returned Him to Pilate.

Back in Pilate's court, Jesus was interrogated but answered nothing. Pilate was amazed. He had often seen criminals accused, and he knew how they responded. But Jesus was not acting according to form. He had complete composure and calm, even though it was evident to all that He was falsely accused and condemned. Imagine the humanity of Jesus. He had just been through the agony of Gethsemane and separation from His Father's love. He had spent a night without sleep and endured the mockery of the trial by night. Now He stood before Pilate with absolute trust and serenity upon His face.

This is no weakling—Jesus was a real man.

Pilate desired to release Jesus. Suddenly a way out appeared. At Passover, it was customary to release a prisoner. He went to the jail, picked out the most notorious prisoner in confinement—Barabbas—and brought him up to the judgment hall. Surely the multitudes would choose Barabbas over Jesus. Then Pilate could save face, release Jesus, and still crucify Barabbas. But when Pilate provided them with a choice, these church-going people of the first century, led on by their religious leaders, cried out for Barabbas to be released and asked Pilate to crucify Jesus.

How often, even in the twenty-first century, we listen too closely to the multitude. If everyone is doing it, then it must be right. We must never forget that the multitude cried out to crucify Jesus and release Barabbas. As the poet James Russell Lowell declared: "Truth forever on the scaffold, wrong forever on the throne."—*The Present Crisis: The Poems of James Russell Lowell*, Oxford University Press: London, 1926, p. 96. When it comes to truth, the opinion of the majority does not count. Truth must be decided on the grounds of scripture alone and not based on the whims of an unstable majority. Otherwise, we might be crucifying Christ afresh today.

When Pilate saw he was unable to release Jesus, he next brought a basin of water, washed his hands in front of the multitude, and declared that he was innocent of Christ's blood. Yet with the next stroke of his pen, he condemned Jesus to be flogged and crucified. There is no neutral ground here. Either one stands for Christ or one is against Him. You cannot wash your hands of the Redeemer. To fail to take a stand for Jesus is to crucify Him. Some people today still try to wash their hands. They examine the truth from all angles. They will declare it to be scriptural, but when asked what they will do with it, they wash their hands, declaring they find no fault in it, yet they do not choose to follow. Such inaction sends Jesus to the cross all over again. We cannot be neutral with Jesus—either we go all the way in obedience to Him, or we end up renouncing Him and crucifying Him afresh.

Pilate sent Jesus to the courtyard, where He was stripped to the waist, His hands tied above His head, and with the long leather scourge that had bits of metal embedded in the ends, He was lashed nearly forty times across His back and chest. This Roman punishment was such a terrible ordeal that many men died just as a result of the scourging. Again, the endurance of Jesus is a tribute to His strong humanity. Having scourged the Son of God, they placed a crown of thorns upon Him, took a reed, and smashed Him on the head, driving the thorns into that tender brow. Jesus was not even able to lift His hands to wipe away the blood, because they were tied behind His back. All this was for you and me, my friend—we who are lost in sin. He did it just for us.

Again, Pilate brought Jesus back to the court and presented Him to the multitude, declaring: "Behold the man" (John 19:5). Behold Him, indeed—the Creator of the world coming to this sin-cursed earth, enduring all this in order to save us. How unimaginable! How impossible! Yet it is true.

Behold the man as the heavy wooden cross, weighing over a hundred pounds, was placed upon his shoulders. Again, we marvel that He was able even to lift it after all He had been through. Yet ultimately, it proved too much, and Jesus fell beneath the load. So Simon the Cyrenian was asked to carry it the rest of the way.

When Jesus arrived at Golgotha's hill, the cross was placed on the ground, He was stripped totally naked, laid against the cross, and one Roman soldier grabbed His extremities to hold them in place while another pounded the nails through His hands and feet, affixing Him to the cruel tree. Then roughly, the soldiers raised the cross with the Son of God hanging on it and thrust it into place, causing the most excruciating agony to the victim on the cross. The cross was the cruelest instrument ever devised by human beings to torture another and at the same time prolong their life of suffering as long as possible. Many men hung on the cross in this agony for days. The pain was so intense that many times the curses and screams of those on the cross caused the Roman soldiers to climb up the ladder and cut the person's tongue out to stop the cursing. But instead of curses, all that proceeded from this man was: "Father, forgive them; for they know not what they do"(Luke 23:34, KJV). What a God! What a man! This is the power of the cross.

Yet Jesus scarcely felt the physical pain. It was not bodily suffering that tormented Him—it was the mental anguish that tore through His body. He was dying the second death, the death of sinners, a death of separation from God. This was unbearable for Him, yet He endured it for the sake of seeing us in the kingdom of God. It was this awful sense of separation from God that forced from His lips that despairing cry: "My God, my God, why have You forsaken me?" (Matthew 27:46). Yes, there He was, forsaken of God and forsaken by those He had created. There He was, dying the death of sinners. There He was, dying in my place. Look—and you can see Him there.

As your imagination takes you to the foot of the cross, look up into those searching eyes of Jesus. As you see the Savior looking down, wondering about you, how will you respond? Will you be able to look Him straight in the eye and declare: "Jesus, You may feel that all people have forsaken You, but there is one thing I want You to know. If You have gone through all this for me, I am willing to do anything for You. I give You my heart right now."

If you had been standing there at that moment, would you have given Him your life? Then give Him your life today. In this closing appeal, I invite you to bow anew at the foot of the cross and present yourself once more to this Jesus who died for you. And if you have never done it, why not do it right now? Don't let anything keep you from following Jesus all the way in full obedience to His truth. Your obedience is not something you do to merit God's favor. Jesus has already done that for you. Your obedience to this Christ simply lets Him know how much you love Him for what He has done for you. How can you say "No" to the One who died for you? Come now and raise the banner of Calvary in your life. Accept the crucified Redeemer as your Lord and your God. Do it now!